S0-CKS-177

The Franco-German Axis in European Integration

The Franco-German Axis in European Integration

Gisela Hendriks

Lecturer in European Studies,
University of Kent at Canterbury, UK

Annette Morgan

Formerly Senior Lecturer in European Training,
Civil Service College, UK

Edward Elgar
Cheltenham, UK • Northampton, MA, USA

327.44
H49f

© Gisela Hendriks and Annette Morgan 2001

All rights reserved. No part of this publication may be reproduced, stored in a retrieval system or transmitted in any form or by any means, electronic, mechanical or photocopying, recording, or otherwise without the prior permission of the publisher.

Published by
Edward Elgar Publishing Limited
Glensanda House
Montpellier Parade
Cheltenham
Glos GL50 1UA
UK

Edward Elgar Publishing, Inc.
136 West Street
Suite 202
Northampton
Massachusetts 01060
USA

A catalogue record for this book
is available from the British Library

Library of Congress Cataloguing in Publication Data

Hendriks, Gisela.
JK   The Franco-German axis in European integration / Gisela Hendriks, Annette Morgan.
      p. cm.
    Includes bibliographical references and index.
    1. France—Foreign economic relations—Germany. 2. Germany—Foreign economic relations—France. 3. Europe—Economic integration. I. Morgan, Annette. II. Title.

HF1544.15.G35 H46 2001
327.44043—dc21   00–055121

ISBN 185898 360 6

Printed and bound in Great Britain by Biddles Ltd, *www.biddles.co.uk*

Contents

University of Illinois
Carnegie Mellon University
Pittsburgh, PA 15213-3890

Abbreviations

ACP	African, Caribbean and Pacific
CAP	Common Agricultural Policy
CDU	Christian Democratic Union
CEECs	Central and Eastern European Countries
CFSP	Common Foreign and Security Policy
CJTF	Combined Joint Task Forces
COREPER (CPR)	Committee of Permanent Representatives
CSCE	Conference on Security and Co-operation in Europe
CSU	Christian Social Union
DG	Directorate-General
DM	Deutsch Mark
EAGGF	European Agricultural Guidance and Guarantee Fund (also known as FEOGA after its French acronym)
EBRD	European Bank for Reconstruction and Development
ECB	European Central Bank
ECOFIN	Council of Economic and Finance Ministers
ECSC	European Coal and Steel Community
ECU	European Currency Unit
EDC	European Defence Community
EDF	European Development Fund
EEC	European Economic Community
EFTA	European Free Trade Association
ELDO	European Organisation for the Development of Space Vehicle Launches
EMCF	European Monetary Cooperation Fund
EMI	European Monetary Institute
EMS	European Monetary System
EMU	Economic and Monetary Union
ENA	Ecole Nationale D'Administration
EP	European Parliament
EPC	European Political Cooperation
ERDF	European Regional Development Fund
ERM	Exchange Rate Mechanism
ESCB	European System of Central Banks
ESRO	European Space Research Organisation

EU	European Union
EURATOM	European Atomic Energy Community
FDP	Free Democratic Party
FRG	Federal Republic of Germany
FRY	Former Republic of Yugoslavia
GATT	General Agreement on Tariff and Trade
GDP	Gross Domestic Product
GDR	German Democratic Republic
GNP	Gross National Product
IFRI	French Institute of International Relations
IGC	Intergovernmental Conference
INF	Intermediate Nuclear Force
KLA (UKC)	Kosovan Liberation Army
MCA	Monetary Compensatory Amount
MLF	Multilateral Force
NAFTA	North Atlantic Trade Area
NATO	North Atlantic Treaty Organisation
OECD	Organisation for Economic Cooperation and Development
OEEC	Organisation for European Economic Cooperation
OSCE	Organisation for Security and Cooperation in Europe
PDS	Party of Democratic Socialism
PHARE	Programme of Community Aid for Central and Eastern European Countries
SAMRO	Satellite Militaire de Reconaissance Optique
SEA	Single European Act
SFOR	Stability Forces
SPD	Social Democratic Party
TEMPUS	Trans-European Mobility Scheme for University Students
TEU	Treaty on European Union
UN PROFOR	United Nations Protection Force
UN	United Nations
USA	United States of America
VAT	Value Added Tax
WEU	West European Union
WTO	World Trade Organisation

Preface

The idea of the book came to us as a result of joint presentations we gave on France and Germany to British Civil Servants at the Civil Service College over a number of years. These presentations gave rise to the realisation that continental perspectives generated both interest and questions and on occasion surprise in our audiences. As a result we decided to develop our theme into book form. We were fortunate to find in Edward Elgar understanding and patient support for our project. The fact that both authors were brought up in their respective countries of birth, but have for many years been residing and professionally engaged in European affairs in Britain, brings a special flavour to a book which can truly be called a Franco-German collaborative effort.

We would like to thank our publisher Edward Elgar, the Civil Service College, the University of Kent and the Royal Institute of International Affairs, which have all in their various ways helped to bring this project about. Thanks are also due to Anna Miller and Chris Keene, both at Templeman library, University of Kent, for unflagging patience and constant readiness to assist in both the research and technical setting up of the book. Special thanks to Roger Morgan who read our chapters and agreed to write a postscript at very short notice.

Gisela Hendriks and Annette Morgan

PART I

The Players

1. Introduction

The History of France and Germany has for centuries seen nothing but a continuous attempt to get closer together, to understand each other, to unite, to dissolve one into the other.   (Ludwig Börne, 1836)

We have reached the end of a century, the first half of which witnessed the decline of European influence in the world, the destruction of continental Europe and its infrastructure and the death of tens of millions of inhabitants. In the context of a precarious stability, the so-called balance of terror, generated by the Cold War, the division of Europe into two mutually hostile camps and the development of weapons of global destruction, a new phenomenon took place, that of European integration which, throughout the latter half of the century, has radically transformed the nature of international relations. Finally, the last decade of the century saw Europe precipitated into further, albeit relatively benign, turmoil by the collapse of the Soviet bloc. On the dawn of the new millennium we must look into the recent past and the current developments to try and detect likely alterations in the configuration of Europe, in other words, to see where the dynamics of European integration might lead us.

European integration is a process by which a number of decisions and policies embodied in treaties, legislation and court judgements crystallise into a new entity now called European Union. This process is made possible by the willingness of states to transfer elements of their national sovereignty upwards to the level of European sovereignty. This has long been confirmed in a judgement of the European Court of Justice of 5 February 1962 (Van Gend en Loos) which established the primacy of European over municipal law within the scope of the treaties, thus creating a new legal order. With the advent of a single currency, economic union is about to be completed. Integration of other broad policy areas is proceeding at a much slower and sometimes erratic pace, but hardly any policy area has remained unaffected.

This process primarily, though not exclusively, motivated by the wish to render war between European states impossible, was allowed to develop thanks to the determination of a number of states, France and Germany prominent among them. By signing in April 1951 the Treaty of Paris creating the European Coal and Steel Community (ECSC), they entrusted a whole panel of their sovereignty to a supranational authority. Since then, together they have initiated virtually every step leading to economic cooperation and now monetary union. While integration is lagging behind in the field of foreign policy and security, it is nevertheless cautiously and patchily proceeding within an institutional framework where intergovernmentalism is resisting erosion.

Despite historical and psychological differences in French and German approaches to Community and world affairs, the disparity in their economic and political philosophy, their divergent interests both at home and abroad, and their repeated disputes which have invariably resulted in intra-Community crises, the Franco-German duo has become the indispensable foundation of European integration. Strong ties, based on geography and political experience, a common destiny and interdependent needs have forged France and Germany into a 'fateful union',[1] whose intricate web of relations has gone beyond the personal ties of their political leaders and has survived any disparities in political and economic philosophy. Geographically (the two countries account for 40% of EU population), economically (they represent 17% of total world trade and produce 50% of total EU output)[2] and politically (an importance derived from centrality and economic strength) France and Germany play a dominant role within the Union largely determining its success or failure.

The history of Franco-German cooperation since the momentous press conference of Robert Schuman on 9 May 1950 is therefore one of broad and determined consensus that the building of Europe is the unquestionable priority, not undermined but sensitised by mutual suspicions of, at best the validity of the other's political principles, at worst the covert motivations of certain actions, leading to repeated episodes of recriminations and difficult negotiations and renegotiations. One need only mention the Hallstein doctrine, de Gaulle's threats of French withdrawal in the Common Agricultural Policy (CAP) negotiations of 1964 and 1965, Brandt's *Ostpolitik*, Mitterrand's flight to Kiev or more recently Chirac's stubbornness over nuclear testing in the Pacific among the more notorious squawks, to realise that Franco-German cooperation is neither automatic nor invulnerable. Yet, in the long term, it looks both so formidable and unassailable that, at least outside France and Germany, one is tempted to refer to a Franco-German axis within the European Union and the most worn cliché is that of the Franco-German tandem as 'the motor of European integration'.

There is an impressive corpus of literature on Franco-German relations, and on Franco-German cooperation within the European Union.[3] The fascination with these two former enemies, now close allies, is easy to understand. The fate of Franco-German relations has been punctuated by spectacular partnerships: those of de Gaulle and Adenauer, Giscard d'Estaing and Helmut Schmidt, Mitterrand and Kohl, all of them committed to the building of Europe. The two countries have enjoyed long periods of economic growth and developed a pattern of trade interdependence which has considerably helped economic integration. They have developed a network of intergovernmental and extra-governmental links which is the envy of other governments.[4] Above all, they are driven by the realisation that France can only maintain her international status through the development of Europe, while Germany can only retain the trust of the international community through the sublimation of her national ambitions into a commitment to European unification (even more so since German reunification).

The ties between Germany and France have been durably cemented by self-interest: the legacy of the Second World War had curtailed Germany's freedom of action. Compared with France, the FRG, particularly during the 1950s and 1960s, was on a very different footing in terms of political status and international respectability. In that sense, the Franco-German condominium has helped to contain Germany's growing economic prowess, not just within the EEC, but on the world stage generally. Embarrassed at their country's own importance, the Germans used the French connection in order to conceal their own reviving strength.[5] Past guilt resulted in a reluctance to oppose the European policies of France and in a greater obligation to consult with Paris over vital issues.[6] Political and economic policies put forward and undertaken under French leadership seem to imply respectability. For instance, it was part of German strategy to let the French take credit for joint initiatives, e.g. the EMS. Though principally the system reflected Schmidt's concern for an area of monetary stability in Europe, it has been presented as a joint Franco-German venture. In that context Franco-German cooperation was of prime importance in German-European relations: indeed the very creation of the ECSC and the EEC was based on the desire to effect a lasting rapprochement with France.

But this is not to say that even the early Community of the 1950s and 1960s bears a French stamp, with Germany being a passive instrument of French strategies. If we look closely for example at the formulation of the CAP, we can see that the Community's key area bears the grand design of the German not the French model. Paris, the more innovative of the two and with its penchant for pioneering, was the guiding rider, usually designing the framework, while Bonn, being methodical and legalistic, made it work. 'But in view of the sensitivity about status of others – not just the French – Bonn could never appear to be Europe's leading power but had to let France lead.'[7]

Relations between the two countries began to change in the 1970s. The world-wide recession had enhanced Germany's economic weight and sharply tilted the balance of power between the two countries in favour of the FRG. Diverging policy lines in the two countries emphasised unequal performances, widening the economic gap between the two countries. The revival of strength on the part of Germany encouraged a more aggressive pursuit of national objectives, even in the face of French resistance. Germany's obligation to atone for its past declined through the sheer passage of time and by the launching of *Ostpolitik*. More importantly, Bonn's political influence was greatly increased by both its economic potential and its role as a fulcrum between East and West. As a result, Germany's relations with its European partners increasingly revealed a tough language, which was openly voiced in the defence of domestic interests. In particular, Germany was no longer willing to adapt its economic policies to the needs of French interests.

The accession of Schmidt in May 1974 as Chancellor and Giscard d'Estaing as President in France introduced new elements into Franco-German relations. Both former ministers of finance, they shared the view that the international economic recession had been due mainly to failing budget and balance of payment discipline in the US or at least that the US had started a process of stagnation. Though a fervent supporter of Britain's entry into the EC and keen defender of the Franco-German axis which had existed since Adenauer's time, Schmidt's Europeanism was nevertheless constrained by the more pragmatic approach of the younger German politician with a weaker perception of past guilt. For him Europe was no refuge, but an opportunity for concerted action against the all-absorbing danger of economic recession and inflation. As Chancellor he continued his battle which he had started when still Minister for Finance in the early 1970s. For the first time German financial assistance was made dependent on simultaneous integrationary programmes. Schmidt warned that even the seemingly inexhaustible wealth of the Federal Republic had its limits.

This 'paymaster' philosophy was there to stay. This new Germany, no longer identified with Adenauer or Brandt, successfully translating its economic potential into political power was no longer prepared to pursue a European policy focused on the past. Examples of unilateral action on behalf of the FRG clearly signalled the end of the time when Germany sought refuge in Community consensus. Bonn's staunch defence of Germany's cereals farmers during the 1985–6 price review and the vigour with which Germany insisted on new and tighter standards for car exhausts to safeguard German forests is a far cry from Bonn's traditional European rhetoric. Thus, while the Franco-German axis has continued, its character has changed. The reasons are not to be found merely in a resurgence of economic and political strength nor in the new flexibility opened up by *Ostpolitik*. It is also because contemporary conflicts are no longer directly linked with German guilt. As a result, the German approach to the solution of such problems is less constrained by historical inhibitions, which during the 1950s and 1960s led to the adoption of a modest position in the Community and a strong inclination to follow the French lead. However, that said, some modifications are necessary to the argument that Germany has become a demandeur vis-à-vis its European partners, in particular France. The major difference from the transitional period, i.e. 1958–69, is that the Community has been given a high measure of cohesion by the Franco-German axis ever since.

The 1990s characterised major political changes in Europe at large which also had domestic repercussions in both countries, particularly in Germany. First of all, if the two countries have had a comparable population (61 million in Germany, 58 million in France), Germany increased its population virtually overnight by 16 million as the result of unification which widened further the economic distance between the two countries. Importantly unification and the prospect of enlarging the EU to include countries from Eastern Europe emphasised Germany's role giving it a bridgehead function as the centre of a new regional bloc. In terms of population, economic prowess and geo-strategic position Germany became power factor number one in Europe, which perhaps needed to be constrained. This proposed a reaction in France 'Vers une prédominance allemande'.[8]

There has therefore been an interesting reversal of the original situation, from 'binding Germany in'[9] to 'binding in France'.[10] This new situation, which for Germany meant equality for the first time since the war, was however perceived in France as a new inequality. France repeatedly attempted to constrain German strength by consolidating the European integration process, particularly evident by French insistence on the inclusion of the EMU chapter in the Maastricht Treaty in return for EU and French support for German unification. However, this is no longer acceptable to the Germans, because firstly it seems it is part of a French European order under French leadership, second because it seems to reflect suspicion and finally it also prevents Germany from 'binding in herself' i.e. depriving her of the right of self-determination.[11]

After the coming into power of President Jaques Chirac Franco-German relations suffered a set-back. In addition, domestic affairs in both countries deteriorated. Juppé's rightwing government was defeated by Lionel Jospin's leftwing coalition, forcing a weakened Chirac into cohabitation. In the Federal Republic Chancellor Kohl had only narrowly won the 1994 general election, thus limiting his margin for manoeuvre during the run-up to the Amsterdam negotiations. Disputes on macroeconomic policies, particularly Chirac's apparent ambivalence over monetary union on the eve of the Amsterdam summit, constituted a major difference to the stimulating role of the Mitterrand–Kohl era during the negotiations for the Maastricht Treaty. The weakness of the Franco-German axis was largely responsible for a compromise treaty, since Kohl for electoral reasons was obliged to block efforts to streamline EU's decision-making. With his soul-mate, Mitterrand, as well as friends Delors and González gone, the German Chancellor had become a lonely and isolated figure on the European scene.

The Franco-German duet is therefore not without its dissonances. Within the grand design of a strong, united Europe there hide, more or less successfully, fundamental philosophical and tactical differences. They give Franco-German cooperation its particular flavour of suspense, periodically allowing the voices of Cassandra to be heard above all others, and accusations of French arrogance and German selfishness to fly across borders. The *sine qua non* condition of and ultimate limit to European integration is that of convergence of national interests. Reduced to its bare bones the issue of national interests is neither a natural nor an objective concept. It is what the ruling governments perceive as national interests. It could be reduced to ensuring the security and prosperity of the state and these notions themselves are open to wide interpretations and risks of obsolescence.

This study of the Franco-German axis in the 1990s is not another book among the many recently published on Franco-German relations. This is both a re-interpretation and assessment of the salient aspects of the 1990s and the changing contours of a unique and fluctuating relationship. Rather than covering a specific period of the European integration process, this study is an issue-analysis (which is of course in part linked to specific periods). The empirical focus of our study are the three momentous issues which illustrate most forcefully the new directions and the stakes of both Franco-German relations and the European Union as the century drew to a close; the launching of a Single Currency, the forging of a Common Foreign and Security Policy (CFSP) and the expansion of the Union into Eastern Europe (Chapters 4, 5 and 6). Although at different stages of development, these three issues are likely to dominate the transition of Europe either towards further integration or towards dilution and, at its worst, fragmentation, and are a real test of the durability of the Franco-German partnership and the vitality of an enlarged European Union. These three chapters are preceded by a brief analysis of the major factors which have shaped French (Chapter 2) and German (Chapter 3) approaches to European issues. The last section (Chapter 7 and the Postscript) concludes with a number of findings.

As the focus of our study is recent events, we faced a dilemma as to the sources available. We have used academic texts to construct the framework and background to the analysis and a variety of sources ranging from speeches by politicians and civil servants to EU documentation down to journalistic comments to interpret contemporary developments. The latter in particular may not have always been without bias. We have tested our findings by interviews with decision-makers and academics. All interviewees have been granted total anonymity. By using such a variety of sources we feel that the outcome of our analysis is reasonably accurate.

Because of the three topics chosen, and for practical reasons as well as constraint in terms of length, we have treated the two countries as unitary actors or as one common actor. We have therefore deliberately ignored the domestic bargaining process in France and Germany in an attempt to simplify decision- and policy-making in both counties. This meant that we were also able to reduce the complexity of the decision-making process at the EU level. Our aim was to identify a pattern of Franco-German cooperation in these three areas and to analyse how and why France and Germany, who may have originally occupied opposite ends of the spectrum, eventually arrived at agreements, i.e. at the 'Franco-German position'. Once established, it became acceptable to the majority of member states.

In researching this topic, we faced several problems. How do we explain this relationship? What analytical framework is there for two actors operating in a regional system and who have within that system developed a sub-system of their own? No agreement either among politicians or academics has been reached on the concept 'Europe' in the integrative sense, nor on the term 'European', though the latter has been mostly used as a synonym for Western Europe.[12] There is also no consensus on the ultimate objectives of the integration process. Since regional integration is a relatively new field of analysis for political scientists, and as a systematic study of an empirically based theory has had a life-span of just over five decades, no convincing theory has emerged explaining the process of European integration, let alone the Franco-German duo. The general conclusion which might be drawn is that the process of European integration has not developed in the way that was expected by theoreticians or that 'events in Europe continue to outpace academic theory'.[13] All major schools of empirical integration research have an ephemeral character and have limited powers of explanation. Integrative activities have declined from time to time, most notably so in the 1970s and again in the early 1990s, when there was a clear spill back to national authority and intergovernmental bargaining, also evident in the Amsterdam Treaty.

The major battle in theoretical terms has been between state-centric theories, which explain the integration process as the combined efforts of two or more states pursuing national interests,[14] and the supranational theories, where the central institutions of the EU are the driving force of the integration process gaining jurisdiction over hitherto 'national' policy domains.[15] The former, i.e. intergovernmental model, emphasises the resilient capacity of national governments to constrain the growth of supranational institutions. Since the term has been universally applied to post-war international political and economic systems and is not exclusive to Western Europe, it seems to appeal to scholars and politicians who have observed the changing image of the EU and for whom the evolution of the EU is still an open question. The approach has its usefulness when describing, for example, the relationship between Council and Commission in terms of the growth of authority of the former, particularly since the 1966 Luxembourg compromise when it became clear that France was unwilling to accept progressively more majority voting in the Council. Intergovernmental interpretations of the process of European integration underline some trends in the evolution of the Community: for example the creation of the Committee of Permanent Representatives (CPR) as an obstructive organ to the decision-making process at transnational level. Periodic summit meetings of heads of governments since 1969 formalised by the creation of the European Council in 1974, seem to provide some evidence in support of intergovernmental interpretations of the Community's development. Joint decision-making was timid and cumbersome in the beginning: the institutional framework as conceived in the 1950s was the result of a compromise between federalists and traditionalist forces, with an unelected Commission and hybrid Council both legislating on common issues and safeguarding member states' national interests with limited use of majority voting. Integrative efforts, particularly in the area of foreign policy, have in the past largely been based on intergovernmental bargaining between member states. Yet for all the flaws in the institutional set-up of the European Community, the intergovernmental approach does not sufficiently recognise the consensus-building mechanism and the use of majority voting which has been applied in the Community, at least since the entry into force of the Single European Act (SEA), nor the development of a Court with power of judicial review. And although the Franco-German axis has received significant attention, the relationship has not been subjected to a systematic analysis and 'not even the "intergovernmentalist" theorists of European integration ... have devoted much energy to divulging its inner workings.'[16]

By contrast, supranational theories emphasise the automatic element in the integration process predicting as a consequence of economic and political 'spill-over' (functionalism) from one political area to another, the creation or development of supranational organs and the demise of nation-state power.[17] There is some evidence of this. The European Union has changed in several ways since its launching in the 1950s: it has long gone beyond the mere regulating of member states' economics. Supranational decision-making now encompasses areas of so-called 'high politics' e.g. foreign and security policies.[18] Not only have policies been added thus expanding the competence of the original EEC institutions, but importantly the inter-institutional relations of the Commission, Council of Ministers, Parliament and Court of Justice have altered and have acquired a more 'federal' character. The three treaties of 1986, 1992 and 1997 and the draft treaty of Nice have been attempts to manage the increasing complexity of the institutional framework. Yet the significant increase in the powers of the directly elected European Parliament has not fully compensated for the lack of transparency of a singularly arcane decision-making process, nor has the Commission succeeded in dispelling European public's mistrust of its commitment to open government and of its management capabilities. This may well be misdirected criticism: the system has survived four enlargements and a vast expansion of policy areas. Nevertheless, the prospect of further considerable and costly enlargements and the apparently growing disaffection of the populace give institutional reform a tone of urgency which can no longer be ignored.

France and Germany, whose declared priority is the achievement of an ever closer union, will procrastinate at their own cost.

The theoretical divide between supranational and state-centric theories dominated the 1990s although, since neither are satisfactory theories, theoreticians have tried to complement these with other theories, such as multi-level structures of governance which offer a model by which competencies are shared between actors at different levels and not monopolised by state executives,[19] or by giving importance to the rise of crossnational transactions creating pressures for supranational governance (transnational exchange theory),[20] or indeed combining elements of the two aforementioned major schools of theory.[21] The question might also be raised whether the EU is unique and requires a theory of its own. But, if it is argued that the EU is a unique political institution, its development and dynamics cannot be generalised by theoretical explanations.[22]

Thus, even if the evolution of supranationalism has been slower to emerge than predicted by neo-functionalists, it is nevertheless proceeding at an erratic pace. Those who believe in the expanding logic of functional integration expected the demise of the Franco-German axis as 'the engine in European Integration'. And indeed it has been observed that the Franco-German 'motor' and its influence on EU decisions has, although still dominant, declined since the 1970s.[23] This view is not however supported by this study: on the contrary, it is argued that France and Germany have engineered and controlled the processes under review, albeit to variable degrees.

Neo-functionalists predicting the demise of the nation-state would disregard the role of the two countries arguing that power has slipped away from them to supranational organs. But if neo-functionalists are right, what explanation can be given for the continuation of the Franco-German axis, which survived despite the end of the Cold War and the collapse of bi-polarity, despite German Unification and despite periodic enlargements of the EU with ever more 'actors' involved in the decision-making and bargaining processes? It has been shown that France and Germany are both capable of power-sharing between themselves, and of surrendering, irrevocably, sovereignty to independent institutions which in turn have grown both in sheer numbers and in terms of competence. Of course the process of setting up a supranational institutional machinery was initiated by France and Germany (among others), sometimes even in the face of considerable resistance from some member states. What came first: the supranational set-up or the Franco-German axis? The Treaty of Rome clearly preceded the 1963 Elysée Treaty, but the Schuman Plan relied on and took for granted Franco-German collaboration. France and Germany were originally the actors by determining the transfer of certain sovereignty to certain new institutions, but beyond that they appear to have had faith that these institutions would safeguard their interests and that in the end the gains would far outweigh any perceived or real loss. As a general rule, the two countries' involvement has been restricted to the launching of institutions or policies. Once the institutions were running and the policies operating, while constant improvements were carried out, there has never been an occasion of 'doing away' with any of them. This may be because the blending process is controlled by both states, though to varying degrees (as we shall see when we compare, for instance, EMU with the CFSP), but there will be a point when the created institution takes on a life of its own.

Thus theoretical approaches to the European integration process have met with scepticism as they have inevitably failed to explain the full complexity of developments in the European Union. Our aim is not to replicate the various integration theories or put forward yet another proposition for a theory of integration despite recent criticism that theoretical interpretations of the Franco-German relationship have been absent from all major studies.[24] On the whole, theories have come up with explanations as to why small states support integration, but the same does not apply to large states.[25] In the case of the Franco-German alliance the focus of political scientists has been the role played by the French Presidents and German Chancellors. This is not to say that theoretical models do not have valuable guides to understanding the trend of integration. Nevertheless the search for a suitable political model to fit present cooperative relations within the Union may not be an urgent task. This is because it appears not only that attitudes and expectations regarding regional integration are shifting, but the Union is developing at a speed sometimes dictated by developments in the international community, caused by external pressures, sometimes generated by its own dynamics. 'Europe and the world live in an era of accelerating political processes and developments which are truly breathtaking'.[26]

While we do not feel that Franco-German relations rest on a strong theoretical foundation, de Schoutheete's theory of a 'sub-system' inside a larger whole is an interesting and helpful model.[27] He offers three categories all of which comprise elements of a 'sub-system'. First is that of a collective leadership, a kind of directoire which emerges when certain actors are called upon to play a leading role. This applies to Franco-German relations in many instances, starting from the ECSC to the EMS but does not cover all aspects of the relationship and above all does not fully explain why the integration process has been initiated in the first place. Secondly, a situation may be described as a sub-system when there are attempts which serve to defend and preserve certain positions acquired prior to the joint effort. This applies to some degree to France which had a position to defend but does it really reflect Germany's defeated post-war situation? And, finally, a sub-system may be designed for those who wish to press forward in a specific field, a situation which has been captured by the term two-speed or variable geometry. Elements of this have been articulated for example by the Lamers/Schäuble paper 'Reflections on European Policy', which defines the Franco-German axis as 'the hard core of the hard core'.[28] But this too has only limited relevance.

The features which make the Franco-German relations a 'classical sub-system' in de Schoutheete's view is that it is (among others) durable. This is self-evident. Early Franco-German attempts at cooperation and integration are often overlooked: a European customs union was already discussed during the late 1920s. During that time Briand, the Foreign Minister of France and Stresemann, his German counterpart and later Chancellor of Germany had been working out a plan on a kind of European federation. And although early attempts came to a sudden halt both by Stresemann's death and the world economic crisis in 1929, a Franco-German committee set up in 1929 continued to function until 1932.[29]

The second most important element of a classical sub-system is its formality i.e. Franco-German relations are legally underpinned by the Elysée Treaty of 1963, which is 'a treaty of friendship which formed the cross-party basis of the unique network of relations between the two countries. Over the years, these relations have acquired an in all probability almost unparalleled intensity'.[30] As has been emphasised cooperation between countries needs to be 'organised', i.e. a zone of agreement has to be created that makes co-operation possible.[31] Third, such a system also has to be effective: '…we knew that the European economies were unable to withstand the turbulence of the international economy. That's why we wanted the collaboration and the common success.' Thus Helmut Schmidt was emphasising that only by pooling resources can governments hope to survive.[32] And finally the Franco-German sub-system has to be acceptable. According to Giscard d'Estaing 'Where Germany and France are in agreement, Europe advances, where Germany and France are divided, Europe stagnates.'[33] This has been echoed by Germany: 'Whenever Germany and France were at odds, both countries, and, an even greater calamity, the whole of Europe were plunged into disaster. Whenever both countries see eye to eye over the past 40 years, the process of European integration was given a decisive fillip.'[34] There is therefore a uniqueness in the Franco-German axis, which also seems to be implied by de Schoutheete. 'This leads to the conclusions that, other than the Franco-German axis, no bilateral relationship can qualify as a sub-system in the European whole.'[35] But although 'no two other counties in the world have developed such close cooperation as Germany and France',[36] it is not clear in what aspects the Franco-German axis differs from other bilateral relationships and the reasons why these two countries play for such high stakes.

Despite the dilemma we faced in explaining the Franco-German axis in theoretical terms, this book is not a defence of the 'sub-system' theory nor is the Franco-German duo perceived as an 'alliance in an alliance'[37] or indeed as

'Siamese twins'.[38] In a sense, it is a 'one off', because can one theorise on a relationship that is unique? We believe that France and Germany have created their own system unique to them, cemented by formal and informal links and based on mutually beneficial bargaining processes often involving trade-offs between the two countries. Thus this study is an attempt to analyse what has been called the 'cooperative hegemony of France and Germany'[39] which may have a particular attraction for declining powers (France) or for those which may be burdened with particular constraints (Germany) and thus are either unwilling or unable to exercise power on their own. The leadership by these two countries is accepted and tolerated so long as it serves the construction of Europe which they initiated, so long as it overcomes hesitation, stagnation and obstacles in this task, so long as it points to solutions and opens new avenues. As long as the relationship remains a key element in Europe's stability the other member states will not be alarmed by the Franco-German directorate. But, having said this, we do not feel we need to prove this hypothesis, as the effectiveness of the Franco-German axis is a long established fact. Indeed, as has been observed, it has become 'so central and obvious'.[40] Our interest purely lies in understanding the Franco-German dialogue of the 1990s when Europe was faced with challenges which are virtually unparalleled. Inevitably however, in an attempt to draw a fuller picture, we frequently referred to the past to point out continuities or indeed to speculate as to the direction the two countries and the EU were heading.

We believe therefore that predictions can be made with reasonable certainty. The Franco-German partnership is based on a like-minded assessment of political issues equally important to both countries: the new and radical phenomenon released by the Schuman Plan is not that the French and German governments no longer perceive their respective national interests as antagonistic, but that they perceive them as complementary. In the final analysis it is not possible for either Bonn or Paris to overlook the other partner's interests in the EU. No effective reform or new ventures can be agreed upon until these two calculate that visible disharmony is more dysfunctional than relinquishing sovereignty in areas where in the short term loss of status, and possibly of earnings at the national level, is a very real deterrent to supranational decision-making. It is for this reason that conflicts have not seriously impeded the evolution of the Franco-German dialogue, although the relations between the two countries suffer from ups and downs as a result of domestic political pressures.

The basis of the Franco-German axis is a shared objective, i.e. a strong and integrated Europe: both countries feel that their respective fortunes are tied up with and safeguarded by the Union. The success of the Franco-German axis does not depend on spontaneous empathy, but on the actors' political will to reconcile divergent positions for the sake of their common objective. It is this shared vision which allows no compromise. In identifying it, both France and

Germany accepted their interlocking needs, arising out of geographical proximity, a shared painful history and a common future. Indeed, at the root of Franco-German relations might even lie a 'shared sense of weakness'.[41] Both countries have needed European integration: France because it wanted to secure a place as a global player in the multi-polar international system,[42] Germany because it perceived the EU as a legitimate vehicle for the articulation of national interests. Certainly this assessment of French and German motives is banal, but nevertheless relevant: both countries, in the 1950s, started from a position of weakness and the joint realisation that the Community was the answer to pressing domestic needs while, at the same time, it would dilute economic (German) and political (French) power in a larger European framework. In that sense integration became synonymous with, as Pedersen put it, 'extension of national power': for both countries the EU has become a tool of influence.

We believe therefore that the process of Franco-German cooperation, that is, the Europeanisation of both institutions and policy-making in the two countries, is irreversible. French and German identity of interests have worked towards a mutual concern to extend and reinforce economic and political integration. Both countries will therefore strive to preserve the achieved in order to ensure their respective economic and political viability in a changing European and world order and they will thus maximise their capabilities within the system that they have helped to create.

NOTES

1. P. Frank, (1983), 'Twenty Years Franco-German Treaty', in *Aussenpolitik*, **34** (1), p. 29.
2. Ernst Welteke (1998), 'Franco-German Economic Relations', in David P. Calleo and Eric R. Staal (eds), *Europe's Franco-German Engine*, SAIS, European Studies, Brookings Institution Press, Washington, pp. 93–4.
3. See for instance Patrick McCarthy (ed.) (1993), *France-Germany 1983–1993. The Struggle to Cooperate*, Macmillan, London. Haig Simonian (1985), *The Privileged Partnership*, Clarendon, Oxford. Roy Willis (1965), *France, Germany and the New Europe 1945–1963*, Stanford University Press, Stanford. Thomas Pedersen (1998) *Germany, France and the Integration of Europe*, Pinter, London and New York. Robert Picht and Wolfgang Wessels (eds) (1990), *Motor für Europa?*, Europa Union Verlag, Bonn. Colette Mazzucelli (1996), *France and Germany at Maastricht: Politics and Negotiations to Create the European Union*, Garland Publishing, New York. Douglas Webber (ed.) (1999), *The Franco-German Relationship in the European Union*, Routledge, London and New York.
4. For details and frequency of bilateral meetings and consultations see Webber, *ibid.*, p. 2–3.
5. See D. Lawday (1979), 'The Odd Couple', *The Economist*, 26 May, see also F. Stern (1980), 'Germany in a Semi-Gaullist Europe', *Foreign Affairs* (1).
6. McCarthy (1993), *op. cit.*, p. 10.
7. Helmut Schmidt (1990), *Die Deutschen und ihre Nachbarn*, Siedler, Berlin, p. 173
8. Title of an article in *Le Monde*, 16 July 1993.
9. See Rainer Zitelmann, Karlheinz Weissmann and Michael Grossheim (eds) (1993), *Westbindung. Chancen and Risiken für Deutschland*, Propylaen, Berlin.
10. *The Economist*, 28 August 1993, p. 14.

11. Ingo Kolboom (1994), 'Dialog mit Bauchgrimnmen?', *Europa-Archiv*, **49** (9).
12. J. Lodge (1983), *A History of Thought on Economic Integration*, Macmillan Press, London.
13. Charles Pentland (1973), *International Theory and European Integration*, The Free Press, New York, p. 146.
14. Andrew Moravcsik (1991), 'Negotiating the Single European Act', in Robert O. Keohane and Stanley Hoffman (eds), *The New European Community: Decision-Making and Institutional Change*, Westview Press, Boulder, pp. 41–8. Moravscik (1993), 'Preferences and Power in the European Community: A Liberal Intergovernmentalist Approach', *Journal of Common Market Studies*, **31** (4), 473–524.
15. See for instance Alberta Sbragia (ed.) (1992), *Euro-politics: Institutions and Policy-Making in the 'New' European Community*, The Brookings Institution, Washington, DC. Wayne Sandholtz (1992), 'ESPRIT and The Politics of International Collective Action', *Journal of Common Market Studies*, **30** (1), 1–22. K. Lenaerts (1990), 'Constitutionalism and the Many Faces of Federalism', *American Journal of Comparative Law*, **38** (2), 5–64.
16. Webber, (1999) *op. cit.*, p. x.
17. Ernst H. Haas (1958), *The Unity of Europe*, Steven & Sons Ltd, London and Ernst H. Haas (1964), *Beyond the Nation State*, Stanford University Press, Stanford.
18. Helen Wallace and William Wallace (eds) (1996), *Policy-Making in the European Union*, 3rd edn, Oxford University Press, Oxford, pp. 16–17.
19. S. Bulmer (1994), 'The Governance of the European Union. A New Institutional Approach', *Journal of Public Policy*, **13** (4), 351–80. John Peterson (1995), 'Decision-Making in the European Union: Towards a Framework for Analysis', *Journal of European Public Policy*, **2** (1), 69–93. F.W. Scharpf (1988), 'The Joint Decision Trap: Lessons from German Federalism and European Integration', *Public Administration*, **66**, Autumn, 239–78. Gary Marks, L. Hooge and K. Blank (1996), 'European Integration from the 1980s: state-centric v. multi-level governance', *Journal of Common Market Studies*, **34** (3), 341–78.
20. See for instance Alec Stone Sweet and Wayne Sandholtz (1997), 'European Integration and Supranational Governance', *Journal of European Public Policy*, **4** (3), 297–317. Thomas Risse-Kappen (1996), 'Exploring the Nature of the Beast: International Relations Theory and Comparative Policy Analysis Meet the European Union', *Journal of Common Market Studies*, **34** (1), 53–80.
21. Robert O'Keohane and Stanley Hoffman in William Wallace (ed.) (1990), *The Dynamics of European Integration*, Pinter, London.
22. Wayne Sandholtz and John Zysman (1989), '1992: Recasting the European Bargain', *World Politics*, **42** (1), October, 95–128.
23. Webber (1999), *op. cit.*, 9–12.
24. Pedersen (1998), *op. cit.*, 5–7. The author attempted to fill this gap by offering his 'realist' interpretation of the relationship, and Mazzucelli (1996) *op. cit.* focuses on the role of new politics-administrative actors in the EU's constitutive politics.
25. Alan S. Milward (1992), *The European Rescue of the Nation-State*, Routledge, London.
26. Klaus Kinkel (1994), 'Deutschland und Europa', *Europa-Archiv*, **49** (12), p. 335.
27. Philippe de Schoutheete (1990), 'The European Community and its sub-systems', in William Wallace (ed.), *The Dynamics of European Integration*, Pinter, London.
28. Karl Lamers and Wolfgang Schäuble (1994), 'Überlegungen zur Europa-Politik', CDU/CSU Fraktion des Deutschen Bundestages, 1 September.
29. Thomas Pedersen, *op. cit.*, p. 70.
30. Rudolf Scharping (1994), 'New Challenges for Franco-German Co-operation', *Aussenpolitik*, **45** (1), p. 3.
31. See Matthias Kaelberer (1997), 'Hegemony, Dominance or Leadership? Explaining Germany's Role in European Monetary Cooperation', *European Journal of International Relations*, Sage Publications, **3** (1), 35–60.
32. Helmut Schmidt (1990), on the EMS, *op. cit.*, p. 220.
33. Valerie d'Estaing, quoted by Schmidt, *ibid.*, p. 288.
34. Scharping, *op. cit.*, p. 3.
35. de Schoutheete, *op. cit.*, p. 112.

36. Klaus-Peter Klaiber (1998), 'Europe's Franco-German Engine: General Perspectives', in Calleo and Staal, *op cit.*, p. 38.
37. This refers to the title of an earlier study on the subject, Robert Picht (ed.) (1982), *Das Bündnis im Bündnis. Deutsch-Französische Beziehungen im internationalen Spannungsfeld*, Severin & Siedler, Berlin.
38. *The Economist*, 26 May 1979.
39. Pedersen, *op. cit.*, p. 6.
40. Gilles Andreani (1998), 'The Franco-German Relationship in a New Europe', in Calleo and Staal, *op. cit.*
41. *Ibid.*, p. 25
42. *Frankfurter Allgemeine Zeitung* (1997), 'Chirac ruft Botschafter nach Paris', 13 April.

2.   French self-perceptions of France's role in Europe: A historical perspective

Unlike Pallas Athene, who was born fully armed from Zeus' head, Europe was not born from Robert Schuman's head on 9 May 1950, although the event marked him and itself for historical immortality. Throughout this last half-century, the construction of Europe has been the single most tenacious political imperative of French foreign policy, enabling France at the same time to reconcile herself to the status of a medium power, and to claim the role of a major international actor through a European Community that might, in de Gaulle's bowdlerised words, extend one day from the Atlantic to the Urals.

Any self-respecting account of the development of the European idea mentions l'Abbé de Saint-Pierre, Michelet or Victor Hugo among others, who dreamt of some form of European unity. Nearer our time it is impossible to omit the then French Foreign Minister Aristide Briand who presented his project to the general assembly of the League of Nations at the ill-fated time of September 1929. The former French Prime Minister Edouard Herriot, in his book *Europe* published in 1930, gives a detailed account of the work carried out by experts as a result of Briand's proposal.[1] An international Federal Commission for European Cooperation was convened and produced a questionnaire of astonishing topicality. On considering the main headings of the enquiry, one cannot help but notice that, with very little updating, they could be applied to the current progress in European integration:

I.

    a) Should one aim to extend European cooperation beyond the field of economics to the field of politics?
    b) If yes, should the political aim be:
       1. A unitary state?
       2. A federal government?
       3. Units included in a broader unit such as they exist in the present system of the League of Nations or the British Commonwealth?

These questions remain pertinent, and are still debated, the general one about 'post-euro' Europe, the more specific ones either in academia or among certain pressure groups, and No. 3 about WEU and NATO and about the Single Market and a broader North Atlantic Free Trade Area.

II.

Should European co-operation aimed at by the Commission include:
a) The Soviet Republic?
b) Turkey?

The current negotiations towards enlargement raise exactly this type of debate.

III.

Should European co-operation aimed at by the Commission include collaboration with:
a) the autonomous dominions of the British Empire and India;
b) the colonies or non-autonomous dependencies of European states which have a representative of government;
c) the colonies or non-autonomous of European states whose government is 'controlled' by the parent state;
d) the United States of America and the other parts of the world?
And what kind of collaboration should be devised?

Although there are no colonial empires any more, collaboration with ex-colonies was explicitly endorsed and codified in the successive versions of the 1975 Lomé Convention.

IV.

Should one consider setting up regular meetings of Foreign Affairs ministers in Geneva, under the auspices of the League of Nations, in order to deal with issues of European co-operation?

The very evolution of political cooperation into the present Common Foreign and Security Policy is an exercise in European cooperation.

V.

Do you approve of:
a) the recommendations of the 1927 World Economic Conference?
b) The proposals for a customs truce of the 10th session of the League of Nations?
Can we envisage the conclusion of collective trade treaties open to European states?
What would be the most appropriate means to reach this aim?

The creation of a customs union by the Treaty of Rome is the direct consequence of the lessons learnt from the poor results of the 1927 World Economic conference and the entrenchment behind tariff walls in the 1930s.

VI.
>   Additionally to economic issues, should the scope of European co-operation aimed
>   at by the Commission include:
>   a) issues of public and private law;
>   b) public education;
>   c) earth, water and air transit and communication;
>   d) post office, telegraph, telephone and radiophone;
>   e) public works;
>   f) credit and currency;
>   g) public health, physical and moral welfare;
>   h) police;
>   i) agriculture and fisheries, including economic biology;
>   j) immigration;
>   k) working conditions;
>   l) remaining administrative issues, to be specified

These chapter headings resurface almost literally in the Treaties of Rome (agriculture and transport), Single European Act (SEA) (environment, education, sea and air transport, telecommunications, procurement), Treaty on European Union (TEU), First Pillar (currency, public health) and Third Pillar (police, immigration).

VII.
>   In order to scrutinise these issues more closely and to co-ordinate the results of
>   such a scrutiny, should one attempt to create:
>   a) a research body;
>   b) in that case, should the financial support of governments be sought for that
>   body;
>   c) would it then be wise to ask one or two people to prepare a report on the issues
>   detailed above;
>   d) do you wish to suggest other proposals, in preference to those mentioned above
>   in a) b) and c), for the examination of these problems

It is quite fascinating to realise that, once allowance is made for historical change that makes reference to the League of Nations, the Soviet Republic, colonies or dependencies redundant, virtually every single one of the issues mentioned in the questionnaire has either been dealt with in the Treaties, from the competences of the European Commission to the Lomé Conventions, or has lost nothing of its topicality and sensitivity, such as relations with Russia or the creation of a North Atlantic Free Trade Area (NAFTA). Throughout this century, mostly because of the two world wars, but also because of the evolution towards a global economy, there has been a sometimes slow, sometimes accelerated maturation of the concept of European unity.

In response to the questionnaire, a committee of French experts advocated not just economic, but political, administrative, intellectual and moral (*sic*) cooperation. It also considered that such a creation would only be possible if framed in a general programme of solidarity and justice, through the actions of governments and the conclusion of treaties. It added that it was necessary to have an entirely new model, which had yet to be developed. 'Only the future will gradually release the contours of the institutions most likely to approximate the ideal in the name of which we would like to conduct a practical and gradual experimentation of European solidarity.'[2]

In contrast to this lofty, highly abstract and philosophical French ambition, Herriot summarises the views of the corresponding German committee as follows: 'It is advisable to create a federation of European states, the main aim of which must be to guarantee for these states the security and freedom of their economic and cultural development, and to grant them, by means of gradually abolishing intra-European barriers, the same economic advantages that the great indivisible territory of the United States of America offers its population'.[3]

There in a nutshell lies the fundamental cleavage between French and German ambitions for Europe. The French consider European unification, under whatever name and form, as the ultimate guardian of a *European* civilisation based on the principles of the 1789 Declaration of the Rights of Man and Citizen. The implementation of this project must be *formally* codified, through the agency of governments, their commitments enshrined in treaties. The concept being entirely new in essence, the constitutional institutions entrusted with its realisation can only *gradually* be shaped following the perceived needs as they emerge. Conversely, the Germans go for the model they know best – federalism – even though they mention the USA and not the previous constitutional forms of their own protean territory. In a pragmatic manner, they advocate as a first step what amounts to a common market, and have in mind the economic and cultural development of the new entity.

The French had little chance to implement Briand's proposals. In France, the 1930s were a time of parliamentary disintegration, of timidity approaching cowardice in foreign policy, of economic protectionism. Ideological jousts provoked both by the communist and the fascist camps endangered parliamentary democracy and eventually precipitated its downfall as much as the military defeat of 1940. A Hitler-dominated Europe appealed only to an insignificant minority – as testified in such documentaries as 'Le Chagrin et la Pitié'[4] – whereas the French and other European resistance movements signed and published in Geneva in July 1944 a *Manifesto of the European Resistance* calling for a federal Europe which would include Germany.[5] After 1945, enthusiasm for a federal Europe, in France mostly prevalent amongst political elites, did not survive the debate that divided 'Carolingian' continental pro-federal Europe (minus Germany, not yet a state then) and 'Anglo-Saxon' Nordic anti-federal Europe. However, the threat posed by the Cold War and the emergence of a new, democratic, 'American-sponsored' Germany, concentrated minds on narrowing options for French foreign policy.

Interestingly enough, two decades after the Briand Memorandum, the Schuman Declaration of 1950 stated that Europe could only be built through 'concrete steps', the first one being a common market in the field of coal and steel production and distribution. It also stated that the ultimate aim was a European federation. In other words, the Schuman Declaration, directly inspired by the pragmatist banker and international civil servant Jean Monnet, was much closer to the German than to the French previous comments on the Briand-generated questionnaire.

That evolution probably occurred as a result of the French obsession since the beginning of the century: security. Both Schuman (born 1883) and Monnet (born 1888) were men of that epoch, witnesses, and, in the case of Schuman, a victim of repeated Franco-German hostilities. The sham victory of 1918 produced the pan-European convictions of Aristide Briand. The military and political collapse of France in 1940 produced the commitments of a Jean Monnet, a Robert Schuman and, incidentally, of a François Mitterrand. That Briand was unsuccessful is due mostly to the 1929–39 international economic and political tensions, and to the nationalistic reflexes thus induced. That Monnet and Schuman were successful is of course due to the hard lessons learnt from the trauma of defeat and occupation, and the realisation that 'France was not at Yalta, and must therefore find a new partnership to ensure first of all her security, then her prosperity and international status. Her ambition went back to the Briand project: peace and security through economic integration. Another consequence of what might be called 'the 1940 plus Yalta syndrome', in other words a profound national humiliation, was the resentment against what was often perceived as dancing to the American tune, notably under the IVth Republic. That was picked up with particular acuity by de Gaulle and the Gaullists, and it echoed with immense resonance in the national psyche. Hence the continuing obsession with independence, which explains both the IVth and the Vth Republics' concern to develop the 'force de frappe' and France's dramatic and generally popular withdrawal from NATO's integrated command in 1966.

France's progress towards European unification is indeed characterised by repeated attempts to reconcile contrary principles. In a country that is the traditional home of cartesian rationality, that progress looks extraordinarily chaotic. The first set of contrary principles is the coexistence of federalism and 'souverainisme', resulting in what one might call, after Richard Mayne in a slightly different context, the Echternach dance: five steps forward and three steps back.[6] That was already apparent in Briand's speech to the Assembly of the League of Nations, when he stated: 'the federal link, which would leave the sovereignty of any nation entering such an association untouched, can be beneficial.'[7] After the war, France, still in a weak position and struggling to rebuild her economy, but above all concerned about her security, was prepared to surrender some degree of sovereignty as stated in the Preamble of the Constitution of the IVth Republic: 'On condition of reciprocity, France will accept those limitations to her sovereignty which are necessary for the organisation and defence of peace.'[8] Indeed, when in the winter of 1948–9 ten Western European governments negotiated the setting up of the Council of Europe, France (together with Belgium) pressed for a strong political organisation of a supranational character, but was defeated by Britain, with the result that the Consultative Assembly was essentially a debating forum, even weaker than the weak Committee of Ministers which was strictly intergovernmental, and acted by consensus. This continental enthusiasm for supranationalist – though hardly federalist – solutions still pervaded the Treaty of Paris creating the European Coal and Steel Community, and to some extent the Treaty of Rome. But when de Gaulle took power, he made it absolutely clear that the protagonists in intra-European politics as well as in the wider international environment, were the states.

The maligned IVth Republic had accomplished a fundamental task for which it received little recognition. It had overturned the French traditional view of Germany as 'l'ennemi héréditaire' and made Germany the most favoured partner,[9] and it had initiated the long march towards European economic integration. It was de Gaulle, however, who put the weight of his immense prestige and authority into redefining the terms and setting the limits of France's contribution to the construction of Europe. De Gaulle was profoundly influenced by his own reflections on history, and the Gaullist language is highly charged. Words such as rank or independence were not to be taken lightly, but were genuine beacons lighting his political itinerary. Economic integration, because it had been set in train, would not be upset, but the real task was to build a union of European peoples, a 'European Europe', i.e. without Britain who would only have turned Europe into an Atlantic system. This European Europe must include Eastern Europe, though of necessity in an indeterminate future. In order to build this Europe, German cooperation was essential, because 'at the heart of the problem and at the centre of the continent, lies Germany. It is her destiny that nothing can be built without her.'[10]

This Franco-German partnership was sealed in the 1963 friendship treaty, which has endured to this day in spite of inauspicious beginnings. Although neither de Gaulle's plan for a political union nor his plan for a Europe that would reach to the Urals came to fruition in his life time, the first one is being slowly developed, and the second one figures prominently in the present enlargement agenda. What de Gaulle achieved was to make the partnership with Germany not just acceptable, but popular with French public opinion. At the same time, by reasserting the possibility, indeed the necessity of French independence, he raised the morale and the pride of the French electorate, so badly damaged by the dramatic events of decolonisation and the discomfiture of the IVth Republican State. And here we meet the second set of contrary principles which beset France's views of European integration: French independence within European interdependence. For de Gaulle it was axiomatic that Gaullist France, while working for the benefit of France, was working for the good of Europe, and indeed for the good of the world. For France's partners, that was not axiomatic: hence the failure of the Fouchet Plan (see Chapter 5). Hence too Germany's preference for the Washington nuclear umbrella, infinitely more credible and therefore more comfortable than France's dwarf nuclear force, the first French atomic weapon being derisively nicknamed 'grapefruit' by the French themselves!

Predictably, there was a cool international reception of de Gaulle's announcement in March 1966 that France was withdrawing from NATO's integrated command. That policy, however, continued to be upheld by de Gaulle's successors, because it enhanced France's independent position and in addition successfully stimulated French efforts to develop her deterrent force to the point when it eventually overtook Britain's in the 1990s.[11]

Nevertheless, this insistence on narrow cooperation within the European Community, which in practice meant acceptance of French political leadership, while maintaining a defiant stance of independence within the Atlantic Alliance, could lead to accusations of inconsistency, if not two-faced behaviour. Moreover, de Gaulle's attempt at a rapprochement with Moscow from 1966, which he might have conceived as an elegant way of eventually solving the German problem, could also be viewed by France's partners as a threat to the cohesion of the Atlantic Alliance and more obviously designed to challenge the position and resolve of the United States than to ensure the protection of Germany. Indeed, de Gaulle's repeated warnings that the United States might not forever be willing to maintain their military commitment in Europe could be suspected of becoming a self-fulfilling prophecy. De Gaulle's questioning of the justification for and immutability of the bi-polar world had a rationale of its own for France and perhaps also for Europe, except that it seemed somewhat foolhardy to upset the balance thus maintained without having first established a solid European security system. That, however, never even reached the drawing board stage. By 1969, in any case, de Gaulle's popularity had long been on the wane. Not only had he failed to convince Germany to embrace his views on European security, but his own electorate was deserting him, and his authority was undermined beyond repair by the 1968 student rebellion which engineered the strike of 10 million people, from the workers of Sud-Aviation to the actors of la Comédie Française. It was not de Gaulle, but his Prime Minister Georges Pompidou who engineered the restoration of public order, himself succeeding to the Presidency of the Republic in June 1969.

Dying just under five years later, and very ill for the last two, Pompidou made less of an impact as President than he had done in his six years as Prime Minister. In other words, he was more versed in internal than in external politics. Nevertheless, he acted decisively in a direction that went straight against Gaullist doctrine by announcing at the Hague Summit meeting of December 1969 that France would no longer object to British membership of the European Community. In fact, Pompidou, who had been a banker until de Gaulle appointed him Prime Minister, took a pragmatic view of politics, and, in contrast to de Gaulle, was more interested in economic than in political integration. He would find in Britain a strong supporter of the maintenance of the nation-state and therefore of intergovernmental procedures, and a useful counterweight to Germany's growing assertiveness as examplified by Brandt's *Ostpolitik*. As a consequence of his interest in the industrial regeneration of France in general and his attempts to safeguard France's monetary stability, he tended to consider Germany more as a rival than an ally, although well aware of France and Germany's unquestionable interdependence in European matters.[12] The situation was not helped by the presence of a brilliant but cantankerous Foreign Minister, Jobert, who famously battled with the American Secretary of State Henry Kissinger and who dissociated himself from Germany on energy policy (in fact isolating France), and a vindictive Agriculture Minister (Helmut Schmidt called him brutal and 'impertinent in the pursuit of French peasants' interests'[13]), one Jacques Chirac, who accused his German counterpart of duplicity on possible reforms of the Common Agricultural Policy. Within the difficult international environment of an unstable monetary order and a serious oil crisis unleashed by the Yom Kippur War, the presence at the helm of the state of personalities with very strong nationalistic instincts projected an image of a France more concerned to lay down her law than to nurture European solidarity.

Pompidou's France had been a conservative bourgeois country aiming at prosperity in preference to grandeur. Giscard d'Estaing, 48 years old when elected to the Presidency in the spring of 1974, wanted to add a youthful streak to this image while anxious to maintain France's 'dignity and independence.'[14] He also wanted to put an end to what he called the country's 'moroseness'. One of the key words of Giscardian rhetoric was 'décrispation', which translates more or less as 'loosening up', and Giscard's personal style would alternate between relaxed and regal. His first Foreign Affairs Minister, Jean Sauvagnargues, was the former French Ambassador to the Federal Republic, and the third one, Jean François-Poncet, formerly general secretary of the Elysée, well-known for his pro-European views, was the son of André François-Poncet, the eminent diplomat who had been ambassador to Berlin in the 1930s.

Clearly Germany was at the forefront of Giscard's international agenda. His friendship with Helmut Schmidt, dating from the time when both of them were Finance Ministers, would help iron out many a disagreement, political or otherwise. Both coming to power in May 1974, they would actively cooperate for a full seven years, and remain friends long afterwards, probably to this day. Chancellor Schmidt's first foreign visit was naturally on French soil. After the turmoil and misunderstandings of the previous five years, the air needed clearing. The press called the visit 'Europe's last chance... they must reflect on the rescue of Europe'.[15] Inheriting from de Gaulle a constitutionally robust France and from Pompidou a modernised economy, Giscard was intent, on the one hand, upon making friends as widely as possible, on the other, making France's voice heeded and respected throughout the world.[16] Under his presidency, France's policies would focus primarily on Europe and Africa. The two aspects were actually combined to produce the Lomé Convention codifying privileged trade relations between the European Community and African, Caribbean and Pacific countries, the negotiations for which had actually been started before 1974. The still unresolved oil crisis suggested the pursuit of a North–South dialogue between oil producers and consumers through which Giscard wanted to inaugurate a 'new international economic order', but which found little echo among France's partners. Giscard more fruitfully initiated the institutionalisation of European summit meetings into a European Council, and the formalisation of meetings of the most industrialised nations which were to become the G7 meetings. It was also during his term of office that European Political Cooperation (EPC) developed, and the Nine were successful negotiators in the development of the Conference on Security and Cooperation in Europe (CSCE). He was proud of having overseen France's military power to the third place in the world, and her export performance reached fourth place. No federalist, he nevertheless encouraged the holding of direct elections to the European Parliament. His most lasting monument to the development of European integration was undoubtedly the setting up, jointly with Helmut Schmidt, of the European Monetary System (EMS). This answered Giscard's determination to ensure the progress of European integration without compromising French formal sovereignty.[17] And this, in his opinion, would be best achieved by the closest of alliances with Germany, perceived not as the rival feared by Pompidou, but as the most powerful and steadfast partner, thus adding to rather than diminishing France's weight in the world.

There were, however, some areas of foreign policy, indirectly connected with the development of Europe, where the close Franco-German partnership was put to the test. French forays into African internal conflicts such as periodically erupted in Zaire and Chad, without prior consultation within the European Political Cooperation machinery, was a stark and not particularly welcome reminder that France was also engaged in world politics as a solo performer. Of more immediate concern to Germany, Giscard, like his two predecessors, also signalled to the Atlantic Alliance, and, by ricochet, to the Warsaw Pact countries, that France meant to maintain as far as possible, amicable relations with Eastern Europe. The destabilisation of that area, triggered by the Soviet invasion of Afghanistan, reactivated the Cold War reflex of the West. Giscard, however, tried to play the part of trouble-shooter, and, without any mandate from his European partners, flew to Warsaw in May 1980 to meet Brezhnev, stating the position of the Nine without getting real assurances of a Soviet withdrawal. That particular initiative proved very unpopular with French public opinion, while in contrast Chancellor Schmidt chose to interpret this surprising move as a positive step, easing the way for his own visit to Moscow, after consultation with his European partners, a few weeks later.[18] That summer, contrary to Germany, France sent a team to the Moscow Olympic Games which were boycotted by many Western states.

Destabilisation of Eastern Europe took another dramatic turn that same summer, when the workers of the Gdansk shipyards went on strike and started the Solidarnosc movement demanding a more liberal regime. Another Soviet intervention could be feared, although it did not materialise. In spite of tremendous French public sympathy for the strikers, Giscard adopted a singularly neutral stance, obviously careful to spare the prickly feelings of the Soviet bear. In any case, he was soon to be defeated in the Presidential election of May 1981.

At a time when 'moroseness' had pervaded not only French society, but also and perhaps more worryingly the supporters of European integration, a good deal of reassurance came from the steadfast Franco-German partnership. Helmut Schmidt quoted a French television interview of the French President on 27 January 1981: 'France and the Federal Republic of Germany represent the nucleus of Europe. It is not a matter of exclusive relations: but the Franco-German reconciliation has in the last decade made its mark on the history of Europe. We cooperate very closely with Germany; and this has not altered in any way in the recent past.' Asked by the interviewer whether he had any doubts about the loyalty and solidarity of the German partner, Giscard answered: 'No doubts whatsoever.'[19]

On 10 May 1981, after 23 years in power, the right wing or centre-right wing parties were defeated, and a left wing coalition that included the communists came into power. The new President, François Mitterrand, was no neophyte in politics. He had held his first ministerial office in 1944 at the age of 28, as junior minister for the War Prisoners and Veterans, and had been the candidate of the left for the Presidency of the Republic at every presidential election since 1965 except in 1969. Having attended the European 'Hague Congress' in May 1948, he was a confirmed European integrationist, but he was also elected as leader of the left. Attending his first European Council in Luxembourg in June 1981, he got blank looks from his partners when he advocated the development of a European social space, i.e. an area covered by European-wide social policy. His concern for the underprivileged, this time those of the developing world and particularly Central America, met an equally frosty reception at the North–South Cancun summit meeting in October 1981.[20]

Moreover, France's new experiment in internal social 'solidarity' having had a pernicious impact on the French public purse, Mitterrand found himself confronted by a stark choice in the last week of March 1983: either pursue a policy of economic autonomy in defiance of European Community rules, or accept stringent European economic and financial discipline, which meant curtailing economic measures designed to buttress the social solidarity panel of his political platform. His decision confirmed his lifelong commitment to Europe and the limits of his socialist agenda. And Franco-German relations would continue to be the centrepiece of France's European policy. Having got on well with the socialist Helmut Schmidt, he was going to develop an exceptionally close friendship with the Christian-Democrat Helmut Kohl, and under their joint auspices (buttressed by Jacques Delors in Brussels), European integration would experience a remarkable revival. In his speeches, in his copious writings, President Mitterrand, whose policy aims were generally notorious for their sibylline quality, consistently showed himself a clear and unwavering supporter of European unification, which he saw as the natural historical development of the continent. Again and again, he reiterated the 'fundamental truths', that is that Germany is of Europe, without Germany there is no Europe, without Europe, there will not be, there will no longer be German grandeur.'[21]

The challenge was considerable. Having felt the harsh effects of economic recession in the 1970s and early 1980s, France was undergoing a ruthless economic restructuration accompanied by a policy of financial orthodoxy to support the policy of the 'franc fort' underpinning the implementation of the EMS. The electoral cost was high: the electoral defeat of the left in 1986 brought about a new experience of 'co-habitation' during which Mitterrand had to accommodate the policies of his unwelcome Prime Minister Jacques Chirac. Clashes on the European front were however minimal, due in part to Chirac's conversion to the cause of European integration.[22] While Mitterrand's re-election in 1988 gave him *carte blanche* to pursue his European policies, he was no longer followed by public opinion, which eventually demonstrated its weariness by approving the signature of the Maastricht Treaty by the slenderest of majorities. Not only was the country suffering from European fatigue, disenchantment with the Commission seen as remote and bureaucratic, and discord between those voters who felt that the Treaty was too timid in its institutional initiatives and those who felt that too much of the national identity and economic interests had been sacrificed on the altar of European integration. A section of the electorate was also demonstrating its perception of a powerful Germany which might henceforth impose her will on a weakened French Republic.

This illustrates in a striking manner the relationship between French presidents and the French electorate. The Vth Republican constitution is vague in its prescriptions for the shared power of the President and the Prime Minister. But as early as 1959 a doctrine developed according to which foreign policy and defence are the 'domaine réservé' of the President. De Gaulle, who was keen to confirm his legitimacy by referendums, never held a referendum on foreign policy. Up to Maastricht, the only president who did, revealingly, was Pompidou, and that referendum (1972) was on French approval of British membership of the European Community, though it was judged by political parties to be a covert plebiscite for other policies. The 1992 referendum was the first, and up to the time of writing the only one, in which public opinion was actually consulted on the substance of European integration. Nor did it help much, if at all, that a copy of the treaty was sent to every elector. It is pretty well universally accepted that foreign policy is a matter of relative indifference to electorates. European policy, however, is no longer a matter of pure foreign policy. The Vth Republic has been neglectful of public sensitivities, partly because of the weakened status of the French Parliament and partly because decision-makers tend to deem the technical complexity of European-related issues as beyond the grasp of the average citizen. 'Government by ENA' graduates may be a caricature of reality, but there now emerges a sense that European policies have been nurtured in the greenhouses of the technocrats, revealing a paternalistic and mistrustful attitude towards French citizens.

One issue of foreign policy about which the electorate is more sensitive, however, is that of Germany. Although the two countries have devoted sustained efforts and resources to develop a high degree of mutual knowledge, in particular among their younger generations, it has been thrown off course as it were, by the issue of reunification. Unhealthy fears and resentment were heightened by the additional realisation that the collapse of the Soviet bloc potentially restored in Central and Eastern Europe the economic hinterland which had made Germany so threatening half a century earlier. Without on the whole suspecting any expansionist designs by her eastern neighbour, France was aware of the balance of power gradually tipping towards Germany. Even the prospect of a further enlargement, which included Austria, Finland and Sweden, appeared to add more linguistic, cultural and ideological weight to the germanophone, lutheran and free-trading elements of the European Union.

Mitterrand's pyrrhic victory in the 1992 referendum was followed by an electoral defeat of the left in 1993 which consequently entailed a return to co-habitation with the right in the twilight of the Mitterrand era. The issue of Europe did not figure in the presidential campaign of 1995. However, in an article in the French daily *Libération* of 25 March 1996, President Chirac reaffirmed: 'Since the war, the European enterprise has been – and remains – the guarantor of reconciliation and peace. But in a new environment... Europe needs a major political project... This project rests on a remodelled European architecture, monetary union and far greater account being taken of the peoples' social and cultural aspirations... Identity, efficiency, democracy, enlargement, these must be the catchwords of the reform of the European architecture'. He went on to suggest a number of areas where reforms and new initiatives could take place. Clearly, President Chirac had no wish to let Europe remain stagnant.

A few weeks earlier, two days after Mitterrand's death, the highly respected veteran journalist Jean Daniel emphatically praised Germany: 'Germany is an examplary democracy, whose decentralised administration is flexible and humane. Moreover she is one of the world's countries welcoming the most immigrants. The extreme right is much weaker there than either in Austria or in France. Last but not least, Germany has demonstrated in the course of the last twenty years a loyalty towards Europe hardly found anywhere else. She could well be the country that maintains the most rigorously the tradition and the impulse which Jean Monnet always wanted to create'.[23]

Approaching the end of the new Intergovernmental Conference (IGC), it seemed that the French elites, at least, were aware of the dangers both of European stagnation, and of a loosening of the links which had turned the Franco-German partnership into the much vaunted motor of European integration. A former French Ambassador to Germany noted in 1997 that 'popular support (for Franco-German friendship) is no longer what it was up to 1980'. He continued that economic problems have weighed on French and German citizens, with twinnings going dormant, Franco-German societies in need of rejuvenation, and prejudices once more resurfacing, while mistrust of Europe was spreading.[24]

In such perceptions, however, could be detected the third set of contrary principles in France's progress towards European unification. For France, obsessed throughout the century to maintain security, is European unification an end in itself, or a means to a covert end, which is the control of Germany? In his very last New Year's address to the French on 31 December 1994, one year before his death, President Mitterrand entrusted his countrymen with two precepts: '1. Do not ever dissociate liberty and equality. 2. Never separate the grandeur of France from the construction of Europe. This is our new dimension and our ambition for the next century'.[25] Like the visible face of the moon, this has light and relief, and gives a good sense of orientation. But there could be a hidden face, where speculation wins over certainty. One form of speculation was developed in an article of the *Frankfurter Allegemeine Zeitung* in early 1997, which cleverly analysed the work of the French scholar Georges-Henri Soutou. The author of the article noted that Soutou repeatedly used the word *arrière-pensées*, ulterior motives, when dealing with Franco-German relations. Ulterior motives on both sides indeed, but on the French side the wish to maintain control over Germany. A reunified Germany, a Germany now pursuing national interests openly and almost brazenly, suddenly seems to slip away from the embrace of France, and France is worried. According to Soutou, France, by pushing for monetary union, was trying to maintain some degree of control, however tenuous, and that was worth the sacrifices France was making by conforming to the criteria for membership of EMU, however detrimental to French social policy.

Whatever interpretations and doubts one may entertain, and whatever stresses periodically occur between France and Germany (and the last decade has experienced quite a few) there remains an unquestioned postulate that only when France and Germany conclude a deal can European integration move on. In Amsterdam there was no pre-arranged deal, and no significant institutional reform was agreed. French and German statesmen, whatever their personal inclinations, tend to support each other in times of crisis. In 1996 Kohl loyally abstained from criticising President Chirac's carrying out of nuclear tests in the south Pacific when German opinion did so, and loudly. The new Prime Minister Lionel Jospin returned the kindness to Chancellor Kohl in 1997: at the Weimar Franco-German meeting he gave up his attempt to set up an economic government to control the European Central Bank, which the Germans were opposed to, although he and his party were worried that the ECB might sacrifice growth and employment, two prominent goals in the government's programme on the altar of financial rectitude.

In the three areas on which this book concentrates, France has had to meet considerable challenges, each of a distinctive nature. Monetary union has long been a French ambition, dating back to the times when the economist Raymond Barre, who was Prime Minister when Giscard and Schmidt concluded the Bremen agreement on the European Monetary System, was a member of the Commission. Monetary Union demanded sacrifices from Germany,[26] but was achieved thanks to persistence and mutual concessions. The aims were clear, and the perceived role of the French was to sweep away obstacles to their realisation.

Foreign and security policy is a different matter altogether. Just as close to the heart of national sovereignty as currency, it is far more difficult to circumscribe. Matters are further complicated by the pre-existence of a security system, the Atlantic Alliance, in which France and Germany have behaved in opposite ways: the French wanting to loosen the American grip on it, the Germans to maintain it. Moreover, the very scope of European foreign policy and security needs to be redefined. Foreign policy is inherently sensitive to change in the international system; and for the past ten years, change in the international system has been radical. It has been hard for the French and the Germans to adjust to change and back each other up when their respective national interests and strategies have affected them differently. In that field, the United Kingdom, which was present from the first days of political cooperation, was a very active partner with assets more or less similar to the French (such as a nuclear capability and a permanent seat in the Security Council) and its security principles closer to the Germans (a primary reliance on NATO for national seucrity), all of which further complicate matters. The French were therefore torn between contradictory hopes and fears. The hopes and ambition were to create a European policy of substance making Europe a major international actor *per se*. The fears were that French sacrosanct independence might be sacrificed on the altar of Atlantic security and that Germany might not welcome the prospect of an increasingly active role beyond the confines of the European Union.

Finally, eastward enlargement implies policies which start as foreign policy and end up as domestic European policy. The French have traditionally been hesitant supporters of enlargement. For all of de Gaulle's dream of a Europe from the 'Atlantic to the Urals', the French felt at their most comfortable in a Carolingian Europe, i.e. the Europe of the Six. Having recognised that this was neither practical nor even desirable, they have not repeated de Gaulle's erstwhile rejection of British membership, although they consider the contemporary prospect of Eastern enlargement with mixed feelings. While it is bound to increase German influence and impose enormous financial costs on present member states, it nevertheless is an indisputable way of avoiding political destabilisation in Europe and its attendant human, political and economic costs, which the catastrophe of Yugoslavia has demonstrated *a contrario*. The official French rhetoric is one of full support, provided that Community institutions are first reformed. This reform was at the very core of the Intergovernmental Conference which was concluded by the Nice Treaty in December 2000 at the end of the French Presidency. On financial aspects of enlargement, French behaviour in the preparatory budgetary negotiations of 1999 under the German Presidency has been hard bargaining, particularly on agriculture (see Chapter 6).

Analytically separate, and dealt with by various institutions or various personifications of the Council, all these issues are nevertheless intertwined. Hence the perpetuation of the package deal in European negotiations. Those negotiations are essentially carried out by civil servants. It is interesting to note that, increasingly, experience of and in Community institutions is a *sine qua non* condition of a successful career for high fliers in the French civil service.[27] French interest in European affairs is not on the wane. It is still mostly confined to political and social elites, but these elites are being trained to formulate their points of view on a broader base than that of the Hexagon. And that at the very time when Germany is learning to take into consideration her national interests as possibly distinct from the European interest! Yet again the Franco-German pulse is badly synchronised. The question is whether the lessons of the past, which clearly show that there is no substitute for Franco-German cooperation to keep European integration flowing, retain their topicality. It is a question to which an insight into the development and present handling of policies in the three areas of our concern ought to provide an answer.

NOTES

1. Edouard Herriot (1930), *Europe*, Les Editions Rieder, Paris, Chapter 3, pp. 54–61. Incidentally, it is interesting to note that Herriot, who became speaker of the National Assembly after the war, actually voted against the European Defence Community in 1954. True enough, defence membership, deemed to put the interests of French Mediterranean farmers at risk. This concern was actually shared by other parties, including on the left.
2. *Ibid.*, p. 57 (our translation).
3. *Ibid.*, p. 61 (our translation).
4. 1971 film – originally for French TV – directed by Max Ophuls and Robert Harris, and based on extensive interviews about occupied France.
5. Kevin Wilson and Jan van der Dussen (eds) (1993), *The History of the Idea of Europe*, Routledge, London and New York.
6. Richard Mayne (1970), *The Recovery of Europe*, Weidenfeld and Nicolson, London, Chapter 9.
7. Quoted in Herriot, *op. cit.*, p. 49 (our translation).
8. See text of Constitution of the Fourth Republic, reproduced, e.g. in Philip Williams, 3rd edition (1964), *Crisis and Compromise, Politics in the Fourth Republic*, Longmans, London, Appendix I, p. 479.
9. When Schuman gave his press conference on 9 May 1950, Adenauer responded positively within twenty four hours, and this symbolically marked the emergence of Germany as the privileged partner in the construction of Europe.
10. Charles De Gaulle (1979), *Mémoires d'Espoir*, Plon, Paris, p. 182.
11. André Dumoulin (1996), 'Les Armes nucléaires et l'Europe', in *Memento Défense-Désarmement 1995–96. L'Europe et la sécurité internationale*, GRIP, Paris, pp. 226–226. The following figures are given: UK nuclear weapons systems (beginning 1996): 136 delivery vehicles, c. 300 warheads. French nuclear weapons systems (beginning 1996): 186 delivery vehicles, 512 warheads.
12. Haig Simonian (1985), *The Privileged Partnership*, Clarendon, Oxford, Chapters 4–5.
13. Quoted in Helmut Schmidt (1990), *Die Deutschen und ihre Nachbarn*, Siedler Verlag, Berlin, p. 190 (our translation).
14. Giscard d'Estaing's electoral manifesto, quoted by Alfred Grosser (1989), *Affaires Extérieures*, Flammarion, Paris, p. 256.
15. Helmut Schmidt *op. cit.*, p. 190.
16. John Frears (1991), *France in the Giscard Presidency*, Allen and Unwin, London, p. 95.
17. The French doctrine on supranationality is that the State has exclusive competence, including that of transferring totally or partially certain competences to the European Community Institutions through the Treaties, and that, *stricto sensu*, does not constitute a limitation of sovereignty. Cf. Labouz, Marie-Françoise, (1988), *Le système communautaire européen*, Berger-Levrault, Paris, p. 48-9.
18. Helmut Schmidt, *op. cit.*, p. 207.
19. *Ibid.*, p. 209.
20. Hubert Védrine (1996), *Les mondes de François Mitterand*, Fayard, Paris, p. 189.
21. François Mitterrand (1986), *Réflexions sur la politique extérieure de la France*, Fayard, Paris, p. 95. The book is a reprint of Mitterrand's main foreign policy speeches delivered in France and abroad, preceded by a long introduction which is the author's personal manifesto on foreign policy.
22. In the European electoral campaign of 1979, Chirac's Gaullist or at least strongly nationalist

party had campaigned in fairly violent terms against the German invasion of France by economic means. One of the other elements of dissatisfaction was the prospect of Spain's membership, deemed to put the interests of French Mediterranean farmers at risk. This concern was actually shared by other parties, including on the left.

23. *Le Nouvel Observateur*, 10 January 1996.
24. Jacques Morizet (1997), 'La Coopération franco-allemande après le sommet de Weimar' in *Défense Nationale*, December.
25. Text of Mitterrand's address reproduced in *Le Monde*, 3 January 1995.
26. In his book *Les mondes de François Mitterrand*, Hubert Védrine *op. cit.*, pp. 419–20 records a conversation between Kohl and Mitterrand at the Madrid European Council of 26–27 June 1989:
    FM: You must commit yourself on monetary union...
    HK: Giving up the Mark is an enormous sacrifice for the Germans. Public opinion is not ready yet!
    FM: I know that, but do it! European opinion is waiting. You are going towards German unification. You must prove that you continue to believe in Europe.
27. Cf 'L'éveil européen des énarques', *Le Monde*, 30 June 1999.

3.   The 'German' conception of Germany

BACKGROUND

Germany's restless search for identity and unity has troubled the peace of Europe for two centuries, affecting the destinies of Germans and non-Germans alike and provoking 'some of the longest, deepest, most contorted answers ever given to any question by any branch of humankind'.[1] Within the span of a single lifetime, Germany has experienced imperialism, a post First World War republic, dictatorship, two world wars during which she almost destroyed herself and much of central Europe and total political and moral bankruptcy. The 'German question' or the 'German dilemma', a legacy of both the old Reich and the Second World War partition, has only been partly laid to rest by the ending of the East-West confrontation and German Unification on 3 October 1990. Thus 'the German future makes no sense without the past'.[2] While Germany of today may have little in common with that of yesterday, the search for identity, the typical (German) self-doubt and above all the yearning to be accepted as a 'normal' state has its root in the turbulent history of the country. Once deliberately opting for political and ideological *Sonderweg*,[3] Germany has seen herself as 'a special case';[4] the difference however is that this phrase, once an expression of pride, has become a source of shame.

The reason why Germany or the 'German question' has been and still is paramount in people's mind and intertwined with the fate of Europe is not merely due to Germany's military or economic power. The history of Europe has been marked by the geographical position occupied by Germany and the historical destiny of Germany on a European scale is not just due to economic strength. Far more important than the military clout of *Wilhelmine* Germany and the Third Reich or the economic prowess of the Federal Republic is Germany's geographical position. A hundred years ago Germany occupied the central territory between Latin and Slav countries. Until recently she was on the borderline between two hostile camps with each half of her territory firmly integrated into two opposing blocs. The two Germanys were the focus of the Cold War, the centre of European division, the battle-field between the two superpowers. Today, United Germany has become the moving force in the new East-West collaboration and, as the location of a strategic centre, Germany's fate seems once again to be inextricably intertwined with that of Europe. As Bismarck once said: 'The only constant in foreign policy is geography.'[5]

The search for a stable geographical and political identity has not been an easy one for Germany. In fact, as has been noted[6] 'there are few nations whose history contains as many broken threads as Germany's'. If it is true that 'to have an identity is to know "where you're coming from" when it comes to questions of value, or issues of importance',[7] how could Germany have an 'identity'? Until 1871 she was merely a geographical expression with some recognition of cultural and economic affinity between a confederation of states, i.e. a *Kulturstaat*, but this cannot be said of the (German) consciousness of national existence which may be as old or older than that of England or France. The absence of a truly national state set Germany apart from other countries which had already established their nation-state. And unlike other nation-states the creation of a single state had not been the product of a historical process extending back over several centuries, but state building and national consolidation had been the work of one short decade and one single statesman (Bismarck) who forged unity by means of diplomacy, coercion and several wars (1864, 1866 and 1870). Germany's rise to power was dependent on territorial conquest: the annexation of Alsace and Lorraine following the Franco-Prussian war of 1870–71 resulted in a permanent Franco-German conflict which was only resolved by the Second World War and the establishment of the EEC. 'German unification under Prussian leadership was thus to a considerable extent the product of military victory, and first and foremost victory over France.'[8]

The creation of the new state in 1871 was accompanied by enormous economic expansion. The *Wilhelmine* Empire was characterised by a discrepancy between rapid (though somewhat belated) industrialisation and political immaturity. Between 1871 and 1914 the population increased from 41 to 65 million accompanied by the corresponding growth of large cities at a speed only matched by that of the United States. This enormous economic vitality generated sufficient force to assert German hegemony over Europe. Bismarck's more limited *Realpolitik* ('Until ... the departure of Bismarck the Prussian government showed a certain amount of self-restraint in its pursuit of power'),[9] whose major objective was maintaining Germany's position in the centre of Europe, had given way to *Weltpolitik* under what was to be Germany's last Emperor, Wilhelm II. As Germany outstripped her neighbours both in terms of population and industrial output, she demanded a 'place in the sun'. Yet, the young state was crippled in several ways: as a late-comer both in terms of power and nationhood[10] the new *Machtpolitik* contained ignorance and insecurity. Germany, whose collective memory was still disturbed by both the devastation resulting from the 30 years war as well as the Napoleonic occupation, felt her chance of survival as a nation-state threatened. 'We are compelled to obtain space for our increasing population and markets for our growing industries', 'we now must decide whether we wish to develop into and maintain a world empire, and procure for German spirit and German ideas that fit recognition which has been hitherto withheld from them'.[11] Mistrust of other countries even extended to her toying with the idea of a 'preventive' war[12] thus justifying a *Sonderweg*. Insecurity was replaced by self-assertiveness and self-aggrandisement. 'We must create a central European economic association ... [which] will not have any common constitutional supreme authority and all its members will be formally equal, but in practice will be under German leadership and must stabilise Germany's economic dominance over *Mitteleuropa*.'[13] Thus Germany became a threat to European equilibrium and a disruptive factor in international politics.

Germany's first experience at democracy was hampered by externally imposed restrictions. The condition of the Treaty of Versailles made it difficult for the Weimar Republic (1919–33) to consolidate itself. In the event it proved unable either to meet the strains imposed by the world economic depression or to overcome the deep social division of the Weimar society. The weakness and disintegration of the Weimar system were inextricably tied up with the impact of German anti-democratic sentiments. The Republic disintegrated because it failed to develop a state consciousness. Although there had been first attempts at integration under Gustav Stresemann, the one time Foreign Minister and German Chancellor, who in 1926 shared the Nobel Peace prize with his French counterpart, Aristide Briand, in recognition of their efforts at Franco-German reconciliation, the world-wide crises of 1929 ended the phase of consolidation and led to political radicalisation and polarisation which gradually paralysed democratic institutions. While it would be unfair to argue that the spiritual climate of the Weimar system had underpinned the rise of totalitarian forces, the democratic movement was nevertheless unable to take root and the young republic fell an easy victim to Nazism. The Third Reich (1933–45) deliberately picked up the Prussian tradition, restoring continuity and a historical consciousness by promising a greater and powerful Germany.

It was only after the ensuing catastrophe which ended with the Second World War that Germany experienced a drastic political economic and social transformation. The experience of dictatorship, the impact of expulsion, division and occupation, the effect of post-war dislocation and isolation had a traumatic effect on the German people from which they have never fully recovered. 1945 was a complete break in Germany's history and marked the beginning of revolutionary changes in its political and economic conditions. Germany's complex situation, making her the 'prize, the pivot, and the problem of European politics'[14] shaped post-war economic and political policies. And the creation of the Federal Republic as well as the German Democratic Republic, both of which were devised by others in the absence of any expressed will on behalf of the German people still living under occupation rule was the result of international politics: both were 'artificial products of *raison d'état*'.[15]

This chapter argues that the main factor determining Germany's post-war policies, particularly in terms of the European integration process, has been the German perception of its history. Although this has been more pronounced during the immediate post-war decades and despite significant structural changes since, Germany's '*Europa-Politik*' has nevertheless been characterised by a great degree of continuity. Yet there are three major cycles: first, the 1950s and 1960s being the 'transitional period' as laid down by the Treaty of Rome when Germany sought refuge in EEC (and by implication French) decisions; the second phase, between the early 1970s and early 1990s when Germany began to equate financial and political investments into the Community with the consolidation of the integration process and the third phase, which probably began as early as 1990 and became more pronounced in the later part of the decade and may be characterised by a distinct articulation of 'German' interests and attempts to globalise German foreign policy.

PHASE I: THE POLITICS OF DEPENDENCE

Given Germany's background, it is not hard to see why she has opted, in the late 1940s and early 1950s, to 'submerge in the greater unity of Europe'.[16] It is important to understand that the desire to be part of a European Community, to pass sovereignty upwards to a European level, is laid down in the Preamble of the Basic Law[17] which states: 'to serve the peace of the world as an equal partner in a united Europe'.[18] This decision becomes operational via Art. 24 of the Basic Law which expresses the willingness to transfer sovereign powers to inter-governmental institutions. Founded on the provisions of the Basic Law, the Federal Republic therefore became a member of post-war international organisations, in particular the EEC. This was a conscious renunciation of national power politics as an organising principle reinforced by bitter historical lessons and the recognition that security and international influence were only possible in cooperation with her neighbours, above all with France. Indeed, Germany has been described as the 'first post-national state'.[19] On launching the European Coal and Steel Community (ECSC), Chancellor Adenauer declared: '... nationalism, the inveterate evil of Europe, will be dealt a death blow'.[20]

There were of course also practical reasons for joining the European integration process. Having traded emancipation for cooperation and integration, Germany reaped enormous advantages from integration, both economic and political. The new Federal Republic established by the three Western Allies in 1949 had only very limited and revocable measures of sovereignty. Adenauer, the first Chancellor of the FRG, was determined to return Germany to the cultural and political forces of western Europe, to recover the basis of national power, to rehabilitate the FRG after the atrocities of the Third Reich and to effect a lasting rapprochement with the Allies, which above all included a fundamental reconciliation with France. Membership of post-war international organisations led to a growing acceptance of the post-war West German state because as 'paradoxical as it may sound, the Federal Republic of Germany became sovereign to the same degree that it let itself be integrated into the Western alliance'.[21] Thus questions of 'surrendering sovereignty' never applied, as the Federal Republic could not surrender powers it had not (yet) regained. While Germany as a result of Allied control became the 'most penetrated national system' in Europe, it was able to utilise the penetration channels to her advantage and transmute her dependence into interpenetration and interdependence. This meant that originally one-sided control panels (by the Allies, later her partners) were replaced by integration arrangements.[22]

Thus Germany has invested in the EEC diplomatically, economically and institutionally. The post-war Federal Republic's formative development was bound up with the project of the EEC. No state has gained more from integration in terms of international prestige and influence than Germany: participation in the integration process was a 'low risk/high pay off proposition'.[23] Consequently, support for the European integration process has been one of the major elements of post-war German foreign policy. *Westpolitik* i.e. the integration into Western Europe which had at its core Franco-German collaboration, became a post-war German *Weltanschauung* and became firmly embedded in the political philosophy of German policy-makers at least until German Unification and even beyond that until the change of government in 1998. To that extent it can be argued that integration into the Western family of nations temporarily compensated for the loss of territorial unity and national identity.[24] '… Our identity is so irremediably lost that one may wonder whether we can still speak of a German nation'.[25] The absence of nationhood meant therefore that the Federal Republic was particularly suited to integrating herself into supranational arrangements.

Passionately craving stability and resolutely rejecting risky independent ventures, successive post-war governments have seen the EEC as a means to achieve international respectability. Preferring a sedate conformity rather than old-style superiority, Germany avoided conflict in the EEC by deliberately constraining the pursuit or maximisation of national interests in the Community, at least during the first two decades of the EC's existence. It was typical for all post-war governments to pursue a European policy characterised by modesty in a deliberate attempt to convince EEC partners that the FRG would accomplish very little without her partners. Adenauer, being a somewhat autocratic, patriarchal leader, might have felt that it was necessary to impose discipline and order on his people to prevent a recrudescence of nationalism. The signing of the Franco-Germany friendship Treaty – within days of De Gaulle's veto of British EEC membership in January 1963 – was Adenauer's crowning achievement in his attempts to Europeanise the German people. Thus it was Germany's shameful past which shaped her pro-European policies. In the new post-war culture of restraint, there was a deliberate avoidance, even denial, of solitary leadership. Power, if exercised at all, was mediated by the EEC or by other international fora. Integration had been the road to sovereignty, economic reconstruction, equality at the international level and finally even to German unification. In a curious way the U-turn after 1945 to democracy and moderation was an expression of (German) 'extremism'. Perhaps this is why post-war Germany is still being eyed with suspicion. The sudden change from imperialism and totalitarianism to the establishment of a stable democracy simply seemed too radical to be true.

PHASE II: PERIOD OF TRADE-OFFS

This enduring pro-European consensus dominated subsequent decades despite subtle shifts in the articulation of Germany's *Europa-Politik* during the 1970s and 1980s when national interests were redefined and at times even rigorously pursued.[26] The 1970s were the beginning of a careful cost-benefit analysis by German governments: in an attempt to perpetuate the benefits realised in the two post-war decades Germany began to equate its perceived interests in the EC with financial contributions made to the common budget, the latter was no longer considered as an unavoidable sacrifice to be made on the altar of European integration.[27] Attempts to maximise German interests in a Community framework have therefore, at times, conflicted with European aspirations. Germany has clearly pursued state interests: the *Bundesbank* has repeatedly put German interests above those of Europe's (see Chapter 4). Throughout the 1970s and 1980s Germany insisted on an agri-technical device, Monetary Compensatory Amounts (MCAs), which insulated the German agricultural price level from the effects of national currency changes and kept it some 10% above the common price level. When in the early 1980s the Community faced bankruptcy, Chancellor Kohl, at the June 1983 Stuttgart summit, insisted that increases in the common budget would have to be part of a wider 'package' which included ratification of Spanish and Portuguese membership. He stubbornly refused to 'untie' the 'package' during three subsequent European Council summits: at Athens in December 1983, at Brussels in 1984 and at Fontainebleau in 1984, when the issues were finally resolved to German satisfaction. In 1990–91 Germany unilaterally raised interest rates thus forcing her EC partners to bear some of the unification costs. The currency crisis of 1992 when both the Italian Lira and the Pound Sterling were forced out of the Exchange Rate Mechanism (ERM) only served to underline the leverage the German central banking had attained. An even greater conflict was produced when Germany broke ranks with her Community partners and recognised the two former Yugoslavian breakaway states Croatia and Slovenia.

But perhaps the most striking example of German assertiveness occurred in 1985, when the Federal Republic for the first time in its EC membership evoked the Luxembourg Compromise by refusing to adopt a Commission-proposed reduction in farm prices. Referring to 'vital national interests', the German Agricultural Minister at that time, Ignaz Kiechle, launched an impassioned attack on the Commission: 'I get the impression that the Commission is using a strategy which is clearly directed against Germany .... One must not go against a big Member State which has always been very co-operative.'[28] The German move was of exceptional gravity, because the veto took place on the eve of the meeting of the European Council in Milan, the very aim of which was to call an Intergovernmental Conference (IGC) on institutional reform to do away with the national veto. Instead of which the German action only encouraged to maintain the system, although Chancellor Kohl subsequently undertook a massive effort to restore his country's credentials albeit at the 11th hour.

The story of the German veto highlights the restriction domestic interests impose on European policies. In the case of the 1985 cereals issue Germany found herself in conflict between domestic priorities and European aspirations: the former frustrated the official European line. While continuously articulating a commitment to European integration, Germany nevertheless has, on occasion, orchestrated a highly national response to Community policies. As a result, German policy-makers have displayed at times a confusing pattern of attitudes to the Community. Again, this can be explained by Germany's historical legacy. Attitudes during that time were exclusively dominated by demands of Germany's political system and by strategic and psychological factors. To this end, the FRG imposed a set of priorities on domestic and foreign policy objectives, the nature of which indicates her deep faith in material wealth as a guarantor of social stability and as a strong force against anti-democratic groups. Haunted by the spectre of the failure of Weimar which resulted in Nazi tyranny, all post-war German chancellors have believed that the FRG's much acclaimed political stability was based very largely on economic security which could only be provided and guaranteed by the EC. The stirring of memories about Nazi Germany triggered from time to time, for example by the rise of far-right parties, the debate on Poland's western border in the run-up to German Unification and recently the new wave of claims against German industry and finance by US and Eastern European Holocaust victims, all of which received widespread coverage both in Germany and abroad, has emphasised Germany's obsession to safeguard the survival of its political and economic system. Unemployment, recession, social unrest and political extremism are acutely felt in Germany since it brought about the death of German democracy in the 1930s. '*Stabilität über alles*' and '*Keine Experimente*' remained the hallmark of Germany's policies.[29] This cautious attitude to all issues touching the very nerve of the country's existence explains the vigour with which Germany has at times striven to preserve its economic security and political stability. In that sense German post-war policy-makers have perceived periodic attempts to maximise German interests in a Community framework as perfectly legitimate.

It has been argued[30] that the reasons for Germany's somewhat ambivalent relations to the Community during that time is partly explained by the need to promote simultaneously German Unification and European integration, and partly as a result of its post-war system (e.g. ministerial autonomy, coalition politics and an independent *Bundesbank*). As far as the last is concerned, 'its independence is legendary' and its 'obduracy sends ripples around the world.'[31] There is also evidence[32] that ministerial autonomy and the importance of coalitions in decision-making have had a decisive impact on the formulation of common policy. However, while all post-war German governments have clearly been pro-integrationist, revealing a new post-war *Realpolitik*, the other twin aim of the Basic Law, namely German Unification, has always been viewed as unrealistic.[33] In fact it is argued here that unification was thrust upon a largely unprepared country which had already resigned itself to division. Germans have been all too aware of the fact that, while the Basic Law demands the promotion of unification in theory, a translation into practice of such aims or even worse, its strident articulation would have been decried and disdained.[34] Moreover, these 'twin aims' were not viewed by Germany as objectives which were necessarily contradictory. On the contrary according to former Chancellor Willy Brandt 'only a pan-European rapprochement can and will result in the two parts of Germany being able to come closer together ... there exists no other way to national unity.'[35] Attempts to 'Europeanise' the 'German question' have been the leitmotif and hallmark of Bonn's *Realpolitik*.[36] No attempt has ever been made to settle the 'German problem' in isolation. Even more emphatically,

Chancellor Kohl declared that German Unification and European integration represented 'two sides of the same coin'.[37] He argued that the integration process, while contributing to the demise of the Soviet empire, had also secured Western support for unification.

Germany's ambiguous, almost schizophrenic view of her role within the EC persisted until and beyond the revolutionary development in Eastern Europe which produced far-reaching political changes. The process of unification and particularly the speed with which it was completed induced speculation and anxieties as to Germany's future role in the Community. The Federal Republic, once defeated and occupied, suddenly had several options, not necessarily just membership of the EU. Already in 1991 *The Economist* had warned that the EC could not count on Germany remaining 'good Europeans for ever.'[38] The threat of Germany leaving the Community in the event of unification has its roots in a special note attached to the protocol during the signing of the Rome treaties that the latter would need to be reviewed in the event of unification.[39] Indeed, a survey of main German newspapers following the first and second year of unification revealed a distinctive new flavour in Germany's attitudes to the EC and confirmed that the German public had developed a more critical attitude towards the EU and in particular to monetary union.[40] While in 1990 73% still approved German membership of the EU, by 1995 support had declined to 51%.[41]

The emergence of a united powerful Germany at Europe's centre evoked historical memories and parallels. The (German) search for territorial identity has been resolved by unification. Today's borders largely coincide with the notion of German citizenship, save a relatively small group of ethnic minority in central and eastern Europe no longer regarded as an integral part of the German nation.[42] The price of course has been partition and annexation of formerly German territories legally sanctioned by the 1990 'Two plus Four Treaty'. Moreover, unification or rather the fear that united Germany might be unpredictable and/or dominant has accelerated the process of European integration in an attempt to increase procedural and institutional checks on German power. Since unification, there have been two more major treaties annexed to the Treaty of Rome, a third will result from the IGC 2000. In particular the Treaty on European Union (TEU) with its special chapter on monetary union was very much inspired by and the result of the impact of unification (see Chapter 4). EC member states gave grudging support to German Unification at the Strasbourg summit in December 1989 in return for Kohl agreeing to convene an IGC on Economic and Monetary Union (EMU) to start in December 1990.

At the same time, Bonn was anxious to convince her partners that German European credentials had not been marginalised. Germany's eager attempts to dispel her partners' suspicion has emphasised German support for

European Integration in the hope that this would address concerns of the international community. 'Not a German Europe, but a European Germany', a phrase once coined by the former long-serving Foreign Minister Genscher in the wake of German unification, was also reiterated by his successor Klaus Kinkel.[43] In that sense, the very issue of German Unification was a blessing, since it served as a forum for allaying concern about the FRG's future role in Europe. Indeed, Chancellor Kohl 'went out of his way to meet their (i.e. EC member states') desire for stricter control of a unified Germany'.[44] By doing so, he not only emphasised continuity in *Westpolitik*, but sought to deepen and strengthen the existing web of institutions and legal procedures that tied Germany to supranational organisations offering as the most important sacrifice the Deutsch Mark – symbol of post-war German stability – to be replaced by a common currency as set down in the 1991 Maastricht Treaty. This is clear evidence of German desires to 'bind herself in' or rather to the European network of organisations. By deepening the ties which 'bind' Germany to the EU, the FRG deliberately increased constraints on domestic policy-making. Against the Bosnian conflict, the German Chancellor declared that European integration was 'the most effective insurance against a re-emergence of nationalism, chauvinism and racism in our part of the continent as well.'[45]

There is one exception to the concept of a 'Europeanised' Germany: the European Monetary Union project only went ahead because its institutional set-up was based on the German *Bundesbank* and EMU membership was also conditional on the meeting of strict financial criteria, while the siting of the newly created European bank was to be in Frankfurt to demonstrate to the German public that it was close to the *Bundesbank* not only geographically but above all in stability and spirit. This was one area in which the Germans saw no possibility for compromise. But even then one could argue that it was done to keep both the *Bundesbank* and the German public on the 'European train.'

While the prospect of German Unification had initially fuelled fear and suspicion, the end of the division of the German nation also healed the division of Europe. Germany, which had straddled the border of two dif-ferent and hostile systems, now became a link between East and West. But because unification also restored Germany's former central political and geographical position, Europe's security very much depends on stability in Germany itself. Located in the heart of the new Europe with nine immediate neighbours and 'open borders to all of them', it has become a transit country restoring the old 'land in the middle' angst.[46] As such Germany is very exposed to political and economic instability in the east also in view of the fact that she has borne the brunt of the new mass migration into the EU, turning Germany, which has had an almost total absence of internal ethnic struggles, into a multi-ethnic society. Unification took place not only under the European roof, but also under the tutelage of the Allies. A special 'Two plus Four Conference' convened during the spring and summer of 1990 and on 12 September 1990, almost exactly 45 years after the fatal Potsdam Conference, the 'Two plus Four Treaty' ('Treaty on the Final Settlement with respect to Germany') was signed by the two Germanys and the Four Allies terminating the Allies' rights over Germany altogether. This meant that the Four Powers withdrew from Berlin and Germany as a whole, and all related Four Power institutions were dissolved: Germany at long last had become a sovereign state.

Does United Germany dominate by her sheer size or economic power? She has regained her sovereignty and unity and an increase in population virtually overnight. United Germany no doubt is the economic power house of the Union. It is the second largest trading nation in the world with a GDP equalling that of France and Britain combined; she holds over 40% of total EU currency reserve, has been and still is the largest contributor to the EU budget and remains the second largest (after the US) financier of NATO and third biggest donor to the UN budget. It holds influential positions in the network of European political, economic and military institutions. It is no longer dependent on the US, once her military custodian, because the main threat to her security, the Soviet Empire, has disintegrated. Indeed, unification has given Germany a key strategic role in the new pan-European order: the strength of German banks and credit institutions, its capital resources and industrial technological expertise are seen as crucial for the success of the transition in Eastern Europe. Germany provided some 60% of all payments by the G24 nations to the successor states of the former Soviet Union; this figure excludes humanitarian aid made by the private sector.[47]

Can Germany be feared simply as a result of acquiring additional territories? Why should the end of German division and its geographical enlargement from eleven *Länder* to sixteen be a destabilising factor in Europe and lead to a renewal of a revanchist foreign policy? Anxieties and consternation originally expressed by Germany's partners during the run-up to unification re-emerged during and at the Maastricht ratification process, at least in Denmark and France, and they were, to a certain extent, present in the British parliamentary process. These anxieties found expression both in the kind of misguided views as espoused by Nicholas Ridley, when he called the EMU 'a German racket designed to take over the whole of Europe'[48] as well as in the national and international press; but also academic articles raised some albeit benign concerns, e.g. 'Must Europe fear the Germans' or 'Why Europe should not fear the Germans'.[50]

Yet unification has not altered the German horizontal and vertical diffusion of power. On the contrary, the *Länder* have been able to increase their participation in relation to the formation of Germany's policies in the EU. An amendment to the Basic Law, the new Art. 23 on 'European Union' has been passed, which means that the German government may transfer sovereign powers by law with the consent of the *Bundesrat* (i.e. the *Länder*) provided that the new legal order, i.e. the European Union, complies with the rule of the German Constitution. In the 'Two plus Four Treaty' of 1990, Germany renounced the possession of nuclear, biological and chemical weapons and agreed to a quantitative limitation of her military forces. Moreover, Germany does not have a permanent seat on the UN Security Council, a criterion usually attached to major powers. With no atomic weapons, virtually no raw materials, located in a precarious strategic position, highly dependent on exports and burdened by an enormous historical legacy, Germany is anything but a world power. Here again we are faced with the limitation of theoretical approaches to international politics. Neo-realist predictions, for example, have viewed the emergence of a reunited Germany against the collapse of bi-polarity as a threat to her neighbours or have argued that the rise of a nationalist Germany is just a matter of time.[51]

Developments during the past decade however point to the exact opposite. Despite a new international constellation the German government continued to lead the drive for further integration, while Germany's peculiar constraints were still clearly reflected by the general public and politicians, both of whom were reluctant to acknowledge or even utilise the country's increased significance in the EU. Political thinking was still characterised and influenced by memories of the past. National consciousness has only slowly developed, indeed if it is at all present in some sections of the German population. Germany continued to exercise power only in the area of economics, or by good example, persuasion, reason and through transnational institutions, and above all in cooperation with France. Continuity, stability, moderation and predictability and importantly policy collaboration with France remain post-unification hallmarks. German government policies at least until 1998 were motivated by the conviction particularly pronounced under Adenauer and Kohl that European integration must continue because the alternative might be a possible relapse into old rivalries, even the possibility of another war. Particularly Kohl is said to have followed a pro-European policy with 'monumental doggedness'.[52]

Neither the new political context after unification nor the addition of a new left-wing party, the Party of Democratic Socialism (PDS), undermined the broad consensus among both political parties and interest groups on pro-European policies, revealing a 'shared European orientation'[53] that continued to dominate the European agenda. Germany pressed forcefully for the adoption and realisation of the Maastricht goals despite growing opposition to, or at least scepticism of, a single currency by some groups, in particular by German banks and the public. As Banchoff noted, the debates by the *Bundestag* following the agreement on the Maastricht Treaty were not only carried by a broad consensus across political parties but reflected clearly the influence of Germany's past. Links were drawn between the irreversibility of Germany's integration into Europe by Kohl (CDU), while Rudolf Scharping, chairman of the SPD from 1993 to 1995 viewed integration as the result of 'devastating experience of two terrible fratricidal wars'. This was echoed by Klaus Kinkel who had replaced Genscher as Foreign Minister in 1992. The former saw the integration process not as many do as 'a child of the Cold War' but as a 'reaction to centuries long fratricidal wars'.[54] In sum, the major political parties emphasised Germany's post-national status and the irreversibility of integration. Indeed, Kohl had warned that Maastricht was an opportunity which might not offer itself for another generation.[55] The *Bundestag* on 2 December 1992 ratified the Maastricht Treaty by an overwhelming majority of 543 to 17.

Curiously enough, there is a distinct pressure from Germany's EU partners who periodically express doubts over Germany's European credentials, demanding 'evidence' of German commitment to the integration process. This suspicion periodically surfaced during times of structural change and/ or international conflicts: for example at the launching of Willy Brandt's *Ostpolitik*, during the run-up to German Unification, at the heights of the currency crisis between 1991–3 and as a result of German unilaterally recognising Croatia and Slovenia. In each of these cases, Germany had to convince her partners of continued commitment to the integration process, but no other member state's integrity is ever questioned in this way. One might have thought that the new government in Germany, for all its strident reference to a 'new' Germany, would be an exception, but when it came to conflicts between the Federal Republic and her partners in the EU at the Berlin 1999 summit, the new government felt that it had no alternative but to 'give in' (see Chapter 6).

Clearly the argument is strongly in favour of continuity. Indeed, Germany's original motives for joining the Community have retained much of their validity. First, although equality and legitimacy have been achieved, post-unification Germany feels that her political future is strongly interwoven with that of the EU, the latter continuing to be seen as an anchor of stability. Germany's main desire is to safeguard its liberal democracy and for this it needed the Community as a force for stability and predictability. German policy-makers were still very sensitive to any elements which might endanger the principle of parliamentary democracy and free enterprise. This is one of the reasons why Germany is such a fervent supporter of eastward expansion. It is hoped that integration into the political system of the EU would in theory exclude a possible backlash to authoritarian regimes in those

countries while at the same time it would contain antidemocratic forces in
Germany. The EU is of crucial political importance for the maintenance of
liberal democracy in the FRG and in the new democracies bordering on the
Federal Republic.

Second, Germany still cannot ignore the substantial trade benefits derived
from a common market of 15 countries. Some 30% of Germany's GNP is
exported in the form of goods: economic expansion and full employment
largely depend on the success or failure of its export trade, making every third
job in the FRG dependent on its trade performance. The Community is the
most important market for Germany's industrial produce. In 1958 one third of
its exports went to the EEC; the EU, which has been extended to 15 members,
now takes nearly 70% of all German exports revealing the crucial importance
of Germany's ability to hold on to its market share in the Community. Germany
is also forced to consider the significance of the EU as vehicle for Germany's
economic interests beyond Europe's frontiers. The EU is an important negotiator
in international trade and has established numerous contacts and trading links
with practically the entire world. This network of international trading relations
is particularly relevant to Germany, given its dependence on international
economic exchanges.

Third, the general network of relations and policies built through the EC is
likely to retain its great attraction for the FRG. The Community is a stabilising
element in international politics, a forum for concerted action in the context of
world-wide problems and as such will remain of crucial importance to the
FRG. The EU provides the means to globalise German foreign policy, and the
advantage of collective bargaining is helpful when German diplomacy might
be paralysed by psychological factors. Importantly, Germany's European
foreign policy has made unification possible.

PHASE III: A 'NEW' GERMAN EUROPA-POLITIK?

There are two sides to the coin of 'historical memory'. While on the one hand
Germany's past has been a constraint, on the other, her historical burden has
paradoxically increased national bargaining power: there have been occasions
when Germany's partners have been forced to recognise Germany's special
needs arising from a status of semi-paralysis. Being a country pulled by crucial
ties and burdened with inescapable problems, Germany has enjoyed a 'special
position' in the EU. However, with unification achieved, Germany can no
longer seek refuge into its 'special' status or impose the costs of its economic
and political security on the Community. It also can no longer claim special
concessions (such as detaching herself from military operations outside NATO
domain for moral or constitutional reasons). On the other hand one can argue

that the two basic aims of the German Basic Law, namely integration into Europe and unification have been achieved: Germany would appear to be saturated. With the change of government, composed almost entirely of post-war politicians, in the autumn of 1998 a new and perhaps more strident language became apparent. The relocation of power from Bonn to Berlin in September 1999, the new government's threat of a 'policy of the empty chair' (boycotting all sessions of the Council of Ministers where under Finnish Presidency no German was spoken),[56] and the continued, yet emphasised paymaster policy that Germany 'cannot and will not solve Europe's problems with Germany's cheque books',[57] have been signs that a shift in the 'German perception of Germany' is about to take place. Indeed, already on 2 October 1982, on the occasion of their first meeting in the Elysée, Chancellor Kohl had remarked to President Mitterrand 'I am the last pro-European German chancellor.'[58]

On taking office in the autumn of 1998 the new German Chancellor Gerhard Schröder declared 'My generation and those following are Europeans because we want to be, not because we must be ... that makes us freer in dealing with others.'[59] Germany, he declared, is no longer a late-comer in terms of nationhood. Sovereign Germany is Europeanised, politically and economically, also in terms of identity and Germans no longer need catch up in terms of recognition.[60] There is a distinct willingness to confront history, also reflected by the government's move to Berlin, a city which is evoking German history at every corner, nowhere more so than by the *Reichstag*. During its first parliamentary session on 19 April 1999 Chancellor Schröder stated: 'The move to Berlin is a return to German history, to the place of two German dictatorships, which brought great suffering to the people of Germany and of Europe ... But equating *Reichtstag* with *Reich* (empire) makes no sense ... The federal model of German politics goes on and is not in the slightest danger'.[61]

The deployment of German troops in former Yugoslavia marked Germany's acceptance of a new responsibility beyond that of merely economic ones, although the issue of military action has not only caused conflicts between the coalition parties, the SPD and the Greens, but evoked a division within the SPD itself. However, referring obliquely to German participation in NATO action in Yugoslavia, the new German Chancellor noted 'Germany's role in the world has changed.'[62] This is also echoed to some extent in academic writing: 'Neither apologetic moralising nor humanitarian chequebook aid as a token of goodwill are appropriate; what is urgently needed is a down-to-earth policy which takes account of our interests.'[63] Indeed, it has even been argued that 'Germany will only be able to survive if it can come to accept both the concept and the reality of "nation" and "interest" as legitimate for itself as well.'[64] Post-war foreign policy – since it urged abstinence in world and power politics – is now being condemned as 'short-sighted'.[65] Already in 1995 the then President of Germany, Roman Herzog, advocating the globalisation of Germany's Foreign Policy, declared: 'What are German interests? German interests are first of all our immediate interests such as security and the safeguarding of economic prosperity.'[66] This new political climate is also reflected by the country's literary giants. On receiving the German publishers' peace book prize, the novelist Martin Walser in his address in the Frankfurter Paulskirche declared that Germans should no longer be preoccupied with the shameful events of the 1930s and 1940s and criticised the media's constant presentation of Germany's past. Germans, Walser said, should be considered as 'normal' people.[67]

Thus a distinct change has taken place in the way Germany not only perceives but importantly articulates her interests, but not as many believe as a direct or only result of unification. Calls for a more nationally orientated European and foreign policy have their origin in the new challenges Germany and Europe is confronted with. Developments in the international economy and changed political circumstances have put the FRG in the forefront of international politics. Germany has declared her willingness to engage herself not only politically and economically but also militarily. The Federal Constitutional Court's decision of July 1994 allowing deployment of the German army outside Allied territories confirms this. While the European integrationist zeal is still there, it has been modified by the aim 'to create a Europe that is worthwhile for Germans'.[68] The new German perception of Germany in Europe will play an important role in the new millennium with respect to the choice and formulation of common plans, particularly as issues of novel complexion and wider importance are at stake. Albeit in collaboration with France, Germany will be pivotal in determining the character of the EU. While a strong awareness of their history persists. Germans, although still intensely aware of being 'German', clearly want to be judged by what they are today.

Having said this, two types of constraints remain as Germany entered the new millennium. First, the new 'Germanness' is, on the other hand, toned down: 'Germany has to face up to her new role as a European great power without repressing or forgetting – not to mention repeating – the bungling, mistakes and crimes of the first half of the century, the effects of which can still be felt today. That is the greatest challenge facing the Germans on the threshold of the 21st century and one that it is imperative they deal with sooner rather than later.'[69] Thus in the final analysis historical constraints remain. German politics, despite the change of government in 1998, remain the result of long-lasting conflicts and are still heavily influenced by traditional objectives. Historical memory though to a lesser degree than during the immediate post-war years will influence Germany's policy choices and the inevitable conflict between everyday national realities and European aspirations will continue.

The second category of constraints is usually ignored by 'realist' interpretations of international relations; the latter is, in any event, 'ill-suited to the complex interdependence that characterises modern Germany's relations with the rest of Europe'.[70] Indeed, structural realists appear to 'have had a poor record in predicting Germany's foreign strategy after the Cold War'.[71] The integration process has its own procedural checks on national power imposed by an increasing degree of Europeanisation of German institutions and policy-making is nowhere more powerful and interventionist than in the monetary area (see Chapter 4). Germany, after all, can only be 'as strong as its alliances',[72] constraints which of course Germany shares with the other member states. It is futile and misguided to speculate on German domination which, even when shared with France, is an irrelevance in a functionally integrated Europe. The key elements of the German foreign policy agenda therefore contain traditional essentials, despite new accents. The strategic outlook is a strong support for integration and although Germany 'ought to be backing full integration because we want it and believe in it, not because people must fear us otherwise,'[73] the Federal Republic is 'of the opinion that there is no other rational alternative'.[74]

NOTES

1. Timothy Gordon Ash (1990), 'Germany Unbound', *The New York Review of Books*, **22**, November, p. 15.
2. David Schoenbaum and Elizabeth Pond (1996), *The German Question and Other German Questions*, St. Martin's Press Inc., New York, p. 5.
3. The German Sonderweg became the embodiment of the tradition which had paved the way to dictatorship and the Second World War. See Heinrich A. Winkler (1994), 'Rebuilding of a Nation', *Daedalus*, **123** (1).
4. A.J.P. Taylor (1945), *The Course of German History*, H. Hamilton, London, p. 7.
5. Quoted by Reinhard Stuth, (1992) 'Germany's New Role in a Changing Europe', *Aussenpolitik*, **1**, p. 22.
6. Josef Joffe (1989), 'The Foreign Policy of the Federal Republic of Germany', in Roy C. Macridis (ed.), *Foreign Policy in World Politics States and Regions*, 7th edn, Prentice Hall, New Jersey, p. 72.
7. Quoted by Thomas Banchoff (1999), 'German Identity and European Integration', *European Journal of International Relations*, **5** (3), p. 277.
8. Thomas Pedersen (1998), *Germany, France and the Integration of Europe*, Pinter, London and New York, p. 69.
9. *Ibid.*, p. 70.
10. Joffe (1989) *op. cit.*, p. 73.
11. General Friedrich von Bernhardi (1912) 'Germany and the Next War', excerpts in J.C.G. Röhl

(1970), *From Bismarck to Hitler The Problem of Continuity in German History*, Longman, London, pp. 65–6.

12. Gregor Schöllgen (1998), 'The Berlin Republic as a Player on the International Stage. Does Germany still have its own Political Interests', *Aussenpolitik*, **49** (2), p. 29.

13. Chancellor Bethmann Hollweg's Programme of 9 September 1914, excepts in Röhl (1970), *op. cit.*, p. 73.

14. Pierre Hassner (1971), 'Europe West of the Elbe' in Robert S. Jordan (ed.) *Europe and the Superpowers*, Allyn and Bacon, Boston, p. 103.

15. Christian Hacke (1998), 'The National Interests of the Federal Republic of Germany on the Threshold of the 21st Century', *Aussenpolitik*, **49** (2), p. 5.

16. A. Surminski (1979), *Frankfurter Allgemeine Zeitung*, 28 January.

17. The Basic Law compensated for the lack of a Constitution and was enacted for a transitional period only since the setting-up of the FRG was seen as a Provisorium pending reunification.

18. Quoted in Konrad H. Jarausch and Volker Gransow (1994), *United Germany. Documents and Debates 1944–1993*, Berghahn, Oxford, p. 7.

19. Elizabeth Pond (1992), 'Germany in the New Europe', *Foreign Affairs*, **71** (2), p. 114.

20. Adenauer to the Bundestag on 12 July 1952 in C.C. Schweitzer et al. (1995), *Politics and Government in Germany 1944–1994, Basic Documents*, Berghahn, Oxford, p. 119.

21. M. Saeter (1980), *The Federal Republic Europe and the World*, Universitetsforlaget, Oslo, p. 17.

22. *Ibid.*, p. 5.

23. W.J. Feld and G. Boyd (eds) (1980), *Comparative Regional Systems*, Pergamon Press, New York, p. 518.

24. For a fuller discussion see W. Weidenfeld (ed.) (1983), *Die Identität der Deutschen*, Carl Hauser Verlag, Munich and Vienna.

25. Hans Magnus Enzensberger (1967), *Deutschland, Deutschland unter anderm. Äusserungen zur Politik*, Suhrkamp, Franfurt am Main, p. 9.

26. See for example Gisela Hendriks (1991), *Germany and European Integration*, Berghahn, Oxford.

27. B. May (1982), *Kosten und Nutzen der deutschen EG-Mitgliedschaft*, Europa Union Verlag, Bonn.

28. *Agence Europe* (1985), No 4090, 15 May, p. 5.

29. See for example Michael Mertes (1994), 'Germany's Social and Political Culture: Change through Consensus?', *Daedalus*, **123** (1), Winter, 1–23.

30. Emil J. Kirchner (1992), 'The European Community: Seeds of Ambivalence' in Gordon Smith, William E. Patersen, Peter H. Merkl and Stephen Padgett (eds), *Developments in German Politics*, Macmillan, Basingstoke, pp. 172–84.

31. David Marsh (1993), 'The German Central Bankers Controlling Europe's Economy', *World Policy Journal*, **X** (1), 73–77 p. 73.

32. Hendriks (1991), *op. cit.*

33. See Erwin K. Scheuch (1992), *Wie Deutsch sind die Deutschen*, Lubbe, Bergisch-Gladbach here p. 101.

34. Hacke (1998), *op. cit.*, p. 6.

35. Willy Brandt, (1970), *Bulletin der Bundesregierung*, 7 January.

36. See Chancellor Kohl in *Bulletin der Bundesregierung* (1990), 19 January, p. 61.

37. *Bulletin* (1993), 5 February, p. 90.

38. *The Economist*, 27 July 1991.

39. For details see Blumenwitz and B. Meissner (eds), (1986) *Die Überwindung der europäischen Teilung und die deutsche Frage*, Verlag Wissenschaft und Politik, Cologne.

40. Dietrich Rometsch (1996), 'The Federal Republic of Germany' in D. Rometsch and W. Wessels, *The European Union and Member States*, MUP Manchester.

41. *Euro-Barometer* (1997), Table 2.

42. Although the opening of borders in Eastern and Central Europe had resulted in an unprecedented wave of migration when millions of 'ethnic' Germans emigrated to West Germany in their search for a better life.
43. Klaus Kinkel (1994), 'Deutschland and Europa', *Europa-Archiv*, **49** (12), p. 336.
44. Wolfgang Krieger (1994), 'Towards a Gaullist Germany?', *World Policy Journal*, **XI** (1), Spring, 26–38 p. 29.
45. Bundestag address 27 May 1994, quoted by Thomas Banchoff (1997), 'German Policy Towards the European Union: The Effects of Historical Memory', *Germany Policy*, **6** (1), p. 63.
46. Much is made of the fact that Germany has so many neighbours, see for instance Schoenbaum and Pond (1996), *op. cit.*, p. 55 and Goldberger (1993), *op. cit.*
47. For details see G-24 (1995), *Scoreboard Assistance Commitments to the Countries of Central and Eastern Europe, 1990–1994*, European Commission Directorate General IA, Brussels, March.
48. Nicholas Ridley, quoted by *The Spectator*, 14 July 1990, 'Saying the unsayable about Germany', p. 8.
49. See for example Conor Cruise O'Brien (1989), 'Beware the Reich is Reviving', *The Times*, 31 October.
50. Andrei Markovits and Simon Reich (1991), 'Should Europe Fear the Germans?' *German Politics and Society*, **23**, pp. 1–20. Bruce N. Goldberger (1993), 'Why Europe should not Fear the Germans', *German Politics*, **2** (2), 288–310. See also Wilfred von Bredow and Thomas Jaeger (1993), *Neue Deutsche Aussenpolitik*, Leske and Budrich, Opladen. Caroline Thomas and Klaus-Peter Weiner (eds) (1993), *Auf dem Weg zur Hegemonialmacht?*, Papy Rossa Verlag, Cologne. Arnulf Baring (ed.) (1997), *Germany's new position in Europe*, Berg, Oxford. Timothy Garton Ash (1994), 'Germany's Choice', *Foreign Affairs*, **73** (4).
51. John Mearsheimer (1990) 'Back to the Future; Instability in Europe after the Cold War', *International Security*, **15** (1), 5–56. Kenneth N. Waltz (1993), 'The Emerging Structure of International Politics', *International Security*, **18** (2), 44–79. Elizabeth Pond and Kenneth N. Waltz (1994), 'Correspondence: International Politics, Viewed from the Ground', *International Security*, **19** (1), 195–9.
52. Hermann Rudolph (1990), 'Von monumentaler Unbeirrbarkeit', in *Süddeutsche Zeitung*, 3 April.
53. On the 'continuity' of Germany's European policies see Banchoff (1999), *op. cit.*, pp. 272–3.
54. *Ibid.*, p. 273.
55. Helmut Kohl cited by *Der Spiegel* (1991), **49**, p. 36.
56. *Die Zeit* (1999), **28**, 8 July, p. 1.
57. Gerhard Schröder (1998), 'Policy Statement to the Bundestag', 12 December, www.germany-info.org/govern/schröder.
58. Quoted by Kenneth Dyson (1998), 'Chancellor Kohl as Strategic Leader: the Case of Economic and Monetary Union', in *German Politics*, **7** (1), 37–63, p. 42.
59. Quoted by *Financial Times* (1998), 'Integration drive set to start', 10 November.
60. Schröder (1999), *Bulletin der Bundesregierung*, 13 October, p. 662.
61. *Financial Times* (1999), 'Reichstag opens under the shadow of its bitter past', 20 April.
62. *Ibid.*
63. Hacke (1998), *op. cit.*, p. 8.
64. *Ibid.*, p. 6.
65. Schöllgen (1998), *op. cit.*, p. 32.
66. *Bulletin der Bundesregierung*, 15 March 1995, p. 164.
67. *Financial Times* (1999), Survey VII 'Historical Dilemma Sparks Strong Reactions', 1 June.
68. Quoted by *Financial Times* (1999), Survey VI 'Horsetrading on EU finance', 1 June.
69. Quoted by Hacke (1998), *op. cit.*, p. 23.

70. Bruce N. Goldberger (1992), 'Why Europe should not Fear the Germans', *German Politics*, **2** (2), 288.
71. Matthias Zimmer (1997), 'Return of the Mittellage? The Discourse of the Center in German Foreign Policy', *German Politics*, **6** (1), 33.
72. Schoenbaunm and Pond (1996), *op. cit.*, p. 51.
73. Gerhard Schröder (1997), *The Economist*, 8 March, p. 38.
74. Gerhard Schröder (1999), *Bulletin der Bundesregierung*, 8 December, p. 808.

PART II

The Policies

4. Economic and Monetary Union (EMU): a Franco-German compromise?

The EURO will ... unite the peoples of the European Union in an order based on peace and freedom. (H. Kohl)[1]

INTRODUCTION

Nothing – short of a construction of the United States of Europe – demands a greater transfer of sovereignty than the resolution of member states to commit themselves to Economic and Monetary Union (EMU) which, next to eastward enlargement, is the key issue the European Union (EU) is facing at the threshold of a new century. Described as a 'grand vision that may radically change the economic and political landscape in Europe',[2] it is not only the most daring and visionary project the EU has undertaken since the Treaty of Rome, but is of far-reaching implications for the countries involved requiring renunciation of sovereignty in an area where loss of status is very real. It thus triggers a degree of integration well beyond the economic rationale of monetary union. The introduction of a common currency implies the loss of exchange rate instruments to absorb huge external shocks, while the Stability and Growth Pact designed to ensure ongoing budgetary discipline constrains (national) fiscal policy-making. The countries participating in the EMU project, to all intents and purposes, have ceased to exist as macro-economic entities. No historical precedent exists to make reliable predictions as to the impact of EMU, but observers are agreed[3] that a large financial market equal to that of the dollar will emerge making significant changes to the international financial system.

It is no accident that this unique experiment of setting up a common monetary system owes its existence primarily, though not exclusively, to France and Germany. This chapter traces how, despite a deep division in terms of economic and political philosophy, a synthesis has developed between French desire to develop an 'EU identity' thus ensuring independence, particularly from the US, as well as 'binding in Germany', and the German objective of arresting, through the introduction of a single currency, a retreat into national self-interest as well as securing her image of a 'European' Germany. It is argued that, although there has been a clear convergence and identity of aims, Franco-German collaboration on EMU, both before and after its launch in January 1999, has not been without dissonance: divergences on monetary matters, already present at the beginning of the 1970s, resurfaced dramatically during the 1990s, as the two countries attempted to influence the design of the EMU project and are now trying to seek some control over its operation.

This chapter is divided into three sections: the first, after a brief background to EMU negotiations, examines the analytical thrust of the French and German input into the EMU set-up, i.e. the institutional framework and policy tools. This section therefore identifies the level of congruence between the two countries' approach to monetary union. This is followed by an examination of the meaning of these findings in terms of the processes and outcomes of setting up EMU: how does Franco-German collaboration facilitate the operation of the EMU; what conflicts remain or have resumed? The concluding section is a somewhat speculative analysis of Franco-German relations after the change of government in Germany in the autumn of 1998 and the impact this has, if any, on continued Franco-German collaboration on monetary matters.

EMU: SETTING THE FRAMEWORK

Historical Background to EMU: from the Werner Plan to the European Monetary System (EMS)

EMU is a project without precedent and yet its origin is rooted in the Treaty of Rome. The Community's main preoccupation during the 1950s and 1960s had been the establishment of the customs unions and the definition of the Common Agricultural Policy (CAP) which were being the most significant landmarks of the treaty and only seven of the 240 articles deal exclusively with economic, monetary and exchange rate policies (Art. 99-111, ex Art. 103-9).* Indeed, the term 'monetary policy' was mentioned explicitly only once, in Art. 105. One might think that this was a rather surprising lack of attention in a treaty laying down the foundation of economic union, but perfectly understandable in view of the stable international monetary conditions which prevailed at that time provided by the Bretton Woods Agreement of 1944 of fixed exchange rates to which all West European countries adhered. Hence

---

* In dealing with treaty articles, we quote the articles according to the new numbering of the Consolidated Treaties followed by the former numbering as in the original treaties.

there was as yet no need to press for common policies in this area: the international monetary system was well structured.

This situation changed dramatically when in the late 1960s the post-war boom gave way to an international recession. Problems began with the gradual erosion of the foundation of the Bretton Woods system and European countries were caught by speculative pressures. In August and October 1969 respectively the French Franc was devalued and Germany announced an upward float of the Deutsch Mark. Fears began to emerge that monetary instability might compromise the extent of liberalisation in intra-EC trade already achieved. In particular, the working of the CAP and the Community's common agricultural price level depended on firm exchange rates.

As a result of these developments, the Community, during the Hague Conference in December 1969, agreed that a plan should be drawn up with a view to the creation in stages of an Economic and Monetary Union (EMU). A committee was set up under the chairmanship of Pièrre Werner, the Prime Minister of Luxembourg, which in October 1970 submitted a plan defining a three-stage transition to monetary union with progressive convergence of economic policies.[4] However, while the European Council in March 1971 endorsed the Report, the summit's conclusions did not go beyond general guidelines for a first stage. Nevertheless three important decisions were taken. In April 1972 the 'snake' was created (see below). This was followed by the creation and setting up of the European Monetary Co-operation Fund in 1973 and finally the adoption of a Council Decision (on the attainment of a high degree of convergence of economic policies) and a Directive (on stability, growth and full employment) in 1974. However, despite these initial legislative implementations, the Werner initiative was short-lived. International events, well documented, altered the economic and political environment in which the Report, written against the background of reconstruction and post-war boom, had been expected to be implemented. Intense speculation in the spring of 1971 put the dollar under pressure with Germany having to revalue her currency against the American currency, followed by the Dutch guilder, while France maintained its parity with the dollar but established a dual foreign exchange market.

The Bretton Woods international monetary system collapsed with the announcement on 15 August 1971 that the US Treasury would no longer convert dollars into gold. In an attempt to rescue some aspects of the Werner project, a currency band (snake) was created to tie European floating currencies together and was tightened the following year by defining a common band against the US dollar (snake in the tunnel). The scheme was however diluted with currencies leaving and rejoining the 'snake' and progressively unravelled during the mid and late 1970s. In reality however, the project had foundered not only as the result of the breakdown of the

Bretton Woods system and the oil crises, but because of unresolved differences in approaches to the economic crises and the unwillingness of member states to subordinate their policy responses to a common objective. The Werner Plan, being ahead of its time in objective and idea could not materialise because, based on a political design, the plan was out of touch with the actual state of integration that existed at that time. On the other hand, it has been argued that it failed because it suffered from an absence of flanking political institutions.[5]

It was against this background that new moves towards monetary stability started. The concern of both the French President Giscard d'Estaing and the German Chancellor Helmut Schmidt for monetary stability led to the reactivation, in 1979, of the Werner Plan, when the European Monetary System (EMS), a less ambitious scheme than the Werner Plan, was created based on a Resolution of the European Council, confirmed subsequently by a Decision of the Council of Ministers and an Agreement between participating banks. The main features of the system was a European Currency Unit (ECU) based on a basket of national currencies, plus an Exchange Rate Mechanism (ERM) whereby participating currencies moved within a narrow margin of plus/minus 2.25%. Italy was originally permitted to join at the permissible fluctuation band of plus/minus 6% (the United Kingdom, Spain and Portugal also joined later at the expanded margin).

Although a less ambitious scheme than the Werner Plan, the EMS has served as focal point for improved monetary policy coordination with increasingly close cooperation among central banks. It has also been argued that the 'system has benefited from the role played by the Deutsch Mark as an "anchor" for participants' monetary and intervention policies'.[6] The EMS developed without an institutional framework, but served as forerunner and constructional basis for EMU as reflected in the adoption in 1985 of the Single Market programme and the signing of the Single European Act (SEA). For a while the system worked well: countries participating in the ERM moved towards genuine convergence in terms of inflation and interest rates and realignments – after an initially unsettled period – were infrequent. However, both founding fathers of the EMS fell victim to political change. In 1982, the liberals in Germany decided to switch coalition and thereby brought Schmidt's government down. In France, the centre-right were replaced by Mitterrand's socialists in 1981. The French economy weakened and the French Franc came under pressure. Between 1979 (the start of the EMS) and 1987, there had been six bilateral devaluations of the French Franc against the Deutsch Mark, with a cumulative devaluation of 45.2%. Unlike under the previous 'snake system', the ECU divergence indicator in the EMS was designed to share the burden of economic adjustments between 'weak currency' and 'strong currency' member states.[7] In March 1983 a realignment in the EMS had become a necessity, a move which had a profound impact on the countries' macro-economic strategies, since the compromise involved a revaluation of the Deutsch Mark of 5.5%, while limiting the devaluation of the French Franc to 2.5%. Thus Germany accepted the larger share of the burden of adjustment.

This event, although painful for France who complained about the 'arrogance and incomprehension'[8] of the German financial élite and un-welcomed by Germany which, as the world's second largest exporter has always been reluctant to revalue its currency, nevertheless marked the beginning of an era of macro-economic convergence. First, it indicated a watershed in economic thinking of France's socialist government and an acceptance of the need to adjust to the constraints of international and European financial markets.[9] Effectively abandoning socialist democratic principles, Mitterrand adapted national economic strategies to the 'German model' and converted to a 'sound' money policy (he was not the first: already Giscard d'Estaing had pointed to Germany as an example of price stability.[10]) Although the French President had been advised to adopt import controls and allow the Franc to float, France gave priority to continued ERM membership rather than withdrawing from the system reflecting a degree of high commitment to Europe and, by implication, to the Franco-German partnership. To mute critics the French President tried to counter-balance this shift in policy by emphasising at the European level the concept of a 'European Social Space'. It so happened that the monetary instability coincided with a major crisis between NATO members and renewed East-West tensions. The French President seemed concerned that a large section of the German population – quite uncharacteristically – had demonstrated in protest against the controversial NATO double track decision on the deployment of Intermediate Nuclear Force (INF) missiles. It was necessary to keep Germany on board the European train. Faced with the choice between continuing his 1981 election programme of a relatively self-contained national model outside the EMS or continued membership of the system, the French President chose the latter but at the price of major policy changes. This has been interpreted as the 'single most important decision of the Mitterrand presidency and the turning point that began movement to EMU'.[11]

Moreover, the 1983 realignment also marked the beginning of a new French strategy in future EMU negotiations: France realised that from now on it had to adopt a low profile and be Germany's 'junior partner', not only because of the gap in economic strength between the two countries, making Germany's prominence in monetary matters more credible, but also because France realised that the German government would not be able to win over the German public for monetary reform unless its mechanism was based on the German model. It has been argued[12] that Mitterrand's decision (i.e. to give up a French leader role in the EMS) was 'probably the most important in his presidential career'. It seems to have paid off though: index prices for private consumption fell from 9.2% in 1983 to 2.7% in 1990 (in Germany the equivalent figures were 3.2 to 2.7%). On the other hand, however, major differences in budgetary traditions and industrial background, savings and investment policies implied that France could never quite match German economic strength. France knew of course that it was being stronger in other areas, particularly foreign policy and hoped that a linkage between issue areas could be exploited to French advantage (see Chapter 5).

The Making of EMU

The third and most concrete realisation of the original objectives in monetary co-ordination crystallised during the latter part of the 1980s, when it became intellectually fashionable to focus discussion once again on EMU. It had become clear that the imperfection of the common market caused by the slow-down in member states' economic performance and the international economic crises combined with the political inertia of member states to move out of the recession, could no longer be tolerated. The political and economic environment at that time was favourable for a 'relaunch' of the integration process. With the publication in 1985 of the Commission Paper 'Completing the Internal Market',[13] the implementation of which by 1992 was set down in the before-mentioned treaty, the SEA, a large legislative agenda was unleashed setting into motion other unforeseen processes. The coming into force of the SEA in 1987 provided the EC with instruments to complete the Rome Treaty provisions and remove final obstacles to trade. In the event, the SEA turned out to be more than an instrument of economic expansion. The functional logic between the Single Market and EMU (particularly evident after the abolition of capital control) was compelling, as periodically pointed out by the Commission which since 1985 had been under a new and strong leadership.[14] The SEA thus not only set the stage for the Single Market project, but it accelerated the momentum towards EMU illustrating forcefully the spill-over dynamics the Single Market has created.

In January 1987 the French Franc came under renewed pressure which led to the 11th and highly acrimonious parity realignment in the ERM with France blaming this on the Deutsch Mark's under-valuation affording Germany structural gains rather than the Franc's over-valuation. As a result, the French government deliberately let the currency fall through its floor against the Deutsch Mark thus forcing the *Bundesbank* to intervene and the German government to re-value.[15] France complained about the EMS 'asymmetric system':[16] the burden of intervention and adjustments, it was argued, had to be carried by the weak currencies, which were not necessarily to blame for imbalances. In an attempt to regain some control over monetary policy or at least to participate in European monetary decision-making and prompted by the January crisis, Edouard Balladur,[17] the French Minister for Finance and Economics, signalled a readiness to consider a European Central Banking System replacing the EMS.[18] France was supported in her efforts in particular by Italy, whose finance minister Guiliano Amato on 23 February submitted a memo of his own to his EC colleagues calling for a reform of the EMS system.[19]

France had two motives for supporting moves beyond the EMS: first, it wanted to shield Europe from volatile dollar movements as well as ending the asymmetry within the EMS between weak and strong currencies. The country, during that time, provided an interesting parallel to Germany in the 1950s. As has been argued in Chapter 2, German support for the EEC in the 1950s had been the result of a convergence of domestic considerations and foreign policy objectives only achievable within the framework of wider policy co-ordination among European states.[20] Similarly France, which had recognised since the 1980s that national strategies were becoming too costly, used the Community as a means to recover or maximise her economic strength and define a more international identity. Moves towards EMU were thus a way of redefining French interests; the country, no longer a world power, perceived the Community as a convenient niche for French ambitions.[21] Economically speaking, closer monetary integration made sense since a single currency would underpin the success of the Single Market.

Secondly, France was loyal to its eternal theme of post-war strategy, namely her desire to 'bind Germany in'. The end of the post-war boom and the onset of upheaval and change since the early 1970s has had a profound impact on the two countries' international standing, shifting the balance of power between the two countries in favour of the Federal Republic. Germany's rise to international actor both in terms of her economic potential and geo-strategic position and France's increasing economic dependence on the Federal Republic had reversed the role of the two countries. The latter's growing economic strength which was needed by a weakening France (the country had a long-standing trade deficit with the Federal Republic)[22] had increased Germany's flexibility and room for manoeuvre. France objected to the *Bundesbank* having become Europe's *de facto* central banker and having to follow German monetary policy and changes in interest rates with no or very little warning. Although somewhat disguised, this was clearly reflected by the Balladur Paper: by demanding that the EMS be reformed, it would 'prevent one country from determining the objectives of economic and monetary policy for the group as a whole'.[23]

In an attempt to arrest Germany's growing economic significance enhanced even further by the opening up of Eastern Europe, France favoured the introduction of a single currency to 'nip Deutsch-Mark nationalism in the bud'.[24] Thus France was prepared to relinquish some degree of control over its economic policies, first to the Banque de France which because of EMU requirements had to become independent from national government control and later to the new European Central Bank (ECB). It was therefore somewhat coincidental that French desire to maintain some control over its monetary policies helped to create arguably the most independent of all EU institutions. So, for whatever reasons, France has been at the vanguard of efforts to create a common monetary system, not in an attempt to surrender more sovereignty to supranational institutions, but to undermine the control of the *Bundesbank* over Europe's monetary affairs.

On 26 February 1988 the then Foreign Minister Hans-Dietrich Genscher published a memorandum calling for the creation of a European Monetary Space and a European Central Bank[25] based on the principles of the *Bundesbank Act*.[26] He tried to persuade the German Chancellor to make the setting up of a special committee charged with mapping out a blueprint for EMU a programmatic focal point of the Germany presidency at the June Hanover summit meeting. Kohl, however, temporarily resisted supporting Genscher's plan. The German Chancellor was satisfied with the EMS: the Exchange Rate Mechanism provided sufficient macro-economic autonomy, while the *Bundesbank* set its own monetary policy goals. However, two factors changed Kohl's mind: first, he feared that the removal of capital controls in the EC (as required by SEA and as confirmed by an EC decision on 13 June 1988) might jeopardise the stability of the EMS and secondly Delors, the President of the Commission, in a series of private meetings, advocated reform of the EMS as a corollary to the Single Market programme. In the event, a special committee, chaired by Jacques Delors and consisting of the 12 EC central bank governors, two commissioners and three appropriate advisers was set up in June 1988 to study and propose concrete stages leading towards the progressive implementation of monetary union and examine the conditions under which such a union could be viable and successful. The conclusions of the (German) Presidency after the meeting of the European Council in Hanover on 27 and 28 June 1988 stated:

> They [the member states] decided to examine at the European Council Meeting in Madrid in June 1989 the means of achieving such a union [EMU]. To that end they decided to entrust to a Committee the task of studying and preparing concrete stages leading towards this union.[27]

As has been noted, it is striking that the main push emanating mainly from Paris, Brussels and Bonn was political not economic.[28] If both the Werner Plan and the EMS had been a direct response to the currency crises and international challenges, the EMU project, by contrast, was launched in a climate of relative economic buoyancy. Monetary union was no longer a question of *whether* but had become one of *how*.

Negotiating the Delors Report

Cooperation on EMU between the two countries assumed a major significance, replacing to some extent the importance of earlier collaboration on the CAP. For Franco-German negotiations to be successful, it was however necessary to keep control of the process and by implication to take charge of it. This made agreements on the bilateral level of paramount importance: history has shown that once the two countries have agreed most of the other member states would follow the Franco-German lead. To quote former Chancellor Brandt 'Nothing is possible in Europe if impossible between the FRG and France'.[29]

As so often before, a somewhat unholy alliance developed between France and Germany at this point vis-à-vis the role of the Commission. The Germans, in an attempt to safeguard the independence of the bank, wanted to conduct EMU negotiations without the Commission's participation, a desire shared by France, but for different reasons. French objectives in keeping the Commission at bay was historic and rooted in traditional French suspicion of the Commission's 'supranational' ambitions. In the 1960s this was reflected by de Gaulle's insistence on the national veto and by institutionalising regular meetings of heads of state and of government as a counterbalance to the Commission. Although the Commission, when led by Delors between 1985 and 1995 had been, next to France and Germany, the most important policy actor in EMU, Delors' role in these negotiations is not altogether clear. On the one hand it has been argued that, rather than acting in his capacity as Commission President, i.e. as the 'honest broker', Delors' role was that of a European activist with very pronounced interests,[30] but on the other[31] that Delors had acted as a mediator between Mitterrand and Kohl, both of whom 'listened to him'. The use of English as the medium had actually been suggested by Delors who felt that this would speed up the discussion.[32] The attempt by the two countries to control the monetary process is also supported by Pedersen who reports that Pöhl had commented: 'His [Delors] contribution was small, but we made him famous.'[33] It is possible that Delors, in order to ensure the success of EMU and despite the fact that this gave the project a Community varnish, might have underplayed his role as President.

Whatever the truth of this might be, it is clear however that at one stage Germany seized full political leadership of the EMU process. Having agreed in principle on the necessity of monetary union, its framework of operation, and the policy tools and speed with which it was to be implemented had to be negotiated and Kohl was determined to safeguard EMU's future design. The *Bundesbank*'s full participation in, even leadership of, the project provided Kohl with the support he needed to sell EMU to the German public.[34] Germany was thus able to turn a major domestic political constraint to her advantage: by exploiting the reservation of the *Bundesbank* to the EMU project, Kohl was able to push for an independent central European bank as a precondition of negotiations as will be seen later. It was a *tour de force* on Kohl's part: he managed to convince the French, that EMU was in their national interest and the German public that the *Bundesbank* would ensure that any future monetary arrangement at European level would be based on the German model. The *Bundesbank* paper (by Karl-Otto Pöhl) was the most comprehensive and detailed contribution (25 pages) submitted to the Delors Committee compared for example to the eight page paper by Jacques de Larosière (Governor of the Banque de France): subsequent negotiations revolved primarily around the German text.

In this discussion paper Pöhl named (among others) two overriding principles of a monetary order: first that of price stability to be pursued by the common central bank and secondly that the overriding commitment to maintaining price stability must be safeguarded through the central bank's independence.[35] By contrast, the Governor of the French Bank, Jacques de Larosière, in his discussion paper was far more cautious in institutional terms. 'The European Reserve Fund' (i.e. forerunner to an European Reserve Bank, which he sees as a permanent body for joint action) 'would be given certain functions in the foreign exchange and the monetary sphere.' Clearly he intended that national governments would remain in charge or at best delegate certain tasks to the Reserve Bank. This is clearly reflected by his subsequent comments: 'one of the important questions that would have to be dealt with would concern the relationships between the European Reserve Bank and the political authorities in charge of setting exchange parities and framing the main lines of the economic policy of the Community. In this respect, it would seem that the role of the Council of Ministers would have to be decisive.'[36]

A deep intellectual divide (already present during the 1960s) resurfaced between France and Germany reflected by the battle between two camps: the 'economists' (Germany and supporters) who regard economic convergence as a prerequisite for a pegged-rate monetary zone and the 'monetarists' (France plus allies) advocating pegged rates in order to force convergence. The former rely on market forces, the latter favour administrative intervention. This division resurfaced during negotiations following the Hanover mandate when a sharp conflict emerged between the German representative of the *Bundesbank*, Karl-Otto Pöhl and Jacques de Larosière, the latter advocating a fast movement towards EMU but without new institutional arrangements. He was vigorously opposed by Pöhl, who thought that French proposals for the immediate creation of a European Reserve Fund might be ducking the institutional issue of an independent bank and economic convergence. Pöhl demanded nothing less but a *Bundesbank*-style ECB which would have sole responsibility for monetary policy. One might argue that the conflict which reached a climax in the penultimate stormy session in March 1989 has continued and resurfaced from time to time ever since.

The Delors Committee published its report in April 1989 recommending the earlier Werner Report proposal for a three-stage approach to EMU.[37] This entailed (Stage I) the completion of the 'Single Market' and membership of the EMS, (Stage II), the founding of new institutions and the gradual transfer of monetary responsibility to the new institutions and (Stage III), irrevocable locking of exchange rates. While all three stages constituted an integrated whole, the last two were unspecified in terms of a deadline. There is a remarkable continuity of ideas and economic logic between the Werner Plan and the Delors Report. Two principles were overriding: that the road to monetary union would be gradual (the Werner Plan recommended 10 years in three stages, while the Delors Report made transition from one stage to the next contingent on progress in the prior stage) and that there must be convergence of economic policies, assisted by sanction procedures, as a precondition or concomitant to monetary union. However, the institutional underpinning – absent in the previous attempt – is noteworthy. The Werner Plan, while referring to the need for institutional reform, does not call implicitly for the creation of a monetary institution. It notes however, that the realisation of EMU demands the creation or the transformation of a certain number of Community organs. The Delors Report on the other hand emphatically states that 'a new monetary institution would be needed' ... and that the 'domestic and international monetary policy-making of the Community should be organised in a federal form ... because a single monetary policy cannot result from independent decisions and actions by different central banks'.[38] Thus the major goal involved transfer of powers from national governments to a new monetary supranational entity signifying a clear shift from the intergovernmentalism of the 1970s. Most importantly the Report states that the status of the new institution should be independent.[39]

Neither report explicitly calls for a single currency. The Werner Report gives preference to the replacement of national currencies by a sole Community currency[40] as indeed does the Delors Report: 'although a monetary union does not necessarily require a single currency, it would be a desirable feature of a monetary union'.[41] It was expected that all member states would eventually join but, although all member states were involved in the gradual steps towards monetary union, participation in the final and third stage was only open to those member states which had satisfied certain convergence criteria or, as it has been in the case of the UK and Denmark, negotiated an opt-out clause (see below).

The Delors Report of April 1989 was clearly dominated by the *Bundesbank*'s paper and was a victory for the German position. The president of the *Bundesbank* had been central to the way all major arguments were resolved, including the commitment to an independent bank which would demand radical institutional restructuring of the Community and would imply a significant surrender of decision-making from national governments to the new bank. Indeed Chancellor Kohl had acknowledged that the institutional design of the EMU chapter as it was incorporated into the Maastricht Treaty bore a striking resemblance to that of the *Bundesbank*.[42] If it is true that, as has been argued[43] German foreign policy employs the 'power of diplomacy, economic power, the power of a good example and of reasonable argument', then the EMU is a case study *par excellence* for Germany's European and foreign policy.

On the other hand however, and in consideration of France, the Delors Report is, like the Werner Report, ahead of its time and to some extent an abstract design, since it decouples monetary integration from political union. Undoubtedly this was a major concern for Germany. The discussion paper, which the *Bundesbank* President Karl-Otto Pöhl submitted to the (Delors) Committee for the Study of EMU reflects this concern:

> ... it should be made clear that monetary integration cannot move ahead of general economic integration since otherwise the whole process of integration would be burdened with considerable economic and social tensions. Moreover examples from history demonstrate that new nations did not confer a uniform monetary order on themselves until after the process of unification was concluded. Any durable attempt to fix exchange rates within the Community and finally to replace national currencies by a European currency would be doomed to failure so long as a minimum of policy-shaping and decision-making in the field of economic and fiscal policy does not take place at Community level...' (pp. 131–2)

and later 'at all events, within a monetary union, monetary policy can only be conducted at a Community level' (p. 136). Undoubtedly Pöhl had been aware that the loss of national sovereignty would be serious and that no monetary union in the past had led to or brought about political union. The creation of the Reichsbank in 1875 – *following not preceding Bismarck's unification of Germany in 1871* – must have been a poignant memory playing on his mind.

At the Madrid European Council meeting of June 1989 the member states agreed in principle to convene an IGC charged with negotiations on treaty changes necessary to put EMU into operation and for the first stage to be launched on 1 July 1990. In the event external pressures and historical events accelerated further developments. France, who took over the rotating EC presidency in July 1989, was determined to make EMU a priority of French presidency. However, having been initially the force behind the Delors Plan, the German Chancellor, preoccupied with domestic issues, began to back-track, risking a rift with France when he resisted attempts by the French President to set a definite date on the convening of the planned IGC on EMU. Already at the Madrid summit in June 1989 Kohl had supported the British Prime Minister Thatcher in resisting the fixing of a deadline for the second and third stage of the Delors Plan. This hesitation became more pronounced during the period between the collapse of the Berlin Wall on 9 November and the December summit in Strasbourg. Kohl's sudden reluctance towards pushing ahead with EMU can partly be explained by his desires to de-couple negotiations on monetary policies from the forthcoming parliamentary elections (in the event the first elections to be held in unified Germany), but partly it reflected Germany's traditional concern already present during the Werner Plan negotiations that monetary union should be the crowning of economic union and not the other way round: Kenneth Dyson calls this the 'coronation' theory.[44] Moreover, Kohl genuinely felt uneasy about alienating the German public by rushing towards EMU.

Circumstances presented France with a welcome leverage. In the autumn of 1989 'the German problem' though only briefly, leapt to the top of the European Agenda. The fall of the Berlin Wall on 9 November added a new dimension to the process of the EC. The prospect of unification reignited old fears of Germany achieving hegemony over Europe. Germany needed the Community and above all French support for unification. As a result, a linkage between German Unification and deeper integration emerged clearly for the first time at the summit meeting of the European Council in Strasbourg in December 1989. At this crucial point the Dutch, who had hitherto supported Germany in a gradual approach to EMU, switched sides and supported Mitterrand for rapid transition to EMU. Finally, and only after the intervention of Delors, a deal was hammered out. In return for the Community's somewhat grudging support for German Unification, Kohl accepted Mitterrand's proposal for convening an IGC prior to the German election in the autumn of 1990.

At the Rome I European Council summit on 27/28 October 1990 Kohl also consented to an ambitious negotiating mandate for the IGC on EMU, including a date for Stage II to start on 1 January 1994 despite British objections.[45] During the course of 1991 the basic structure of EMU was elaborated and was incorporated into the Treaty on European Union (TEU) and was also included in various Protocols and Declarations attached to the treaty making the EMU objective – by giving it a definite time-table i.e. 1 January 1999 – an irreversible reality.

The objective of Stage II was to continue economic, fiscal and monetary convergence among member states thus creating conditions for the transition to the final stage. During this stage, responsibility for monetary policy remained at the national level. But a new institution, the European Monetary Institute (EMI) would be set up which would take over the role of the Committee of Governors of central banks the latter being dissolved at the start of Stage II. The EMI would submit annual statements assessing the progress of member states' economic convergence and make recommendations to member states concerning the conduct of their monetary policies. Stage II was to remain in effect until a decision had been made to enter into Stage III which according to the TEU might have occurred on 1 July 1997 if a majority of member states had satisfied the convergence conditions (see below). However, in the event only five of the member states were forecast to satisfy these criteria and the 1 January 1997 starting date was abandoned. Nevertheless Stage III was to begin by 1 January 1999 irrespective of whether a majority of member states had achieved the criteria. The number of member states was not specified in the treaty, but it has generally been assumed that a minimum of two might be sufficient (probably France and Germany with perhaps a few of the smaller states joining), i.e. the 'ins'. The non-participating member states would have an obligation to meet the convergence criteria as soon as possible, i.e. the 'outs'. Stage III entailed the launching of the EURO, the single currency, on 1 January 1999 and the establishment of the ECB with the primary goal of maintaining price stability.

While it has been argued here that the fall of the Berlin Wall has accelerated the process in terms of a time-table, it is not suggested that German Unification was the momentum behind EMU. Since the project had been on the agenda since 1971, revitalised by both the EMS and the SEA, it was a combination of circumstances and internal and external catalysts, not least the Single Market and a dynamic leadership in the Commission, all of which had preceded German Unification, that added pressure for a single currency. Nevertheless, as far as the design of EMU was concerned, Germany's hegemony was well established. Her outstanding role as an exporter, the prestige of the *Bundesbank* and the leading position of the Deutsch Mark, both in the ERM and also in the international economy, being the only currency which never had to be devalued, appeared to justify the use of Germany as a role model. As has been argued[46] 'structural power' has shifted towards Germany. In the end France conceded that an EMU zone even if based on the German model was preferred to a *Bundesbank*-dominated Deutsch Mark zone. So France opted for a low profile and instead of constructing EMU on the French model, Paris had kept a hand on the German steering wheel, thus seeking to salvage as much as possible on the direction of the project. 'It [EMU] will happen if, but only if, the Germans are willing, and the French are able.'[47]

So what had been German motives for supporting the plan? For Germany the EMU firstly embodied the crowning of the Single Market ('Whoever heard of a Single Market with 11 currencies?' Helmut Schmidt) and consolidated further the process of European integration in which Bonn has a major stake. The October 1987 financial crash demonstrated the need for closer monetary cooperation. It has been conventional wisdom to argue[48] that EMU would not be good for Germany. However, economically, the EMS has certainly been of benefit to Germany, protecting the Deutsch Mark to some extent from pressures to revalue. An EMU would improve on this: there would be no competitive devaluations within EMU and no possibility that, once in place, members particularly France would leave the system or pursue independent policies.

Kohl's support for EMU as had been Adenauer's for the CAP was blatantly political in motivation and purpose. Monetary integration was the next major logical step in the consolidation of Europe and the new key area in Franco-German relations. In that sense, Germany had to take account of French interests in the new venture. In addition, Kohl wanted to show that even a united Germany would remain committed to European integration. EMU was launched in the midst of the euphoric development in Eastern Europe and German Unification. The new dialogue with the East (of significant importance to Germany as the 'borderline' country) had to be complemented by a reassuring initiative directed at the EC. It was necessary to demonstrate that a unified Germany was a European Germany.[49] What better proof of this than to surrender the Deutsch Mark to a Single Currency and to pass decision-making power from the prestigious *Bundesbank* to a new common European bank? Germany thus assumed a 'flagship function' for EMU feeling a 'special responsibility for the completion of monetary union'.[50] The political price was a transfer of sovereignty and decision-making over monetary policies, but only after the design of the project had been overseen by Germany. This attitude and course of events with regards to EMU negotiations and outcome bears a striking resemblance to Germany's position in CAP negotiations.[51]

EMU: A *Bundesbank* Model

Historically France and Germany have pursued fundamentally different monetary policies. One of the reasons for this was the degree of central bank independence in the two countries. In France with a dependent central bank, evidence of economic manipulation was found in several presidential elections. In Germany, by contrast, with an independent central bank, there was an absence of influence on monetary policy by German governments strikingly demonstrated under the forceful government of Chancellor Schmidt.[52] Sensitive to inflation, Germany has always pursued a restrictive, export-led monetary policy, while that of France was expansive and orientated towards a strong exchange rate. France has also been more relaxed in terms of trade-offs between inflation and employment objectives.

During EMU negotiations Germany had insisted on (and France had accepted) three conditions: first, that the new bank would be independent, second, that a series of strict so-called 'convergence criteria' which had to be met by any member state wanting to join the EMU project would be attached to the treaty and third, that the EMU project should be linked to the declared objective of working towards political union. A fourth condition was added to the above as a 'post-Maastricht or renegotiated Maastricht condition: namely the 'Stability Pact' which was to safeguard stability beyond the TEU treaty provisions.

The most sensitive issue was (and still is) the role and autonomy of the central bank. The decision-making body of the ECB is the Governing Council (members of the Executive Board and the governors of the national central banks) and the Executive Board which implements monetary policies according to the Governing Council's guidelines and decisions. The treaty required each member state to begin a legislative process leading to the independence of its central bank during Stage III.[53] At the beginning of the Maastricht process, only the *Bundesbank* was fully independent, while the central banks of the Netherlands and Austria – the latter had joined in 1995 – as well as Belgium, Denmark and to some extent Italy had a very high though varying degree of independence. The country with the least independent central bank (apart from the Bank of England) was France. The government started to implement TEU provision with the laws of 4 August 1993 and 31 August 1993 to comply with treaty requirements and since January 1994 the Banque de France has had statutory independence.

This issue, which had already divided the two countries throughout the duration of the IGC, continues to be a profound irritation for France. German insistence an the bank's independence contradicts sharply with French frustration at the loss of a very important economic 'policy tool'. French opposition to an independent bank centred on having to surrender sovereignty to a banking system built on German lines, but also reflected French tradi- tional monetary policies orientated towards the exchange rate rather than the inflation rate (a soft Franc would boost exports and promote domestic employment). The Banque de France – before attaining independence – was regarded as an 'agency' of government economic policy and thus received instructions from political authorities. France basically believes in the political direction of economic and monetary policies and demanded that the new European bank should be 'politically accountable'. Originally France had not even aimed at creating a new institution, but had hoped that existing ones, the ECOFIN, but particularly so the European Council (a French invention) or the Council of Ministers would determine broad guidelines of monetary policy or at least act as counterweight to a European bank.[54] As a result, France has repeatedly objected (although rather belatedly) that the independence of the future ECB has been anchored and constitutionally safeguarded by the TEU. Given this background and French pre-occupation with 'political independence', it is somewhat surprising that France – albeit grudgingly – accepted the principle of an independent ECB pledged to price stability as early as December 1988 as a basis for negotiations in the Delors Committee.

Although proclaiming officially its belief in the desirability of the bank's independence, France's basic resentment continues to resurface from time to time and has increased in intensity after the 1995 election of Jacques Chirac as president of France signalling growing tensions between Bonn and Paris. The then *Bundesbank* President Tietmeyer warned that France's aim of creating a political counterweight to 'control or influence' the ECB, did not conform with the treaty.[55] This conflict is also reflected by the acrimonious negotiations surrounding the appointment of the President of the ECB. France had supported the candidature of Jean-Claude Trichet, Governor of the French central bank, while Germany had backed the Dutch Wim Duisenberg, President of the former European Monetary Institute (EMI). A 'time-sharing' agreement was hammered out in early May 1998 which, although securing the appointment of the German favoured candidate, limited it to four years, after which Duisenberg is to be replaced by the French candidate. This compromise constitutes a clear break of the TEU which stipulates that the ECB President must serve a non-renewable term of eight years.[56] Although the ECB President has repeatedly stated that it was his decision whether or not to retire after four years, the French have nevertheless succeeded in politicising the issue.

Arguments questioning the need for the ECB's independence are both unsettling and futile to Germany: unsettling because an independent ECB pledged to safeguard price stability was seen as the core element for a viable EMU and a fundamental principle for (German) approval of the project. In Germany it is generally accepted that price stability which is the ECB's primary objective as enshrined in the Maastricht treaty, is best safeguarded by an independent bank which is not subject to the usual short-term pressures that characterised the political process. 'The *Bundesbank* always decided in favour of domestic price stability and sacrificed exchange rate stability if necessary ... The mandate of the ECB must be to maintain stability of the value of money as the prime objective of European monetary policy.'[57]

Germany's consistent record of low inflation seems to demonstrate the wisdom of following such *Stabilitätspolitik*, when the bank's duty to maintain price stability is more important than its allegiance to political mentors. The question of why the *Bundesbank*, by and large, has enjoyed great trust from the German public is a curious one, but it seems clear that any measures threatening the institution's independent actions would jeopardise Germany's stability culture. Policy-makers in a government controlled central bank seek re-election for their government whereas an independent bank seeks to give evidence of its competence to the public.[58] Consequently, policy-makers of the *Bundesbank* have followed a consistently anti-inflation policy, because it has been felt that this is demanded by the German public. If the *Bundesbank* were to fail to deliver in terms of low inflation and stability it would appear to be incompetent at fulfilling its brief. Thus it appears that it is not formal legal devices but, above all, the favourable public opinion and trust which ensures the bank's continued independence.

Making the ECB formally accountable to governments, would, in the German view, contradict the very notion of full institutional independence embodied in the treaty. Clearly, the desire to ensure the new bank's independence was motivated by a deep preoccupation with inflation and the concern that the bank must be able to pursue a policy of price stability without political interference. The ECB has been given a clear European mandate; any accountability in respect of any national government or national parliament would contradict the logic of a single European monetary policy. Moreover, the new bank argues, it is actually perfectly democratically legitimate for the EU to delegate authority to an institution outside the regular political process. In the case of the ECB a treaty concluded by 15 governments and ratified by 15 national parliaments does imply a solid degree of democratic legitimacy. Once accepted that price stability is a lasting and not a temporary concern then the institution which has been entrusted to safeguard that price stability should also be awarded protection.[59]

Attempts to reverse the role of the ECB by France are also rather futile, because the bank's independence has been guaranteed by the treaty (Art. 108, ex Art. 107). These provisions of the TEU, while clearly based on the *Bundesbank Act* have been accepted during the ratification process for the TEU. Why does this issue therefore periodically resurface? With the benefit of hindsight, France might feel that her prime objective for pursuing EMU has not been achieved, namely to break the dominance of the *Bundesbank*. In its place is now a larger and potentially more powerful institution which, also as a result of Kohl's persuasive attempts at the October 1993 summit in Brussels, is located in Frankfurt and, one might say, is overlooked by the German central bank.[60]

However, statutory independence is seen as insufficient for ensuring price stability. Consequently, having insisted on the new bank's autonomy, Germany demanded that entry to EMU was also conditional on fulfilling (and mandatory unless an 'opt-out-clause' was negotiated for those countries satisfying) certain 'convergence criteria'. These conditions reflect to a large extent the German economists' point of view. Thus a gradual instead of a sudden transition was adopted: since the convergence criteria had to be met *before* a country could enter EMU. Germany obviously feared that, if countries with weak financial discipline were to enter EMU, these states would represent a serious risk for countries like Germany with a strong monetary discipline. But by meeting stringent criteria, weaker countries would demonstrate their willingness and ability to live by the demands of a disciplined financial policy. Only then would the EURO be as strong and as stable as the Deutsch Mark. It is for this reason that during Maastricht negotiations Germany had opposed the qualified majority voting rule for membership of EMU and had demanded unanimity instead thus allowing the German government to veto the admission of any country whose economic policies might not satisfy Germany. Already at this stage Germany advocated automatic imposition of large fines on member states whose budget deficit and public debts exceeded certain levels. Germany was outvoted on both issues but she reintroduced the 'automatic sanctions philosophy' in the 'Stability Pact' of 1995 (see below).

These convergence criteria, recommended by the Delors Report, also have a long history: The Werner Report of 1970 states: 'in particular the development of monetary unification must be based on sufficient progress in the field of convergence and then in that of the unification of economic policies.'[61] Entry conditions are based on inflation, interest rates, participation in the ERM and evidence of an absence of an 'excessive deficit' in the countries' budgetary position.[62]

- The average rate of inflation must not exceed by more than 1.5 percentage points that observed in the three best performing member states.
- The ratio of government deficit to GDP and that of government debt to GDP must not exceed 3% and 60% respectively.
- Participation in the ERM means that a member state 'has respected the normal fluctuation margins provided for by the ERM of the EMS without severe tensions for at least the last two years before the examination'.

- In terms of interest rates member states 'shall have a nominal long-term interest rate that does not exceed that of, at most, the three best performing Member States ... by more than 2 percentage points'.

These reference values formed the basis of the Commission's and EMI's report constituting the final decision on EMU membership. The criteria which apply to Stage III of EMU were later supplemented by the 'Stability and Growth Pact' (see below).

It could be argued that the implication of strict convergence criteria and the race between member states to meet them has created a two-speed Europe dividing the 'best-performers' from those unable (or unwilling) to join. When at the December 1995 summit in Madrid EU leaders pronounced that a core group of countries would move to the final stage at the specified time, a 'convergence race' between those member states set on joining in 1999 began. However, even prior to the TEU, attempts at monetary union had resulted in a two-tier Europe: during the 1970s several EC countries were not members of the 'currency snake', while at the same time countries from outside the EC had joined the scheme. The same is true of the remainder of the EMS (i.e. those countries who are not members of the Eurozone), since the ERM does not include Britain and Sweden. Moreover, exchange rates in the EMS before EMU had continued to vary and indeed the diversion had actually increased since the widening of the permissible margins to plus/minus 15 percent.

We do not see it as our task either to question or defend the logic or wisdom of such conditions which have drawn criticism from economists.[64] We are merely emphasising that they seemed important enough (at least to some countries including Germany) to attach them to the TEU. The German Chancellor appears to have demanded these conditions with German public support in mind. If the EMU project was modelled on the *Bundesbank* and if, in particular, the new currency could match the Deutsch Mark in terms of prestige and stability, then public support for the new treaty would be forthcoming, or at least easier to win. In an interview with *Time Newsmagazine*, in 1996, Kohl was asked how he would win the support of his electorate for EMU. He replied that it was not a question of abolishing the mark, but 'of introducing a stable, single European currency. The majority will be in favour if it is certain that the new currency will be stable. That is why there must be no manipulation of the criteria in the Maastricht Treaty.'[65] The insistence on convergence criteria may thus have been a tactical move and a way of saving face and was thus of a political nature, creating pressure and momentum for EMU. However, in pronouncing the TEU compatible with the German Constitutions, the German Supreme Court ruling of 12 October 1993 included a provision insisting on a strict interpretation of the convergence criteria.

Finally, Germany insisted on absolute parallelism between an IGC on EMU and a second conference on European Political Union (EPU). Kohl manipulated French interest in closer co-ordination (with Germany) on security matters to persuade Mitterrand to embark on a process of political union, involving not just CFSP but also institutional reform. The need for a linkage between monetary union and political integration was emphasised by the historical events in the East, but undoubtedly it was also part of Germany's coherent and long-term strategy. However, it is important to realise that the link between monetary and political union had already existed in and since the Werner Plan: 'The economic and monetary union thus appears as a leaven for the development of political union which in the long run it will be unable to do without.'[66] Germany was reluctant to pursue the monetary project – knowing that it would be difficult to 'sell' it to both the German electorate and the *Bundesbank* – unless it was paralleled by equal efforts in the foreign and security area and accompanied by institutional reform. Kohl's 'parallelism' was supported not only by Delors who in a speech before the EP endorsed the German Chancellor's suggestion for a second IGC to address the democratic deficit in the Community,[67] but also by the *Bundesbank*: 'In the final analysis, a Monetary Union is ... an irrevocable sworn confraternity – "all for one and one for all" – which, if it is to prove durable, requires, judging from past experience, even closer links in the form of a comprehensive political union.'[68]

Accordingly, on 19 April 1990, Kohl and Mitterand sent a joint letter to Council's Irish Presidency calling for an Intergovernmental Conference on political union to parallel the one proposed for EMU. The Dublin European Council meeting in June of the same year endorsed the Franco-German request.[69] The second Kohl-Mitterand letter, on 6 December 1990, specified the agenda for political union, which for Gemany was a synonym for transferring more power to the EP and a CFSP. Chancellor Kohl declared to the *Bundestag*: '...the parallelism of the two intergovernmental conferences is of fundamental significance ... As I see it, the only possibility for the Federal Republic is to agree to both at the same time. Both projects are inextricably linked to each other.'[70] Thus the German government and indeed the *Bundesbank* insisted on this parallelism as given. 'Further development towards an economic and monetary union agreed upon in Maastricht is associated with the vision of a Europe politically united as well. The new coordination procedures in both the political and the economic spheres and the increase in Community responsibilities underline the link between the political union and the economic and monetary union.'[71] The linkage between EMU and political union was a political one, an element in a strategy of incremental integration.

However, this having been said, the EMU conference benefited from concrete and well designed proposals, eventually set down under Pillar 1 of the TEU (i.e. the supranational pillar) these proposals, like the customs union in the Treaty of Rome, were given a definite time-table, while the proposals for political and institutional reform were less defined and on French insistence concentrated on strengthening intergovernmental institutions, e.g. the European Council, although of course there had been a significant upgrading of the European Parliament. Thus institutional reforms in the TEU were less far-reaching and less radical than EMU. There was a clear imbalance, a disequilibrium between EMU and political union[72] that is between the two conferences. The negotiations in the IGC on EMU reflected speed, efficiency and a dramatic single-mindedness of purpose, while proposals tabled in the second IGC, i.e. on EPU, drew less attention, the objectives being broader and less defined.[73] In fact Kohl was heavily criticised for not having defended German interests i.e. political union with more vigour.[74]

This fact qualifies to some extent the argument that Germany has emerged as victor from TEU/EMU negotiations. While it is true that the blueprint for EMU clearly reflects German strategies, in particular the independence of the bank and the convergence criteria, and while it was largely on German insistence that a second IGC on political union was convened, Paris could claim that the EMU chapter in the TEU, particularly the attachment of a time-table, reflected the French 'monetarist' views. Thus the TEU, agreed at Maastricht in December 1991, was an example of a classic Franco-German compromise. The French attached primary importance to EMU in a Community framework, which it regards as *sine qua non* for political union.[75] It has been argued that Germany did not have a hegemonic role in the EMS/EMU comparable for example to that of the USA under the Bretton Woods system, because it lacked the resources. Germany's position in EMU negotiations were policy-based deriving from its history of low inflation, a strong currency and a favourable balance of payment position.[76] On the other hand however, there is the view that the TEU 'contracts the pooling of sovereignty in a single currency, a "selling" or "sharing" of the *Bundesbank*, in return for the acceptance of German standards for a stable currency.'[77]

Of course there were other players in this game: Jacques Delors, the Commission President, was one of them. He developed a personal rapport with Chancellor Kohl (much more so than with President Mitterrand) and participated in EMU negotiations not as the Commission President, as perhaps he should have, i.e. the honest broker, but as the policy-maker Delors who passionately believed in EMU, pursuing it for its own sake, but also as a means to an end, i.e political union, an objective he shared with Chancellor Kohl. The entrepreneurial role of the Commission since 1985 when Delors took over as President has been widely documented. Delors, a former finance minister, had ample experience in monetary matters and was largely responsible for the French U-turn in monetary strategies in the early 1980s.[78] His report reflected to a remarkable degree the combined French and German objectives. While proposing a phased approach to EMU, Delors did not specify a time-table, but laid down the irreversibility of the project: 'the decision to enter upon the first stage should be a decision to embark on the entire process.'[79] At the same time, the report emphasises the importance of economic convergence in parallel with technical preparation for monetary union and an independent bank, thus paying due attention to German interests.

There were other countries too which provided occasional leadership as for example the Netherlands. Italy had been a supporter of the 1987 'Balladur' paper, had shared French resentment of the Deutsch Mark as the (undervalued) pivot currency of the EMS system and had argued that German structural surpluses had introduced tension in the exchange system undermining growth in other member states. It was under the Italian presidency in the second half of 1990 that the IGCs were planned and their organisational structure were agreed. Despite these various inputs, however, there appears to be a consensus that it was the *Bundesbank* Council which had designed the institutional parameters of the European Central Bank and the terms for monetary union,[80] although of course it can be argued that the *Bundesbank*'s continued reservation to the EMU project constituted an additional pressure for the German government that other member states did not encounter. While this limited Kohl's freedom to manoeuvre, the German delegation was able, during the negotiations 'to dictate the terms of the Maastricht Treaty related to EMU' thereby ensuring that it reflected *Bundesbank* law.

POST-MAASTRICHT CONFLICTS

Obviously Maastricht could only draw up the framework and set out principles: the interpretation of which had yet to be negotiated including key aspects such as the precise relations between the ECB and national governments and the operation of EMU after 1999. Having settled EMU issues at governmental level, it now had to be sold to the public. Unfortunately, the contradiction between the aspiration of the politicians and actual performance of Europe's economic situation surfaced towards the mid-1990s and was reflected by conflicts over the implications of monetary union at domestic levels, generating a public debate, which surprisingly was not over the ideological wisdom of the project but focused on its short-term costs.

The ratification of the Treaty on European Union (TEU) took place in France on 20 September 1992, when the French President's popularity was waning while the economy slumped and unemployment rose. The German *Bundesbank*'s tough policy on interest rates to counter inflationary pressure as a result of unification created resentment against Germany and further fuelled hostility against what appeared to be a German led EMU project – the centre-piece of the new treaty. Despite an impressive campaign which even included a televised address by Chancellor Kohl on French television to bolster support for Maastricht, the French people narrowly voted in favour (i.e. 51.05%) of the treaty. Franco-German relations became further strained following the serious and prolonged crisis the EMS experienced between September 1992 and August 1993 which not only resulted in the withdrawal of the Pound Sterling and the Italian Lira from the ERM but led to fluctuations in other currencies: the French Franc, the Irish Punt and the Spanish and Portuguese currencies despite massive intervention by the *Bundesbank* in support of the Franc. Speculative activities culminated on 2 August in a *de facto* suspension of the ERM as the permissible fluctuation bands were widened from plus/minus 2.25% (plus/minus 6% in the case of the British, Portuguese and Spanish currencies) to plus/minus 15% of either side of the parity. This was the first sign that the spirit of Maastricht (i.e. to adhere to the exchange rate criterion) had been undermined.

The mid-1990s characterised major political changes in France and Germany. After the coming to power of President Jacques Chirac, Franco-German relations suffered a set-back and caused anxiety in Germany about continued French commitment to EMU. On coming to power, Chirac was rather vague about France's fundamental commitment to European integration in general and in particular whether France would be able to meet the convergence criteria for EMU which now, in the midst of a recession, looked harsher than in 1991 when they had been agreed. Pressures from trade unions led to a wage-push inflation during the early 1990s and in the delay of crucial reforms to both the welfare state and over-regulated labour market. Chirac might have been hoping that Germany in order to ensure French membership of EMU would be willing to soften the criteria. Such hopes were dashed at the first summit of the two leaders in Baden-Baden in October 1995.

Convergence emerged as the major conflict within and between political parties in several member states, particularly so in France. Pressure to meet the criteria now resulted in harsh economic measures by the French government which were unwelcome by the public and led in November–December 1995 to a series of strikes and demonstrations. High unemployment and social unrest triggered renewed anxiety about allowing EMU to turn into a fiscal and monetary straitjacket. In Germany the problem was less about the criteria but rather the strength of the new currency which was in question. It was because of this concern that Germany was determined to insist that there should be no dilution of the Maastricht criteria: Indeed Germany's foreign minister Kinkel insisted that the criteria were sacrosanct and that 'wobblers, delayers and vacillators should have no chance'.[82]

Had EMU originally been an élite-led project, and had public discussion been missing before and during the Maastricht ratification process or had it been subsumed by other issues, debates which had begun with intensity during the mid and later 1990s reached a climax just before the decision was due to be made as to which countries would be participating in EMU and the launch of the EURO in January 1999. The immediate costs of EMU generated public discontent and thus 'nationalised' the debate on EMU which before had been seen as a separate European project under the leadership of governments. As Stage III was approaching a number of important details yet undefined in the TEU had to be settled. Accordingly, the EU set up an ambitious programme put together to carry the Union beyond the provisions of the Maastricht treaty. At the summit of heads of states and of governments in Formentor (Majorca) in September 1995 and at the subsequent Madrid summit in December a blueprint for the introduction of a Single Currency which outlined a detailed change-over scenario to be completed by 2002 was formally endorsed. The German finance minister also secured unanimous support for the name of the new single currency: the EURO. The recommendations reflected key German demands, particularly a long transitional phase in contrast to both the Commission's and France's preference for a swift transition for currency conversion: 'the recommendations [of the EMI] will take account of significant German concerns ... the single currency will only become legal tender once the people have European coins and banknotes in their pockets, that is at the end of a transition period of up to three years'.[83]

Franco-German relations in terms of EMU developments were dominated by two main issues: first, a German inspired 'Stability Pact' and second a French induced special EURO-X committee. The German government had to convince its electorate that the new currency to be introduced in 1999 would be as strong as the Deutsch Mark. To this end and in an attempt to enforce sound management of public finance in the EURO area, the German finance minister Theo Waigel in November 1995 proposed a 'Stability Pact for Europe'[84] as successor to the 'excessive deficit procedure' of the TEU (Art. 104c1). On German insistence, the Commission and the ECOFIN were asked to draft regulations that would clarify the implementation of the excessive deficit procedure to ensure budgetary discipline for those countries entering Stage III. The specification was that annual budget deficits should not exceed 3% of GDP after 1999. This implied permanent obligations binding member states. If a country were to overshoot this target, it would have to produce a credible plan for correcting the imbalance during the subsequent financial year. Failing this and following several Council warnings, fiscal delinquents would face sanctions in the form of a non-interest bearing deposit at an EU institution. The German concern clearly indicated the doubts Germany still had about the institutional framework of EMU and the need to create a stability culture in Europe reflecting yet another guarantee to ensure that EMU would run according to German economic precepts. The pact was viewed as a crucial element in post-EMU arrangements enforcing fiscal discipline in much the same way as the convergence criteria had done during Stage III.

Although all EU states subscribed to the principle of the Stability Pact to enforce budgetary discipline after EMU, only the Dutch were close to the German position. Some countries, in particular France, but also supported by Britain, Italy and Spain, argued that the German approach to budget deficits was too rigid echoing economists' concern that it was rigid, disciplinarian and punitive.[85] Subsequent negotiations exposed a clear divide between German demands for near automatic sanctions against states running deficits in excess of 3% of GDP unless there are defined 'temporary and exceptional' circumstances such as a disaster or a severe recession, and French demands, which insisted on political discretion in applying penalties.[86] The latter mistrusted any kind of 'automatic' decision-making outside the political or parliamentary arena and proposed the creation of a 'stability council' a political body acting in tandem with the ECB giving political direction rather than pursuing purely economic goals and reflecting French views that monetary policies should be subordinated to overall economic policies and subjected to political control. 'The basis of the French position is that we don't want all decisions on economic, budgetary, fiscal and monetary policy to be shaped by a technocratic, automatic system under the sole authority of the ECB.'[87]

Negotiations on the pact became deadlocked and on several occasions German officials threatened to walk out of the meetings, although the threat was generally interpreted as a negotiating tactic.[88] The German finance minister continued to emphasise the creation of a stability culture, while his French counterpart repeatedly referred to 'national sovereignty' clearly reflecting long-term differences in French and German political philosophy and underlying the French view that monetary union cannot be left to independent central bankers but must have a political content. The conflict reached crisis point at the summit meeting in Dublin 14/15 December 1996 during an unparalleled confrontation between Kohl and Chirac ending in a screaming match which shocked their aides rendering them speechless.[89]

In the event, the Amsterdam European Council summit approved the 'Growth and Stability Pact', which is likely to be a deterrent to deficit spending, although as a deviation to the original Waigel paper, there will be no 'automatic' fines. At the same time and as a concession to the newly elected socialist government in France, however, a special Employment Chapter was included in the treaty, demanded by France and agreed by Germany as a counter-weight to EMU. The word 'growth' was added to satisfy some countries (particularly France) to show the priority the EU places on employment and growth. The French proposed stability council was downgraded on German insistence to merely an advisory body.

The Amsterdam summit in June 1997 suffered, if not a crisis, from a low ebb in terms of Franco-German relations which had deteriorated sharply after Juppé's rightwing government was defeated by Lionel Jospin's leftwing coalition in 1997. The new Socialist leader had increased anxiety in Germany over the EMU process, particularly as the election in France had closely followed a dispute between the German government and the *Bundesbank* over the revaluation of the country's gold reserves (in an attempt to meet the convergence criteria). Given the importance of EMU, it is extraordinary that Amsterdam did not engage in a serious debate on this issue. In fact, while the TEU Art. N2 had required the convening of a IGC for 1996–7 to negotiate treaty revision, Mr De Silguy, the Commissioner responsible for monetary affairs, had advised against reopening the provisions of Maastricht in this area presumably to avoid a 'derailing' of the process.[90] This was just as well, because once it had become clear that the original 1997 target for entry into Stage III, i.e. January 1997, had been quietly abandoned, countries entered the race to meet the criteria for 1999 (the economic reference year was 1997) thus splitting the Community into the 'best-performers' and those who were borderline. It seems clear that the Stability Pact has heightened 'the visibility of the linkage between austerity and monetary integration, possibly fanning political discontent with European integration more generally'.[91] Thus criticism about the lack of accountability in EU institutions resurfaced, a fact which prompted France to create a new body, the EURO-X to act as counter-weight to the ECB. In 1997 the French finance minister Dominique Strauss-Kahn proposed a special Committee (consisting of EURO finance ministers only) in an attempt to introduce what became known as an 'economic government of the EURO' causing great alarm in both Bonn and other member states. Germany, anxious that EURO-X might lead to a erosion of the ECB's independence, insisted that the committee should deal with technical issues only. However, since the EURO-X has competence in the areas of exchange rate policy and fiscal co-ordination, it could undermine the ECB's stability-orientated monetary policies, which in any event is considered by Germany an insufficient guarantee for maintaining a near-zero inflation zone. Thus while it can be argued that the introduction of the Stability and Growth Pact (despite French input) has been a clear victory for Germany, the French won on the creation of EURO-X which seems to have developed into the main macro-economic policy arena in EMU.

One explanation of why EMU had not featured significantly at Amsterdam (with the exception of the 'Stability Pact') was that first, the TEU had dealt with the legal framework for EMU and second, that developments relating to EMU were ongoing ones and necessary decisions were in fact taken at European Council meetings. Thus while the Madrid European Council summit in December 1995 had settled among other issues the change-over scenario, member states knew that the biggest question – who would qualify for EMU – would still have to be made. A decision was taken in May 1998 to that effect on the basis of member states' economic performance in 1997. In this second decision process there was no longer any need for a majority of the member states to fulfil the convergence conditions (as had been for entry in 1996). In the event all countries except Greece fulfilled the criteria (Denmark and Britain had secured an op-out clause and Sweden had decided not to 'opt-in'). Chancellor Kohl at the extra-ordinary meeting of the Council on 3 May 1998 told the press: 'these [EMU-membership decisions] will change the face of Europe'.[92] The ECB was established on 1 July 1998, six months before the final start of Stage III and the EMI went into liquidation. Upon transition to Stage III, the right of the national central banks to issue bank-notes was transferred to the Governing Council of the ECB.

Despite these numerous conflicts, particularly on the ECB's status and the Stability Pact, the Franco-German duo survived, even continued to gather momentum on EMU. Both France and Germany felt a special responsibility for the project (as indeed Schmidt and Giscard d'Estaing had for the EMS). France neither wanted to be left out nor risk failure or postponement of Stage III. Germany too did not want to see France failing to meet the criteria. Already in 1995, Waigel, the minister of finance had declared: 'I say that France must be a member of EMU. That is my opinion. I am not alone. The Chancellor has said this. The coalition parties have said this. EMU only makes sense if France and Germany are members.' On the unrest in France, he commented, 'such an adjustment programme produces tensions. But countries would face the need for adjustment, even if European integration was not involved.'[93] On Franco-German relations, Mr Tietmeyer in an interview with a German paper stated: 'I cannot imagine a monetary union either without France or without Germany. Not without Germany because presumably the other countries would have little interest without the participation of the anchor currency in the EMS. Not without France because France is a core country in the European integration process.'[94]

While Jospin's socialist government may have continued to harbour strong reservations against EMU, the French government has nevertheless implemented the convergence criteria with clear determination even when faced with strikes. The budget adopted for 1997 (the qualifying year for EMU membership) provided for a reduction in overall spending in an attempt to meet the deficit target of 3% GDP. At the occasion of the unveiling of 'the most important and closely scrutinised' French budget since 1945, the French finance minister Jean Arthuis declared: 'It is essential not to allow any backsliding either on the criteria, or on the proposed timetable. We want the treaty, all the treaty and nothing but the treaty. I refuse to imagine the hypothesis in which monetary union will not take place.'[95]

By and large both the French and German leaders have been careful not to articulate criticism (in public) of the other partner's approach to the EMUs as both wanted to be perceived, in their own countries, as well as in the Community at large, as sharing a political commitment to a very necessary and worthy cause. During a joint press conference in Brussels for example the German foreign minister and his French counterpart side-stepped questions about German criticism of a French proposal for a political counterweight to the ECB and declined to comment on rumours of a Franco-German deal for the appointment of a President for the ECB.[96] Thus the conflict over the Stability Pact was replaced by a pledge to remain the engine driving political and economic integration. Addressing the German Parliament on 3 April 1998, Kohl declared: 'EMU is ... the most significant decision since German Unification. It is the most profound change in Europe since the collapse of communist imperialism. It is at the same time the most important milestone in the European unification process since the foundation of the ECSC in 1951 and the EEC in 1957.'[97]

THE NEW GERMAN GOVERNMENT AND EMU

There had been one event of importance: the change of government in Germany in the autumn of 1998 which introduced new elements into the Franco-German debate on the EMU regime. With both countries under left-of-centre rule, France and Germany welcomed 'a new chance' and a 'new phase in Franco-German cooperation'.[98] It seems that the new government is more flexible over a trade-off between inflation and employment which might narrow the political gulf between France and Germany over the conduct of monetary and fiscal policies under EMU. Concern in both countries have brought the problem of low growth and employment to the top of the agenda. Indeed, the new German Chancellor, in 1996 when still Prime Minister of Lower Saxony, had argued in 1996 that priority must be given to job creation even at the expense of delaying the EMU time-table, sentiments which were echoed during the French 1995 presidential election which had been run on the same lines. However, the SPD, after a disastrous state election run on an anti-EMU election campaign in March 1996 in Baden-Württemberg and in September 1997 in Hamburg, has been conspicuously quiet on EMU issues which did not feature as an issue in either of the main parties' election campaigns in the autumn of 1998. In any event, the change in Germany's European policy in general and in Franco-German relations in particular is less dramatic than it had perhaps originally been assumed. During the first half of 1999 Germany had taken over the six month presidency of the EU. The new foreign minister and deputy chancellor Joschka Fischer, in a formal presentation of his government's agenda to the European Parliament on 12 January 1999 declared: 'the introduction ... of a common currency is not primarily an economic, but rather a sovereign and thus eminently political act',[99] thus echoing the sentiments of the Kohl government.

Moreover, while German social democrats and French socialists share a greater consensus on fiscal policy, institutional arrangements and the legal administrative environment of the EMU are, of course, regulated by the Maastricht Treaty. This limits the freedom of manoeuvre in the two countries. So far, the ECB, ring-fenced in the TEU – the legal blueprint for EMU – has shown no flexibility in terms of relaxing its commitment to price stability or to demands for greater accountability, although there has been criticism (see below) that the ECB is going soft.

Having said this, the German election on 27 September 1998 meant that 11 out of 15 EU member states had a government led by socialists including those of France, Germany and Great Britain indicating some change in Europe's political climate and virtually coinciding with the launching of the EURO and the entry into force of Stage III, while at the same time the ECB (having already been established) had taken over sole responsibility for monetary policy on 1 January 1999 and the rules of the 'Stability and Growth Pact' came into operation. The newly established EURO-X is to monitor the performance of national governments within the framework of the Stability Pact. One might argue that the clash between social democratic Europe and the principles of EMU, inherited from Maastricht and designed in a different climate and dominated by the traditional German economic model which had shaped the EMU treaty provisions, has already become apparent. Social democratic governments, led by Germany, in the autumn of 1998 and early 1999 pressed for a more policy activist role by the ECB and for the ECB to broaden its mandate to growth and employment. One might have argued at the time that the downward movement of EURO-area interest rates in December 1998 and again in April 1999 (although subsequently reversed several times since) had signalled the weakening of the ECB's independence. Economic figures at the end of 1999 were good: Euroland as a whole is expected to run a budget deficit of 1.7 to 1.8 per cent of GDP going down to 1.4 to 1.5 per cent in 2000. Annual inflation is expected to peak at 1.6 to 1.7 in February 2000 and then to start falling again.[100] These figures should encourage public faith in the ECB, although it might take a little while before economic recovery is reflected in a rise of the EURO's value.

In view of these figures the continuing dramatic decline of the EURO is a bizarre phenomenon, but might have little to do with the EURO-zone economy. Although somewhat speculative, it seems more likely that the present weakness of the EURO is a reflection of the political international and European climate: the war in Kosovo and the unrest in the Middle East, domestic scandals in Germany and the inclusion in 1999 of a far-right party in the coalition government in Austria. Importantly however, and perhaps unexpectedly, the EURO is faced with psychological resistance and distrust at both the European and international level.[101] This is at a time when it seems that interest in central bank independence is increasing: as has been observed, the literature has grown remarkably in this area in the past decade with central bank independence having attained a very high profile.[102]

CONCLUSION

Conventional wisdom has it that Chancellor Kohl has humoured France in terms of launching EMU. However, it has been argued here that monetary union, although originally pushed by France in 1987–8, nevertheless bears the hallmark of Germany. The establishment of an independent bank with its central control of price stability, the aim of the convergence criteria and the post Maastricht Stability and Growth Pact clearly represent German interests. The French republican tradition with its emphasis on political will and direction of economic policy, contrasted at times sharply with German tradition with its stress on an independent institutional framework. France successfully extracted concessions from Germany: changes to the Stability Pact, the creation of the EURO-X committee as a political tool and the compromise over the nomination of the ECB President. If France was successful in imposing its 'fast track strategy' while at the same time attempting to undermine or dilute the independence of the ECB by flanking it with a 'political tool', Germany constantly tightened her interpretation of the Treaty. In addition, the project has been enmeshed and interacted with several factors: the international economy, the collapse of the Soviet empire, German Unification, EU enlargement preparations and finally the change of government in Germany.

Having said this, the impact of EMU is such that it has given the EU a new dynamic element. The existence of the ECB which has already been described as the 'most powerful single monetary authority in the world'[103] with 'more political independence than was previously possessed by the German *Bundesbank*'[104] has transformed the Union to such a degree that even countries as powerful as France and Germany – having entrusted monetary sovereignty to a new monetary authority – may be regarded merely as regional entities. France may have improved its monetary position (albeit indirectly) compared to her pre-EMU standing; while Germany's monetary hegemony has been diluted or Europeanised by EMU, although the new system nevertheless bears distinct German characteristics. Obviously, negotiations about institutional design and policy instruments will be an ongoing one; however, the boundaries between domestic and European affairs, between economic management and political reality, have become increasingly blurred in both countries. EMU is a synthesis of both German and French fundamental philosophies and a compromise between the 'economic' and 'monetary' model. As Henry Kissinger once said: 'Serious students of international affairs know that common policies can endure only if both parties serve their own purposes.'[105] Thus both countries need to feel that EMU is in their national interest, although the definition of 'national interests' and those that are 'communal' is increasingly difficult to define. This dilution of national interests and/or the overlapping of domestic and European affairs is the key to Franco-German collaboration on EMU which was 'carried forth by a strong French-German consensus on the advantages that derive from a more international definition of state identities and interests'.[106] Since Monetary Union is the 'biggest single current component in the process of "Europeanisation",'[107] France and Germany will remain the arbiter of EMU's fate.

NOTES

1. Helmut Kohl, June 1997, quoted by Ralf Zeppernick (1999), 'The EURO – Current State and Future Prospects', *German Comments*, **49**, January, p.63.
2. Manfred Wegner (1998), 'EMU and the World Economy', *European Foreign Affairs Review*, **3**, p.456.
3. Jean-Pierre Landau (1998), 'EMU and the Franco-German Relationship' in David P. Calleo and Eric R. Staal (eds), *Europe's Franco-German Engine*, SIAS European Studies, Brookings Institutions Press, Washington.
4. *Report to the Council and the Commission on the Realisation by Stages of Economic and Monetary Union in the Community 1970* (hereafter called Werner Report) *Supplement to Bulletin 11 – 1970 of the European Communities*, Luxembourg, 8 October.
5. Hans Tietmeyer (1994), 'Europäische Währungsunion und Politische Union – das Modell mehrerer Geschwindigkeiten', *Europa-Archiv*, **16**, 457–60.
6. Committee for the Study of Economic and Monetary Union (1989), *Report on Economic and Monetary Union in the European Community*, Luxembourg: Office for Official Publications of the European Communities, Chapter 1, p.12 (hereafter called the Delors Report).
7. Emmanual Apel (1998), *European Monetary Integration 1958–2000*, Routledge, London and New York.
8. *Financial Times*, 31 March 1983.

9. For a historical background to monetary union see for example Alfred Steinherr (ed.), (1994) *Thirty years of European Monetary Integration from the Werner Plan to EMU*, Longman Group Ltd, Harlow, Essex. Paul de Grauwe (1992), *The Economics of Monetary Integration*, Oxford University Press, Oxford. Daniel Gros and Niels Thygesen (1998) *European Monetary Integration*, 2nd edn., St. Martin's Press, New York. Emmanuel Apel (1998) *op. cit.*

10. K.R. McNamara (1999) 'Consensus and Constraint: Ideas and Capital Mobility in European Monetary Integration', *Journal of Common Market Studies*, **37** (3), p. 468.

11. George Ross (1998), 'The EURO, the "French Model of Society" and French Politics', *French Politics and Society*, **16** (4), pp. 1–10.

12. Guy de Carmony (1992), 'Franco-German Relations in the New Europe', in Robert J. Jackson (ed.), *Europe in Transition. The Management of Security after the Cold War*, Adamante Press Ltd, London.

13. Commission of the European Communities (1985), 'Completing the Internal Market', COM (85) 310 final.

14. Commission (1990), *Economic and Monetary Union*, Luxembourg. Commission (1990), *One Market, One Money. An evaluation of the Potential Benefits and Costs of Forming an Economic and Monetary Union*, Luxembourg. Commission (1992), *From Single Market to European Union*, Luxembourg.

15. David R. Cameron (1996), 'National Interest, the Dilemmas of European Integration and Malaise' in John T.S. Keeler and Martin A. Schain (eds) *Chirac's Challenge*, Macmillan, Basingstoke, p. 340.

16. On the argument of asymmetry in the EMS see Horst Ungerer (1997), *A Concise History of European Monetary Integration. From EPU to EMU*, Quorum Books, Westport, London, Chapter 16.

17. Eduard Balladur (1988), *Memorandum sur la construction monétaire européenne*, ECU No 3, March.

18. Elke Thiel (1989), 'From the Internal Market to an Economic and Monetary Union', *Aussenpolitik*, **1**, 66–75.

19. G. Amato (1988), 'Un motore per lo SME', *Il Sole*, 24 Ore, 25 February.

20. For details see Gisela Hendriks (1991), *Germany and European Integration*, Berg, New York and London.

21. Thomas Pedersen (1998), *Germany, France and the Integration of Europe*, Pinter, London and New York, p. 90.

22. Although France, since the late 1990s, has been able to record consistently higher levels of growth then Germany where real income growth has been weak (i.e. 1.5% compared to 3.3% in France).

23. Eduard Balladur (1988), *op. cit.*, p. 19.

24. Michael Hennes (1997), 'The future of Europe: Monetary or Political Union', *Aussenpolitik*, **48** (1), 11–21.

25. Memorandum für die Schaffung eines Europäischen Währungsraumes und einer Europäischen Zentralbank, Auszüge aus Presseartikeln (1988), *Deutsche Bundesbank*, 1 March.

26. *Europäische Zeitung* (1988), April, p. 30.

27. Delors Report, *op. cit.*, p. 43.

28. Desmond Dinan (1999), *Ever Closer Union*, 2nd edn, Macmillan, London, p. 460.

29. Willy Brandt (1984), quoted in '*Agence Europe*', 27 February.

30. Kenneth Dyson and Kevin Featherstone (1997), 'Jacques Delors and the Re-launch of Economic and Monetary Union', Paper, ECSA Conference 29 May – 1 June , Seattle, USA, ECSA97.DOC 10,346.

31. Pedersen, *op. cit.*, p. 113.

32. Charles Grant (1994), *Inside the House that Jacques Built*, Nicholas Brearley Publishing, London, p. 122.

33. Pedersen, *op. cit.*, p. 126.
34. Mark Duckenfield (1999) 'Bundesbank-Government Relations in Germany in the 1990s: From GEMU to EMU', *West European Politics*, **22** (3), p. 95.
35. *Delors Report, op. cit.*, Part 2: Collection of papers here: Karl-Otto Pöhl (1989), 'The further development of the European Monetary System', pp. 131, 136 and 137.
36. *Delors Report, op. cit.*, Part 2: Collection of Papers, here: J. de Larosière 'First stages towards the creation of a European Reserve Bank', pp. 177 and 184.
37. *Delors Report*, 17 April 1989.
38. *Delors Report, op. cit.*, p. 25.
39. *Delors Report, op. cit.*, p. 26.
40. *Werner Report, op. cit.*, p. 12.
41. *Delors Report, op. cit.*, p. 33.
42. Kohl (1992), *Bulletin*, 7 May, *Bulletin* 22 November, (1990) **136**, *Bulletin* 5 February, (1988).
43. Christian Hacke (1998), 'The National Interests of the Federal Republic of German on the Threshold of the 21 Century', *Aussenpolitik*, **49** (4), p. 15.
44. Kenneth Dyson (1998), 'Chancellor Kohl as Strategic Leader: The Case of Economic and Monetary Union', *German Politics*, **7** (1), pp. 37–63.
45. For details of the conditions see Ungerer (1997), *op. cit.*, p. 217.
46. Kenneth Dyson (1999), 'Franco-German Relationship and Economic and Monetary Union: Using Europe to "Bind Leviathan"', *West European Politics*, **22** (1), pp. 25–44.
47. Ian D.Davidson (1998) 'The political and economic context', in John Arrowsmith, *Thinking the unthinkable about EMU*, The National Institute of Economic and Social Research (NIESR) London, Occasional papers 51, p. 9.
48. See for example Simon Hix (1999), *The Political System of the European Union*, Macmillan Press Ltd, London, p. 293.
49. Hans-Dietrich Genscher (1991), *Wir wollen ein europäisches Deutschland*, Siedler Verlag, Berlin, p. 259.
50. This was articulated in a joint CDU/CSU statement written (among others) by Wolfgang Schäuble, leader of the party, and Karl Lamers (CDU/CSU foreign policy spokeman in the Bundestag) in an attempt to halt the debate on EMU delay which had flared up in Germany. See *Financial Times*, 17 September 1997, p. 2.
51. Hendriks (1991), *op. cit.*
52. John B. Goodman (1989), 'Monetary Politics in France, Italy and Germany: 1973–1985', in P. Guerrieri and P. Padoa (eds), *The Political Economy of European Integration*, Harvester Wheatsheaf, Hemel Hempstead, pp. 179–83.
53. Deutsche Bundesbank (1990), 'Annual Report of the Deutsche Bundesbank for the Year 1989', Frankfurt, p. 32.
54. Conceil des Ministres du 5 decembre 1990, 'Communication: Les propes vers l'Union Economique et monétaire'.
55. *Financial Times*, 20 January 1997.
56. *Financial Times*, 30 April, 6 May, and 10 November 1997.
57. Karl-Otto Pöhl (1995), 'International Monetary Policy: A Personal View', in Yesar Gaidar and Karl-Otto Pöhl, *Russian Reform/International Money*, Cambridge MIT, see particularly pp. 61, 67, 109.
58. Karl Kaltenthaler (1998), 'Central Bank Independence and the Commitment to Monetary Stability: The case of the German Bundesbank', *German Politics*, **7** (2), 102–28.
59. Otmar Issing (1999), 'The EURO – Four weeks after the Start', Speech delivered to the European-Atlantic Group, House of Commons, 28 January www.ecb.int/key/sp990128htm.
60. Pierre Bourdieu (1996), 'Warnung vor dem Modell Tietmeyer', *Die Zeit*, 1 November.
61. Quoted by Hans Tietmeyer (1994), 'On the architecture of EMU', in A. Steinherr (ed.),

European Monetary Integration from the Werner Plan to EMU, Longman, London and New York, p. 31.

62. David R. Cameron (1997), 'Economic and Monetary Union', Center for West European Studies, University of Pittsburgh, Policy Paper, No 4, May.

63. *Treaty on European Union* (1992), Conference of the Representatives of the Governments of the Member States, Economic and Monetary Union, Brussels, 12 February, Art. 109 j (1).

64. See for example P. De Grauwe (1994), Towards European Monetary Union without the EMS, *Economic Policy*, **18**, 149–74.

65. Interview reprinted Embassy of the Federal Republic of Germany (1996), 'Germany Marks Six Years of Unity', Press Release, 3 October, p. 4.

66. Quoted by Hans Tietmeyer (1994), 'On the Architecture of EMU', *op. cit.*, p. 31.

67. John T. Wooley (1994), 'Linking Political and Monetary Union. The Maastricht Agenda and German Domestic Politics', in Barry Eichengreen and Jeffrey Frieden (eds), *The Political Economy of European Monetary Integration*, Westview, Boulder Colorado, p. 72.

68. Deutsche Bundesbank (1990), *op. cit.*, p. 79.

69. There were two summit meetings under Irish Presidency: Dublin I (28 April 1990) and Dublin II (25 June 1990).

70. *Bulletin* 31 January 1991, p. 73.

71. Deutsche Bundesbank (1992), *Monthly Report*, February, p. 44.

72. *Agence Europe* (1992), 11 March, p. 3.

73. For an in-depth analysis of these two conferences, see Colette Mazzucelli (1997), *France and Germany at Maastricht*, Garland, New York, London.

74. *Ibid.*, p. 246.

75. Deutsche Bundesbank (1992), *Monthly Report*, February, p. 97.

76. Matthias Kaelberer (1997), 'Hegemony, Dominance or Leadership? Explaining Germany's Role in European Monetary Cooperation' *European Journal of International Relations*, **3** (1), pp. 35–60.

77. Bernhard Winkler (1999), 'Is Maastricht a Good Contract?', *Journal of Common Market Studies*, **37** (1), p. 41.

78. Dinan (1999), *op. cit.*, p. 454.

79. *Delors Report*, p. 31.

80. Duckenfield (1999), *op.cit.*, p. 95.

81. *Ibid.*, p. 101.

82. *Financial Times*, 23 September 1996.

83. Hans Tietmeyer (1995), *Financial Times*, 14 November.

84. 'Europäischer Einheit- und Stabilitätspakt für Europa', *Bundesministerium der Finanzen* (1995), 8 November.

85. Davidson (1998), *op. cit.*

86. *Financial Times*, 14–15 December 1996, p. 1.

87. Alan Juppé, Prime Minister of France (1996), *Financial Times*, 9 December, p. 2.

88. *Financial Times*, 5 November 1996, p. 3.

89. Reported by *Financial Times*, 29 April 1988, p. 22.

90. *Le Monde*, 25 May 1995.

91. Kathleen R. MacNamara (1999) 'Consensus and Constraint: Ideas and Capital Mobility in European Monetary Integration', *Journal of Common Market Studies*, **37** (3), p. 472.

92. Chancellor Kohl (1998), *Bulletin*, **30**, 11 May, p. 362.

93. *Financial Times*, 11 December, 1995.

94. *Süddeutsche Zeitung*, 28 December 1995, p. 18.

95. *Financial Times*, 18 September 1996, p. 2.

96. *Financial Times*, 21 January 1997, p. 2.

97. *Bulletin* (1998), p. 265.

98. *Financial Times*, 23 October 1998, p. 2.
99. *Bulletin*, 14 January 1999, p. 9.
100. *Financial Times* (1999), 'Euro-Zone Economy', *Quarterly Review,* **3**, December, p. 3.
101. *Agence Europe* (1999), No. 7480, 6 June, Special Edition, p. 6.
102. Duckenfield (1999), *op. cit.*, p. 88.
103. John McCormick (1999), *Understanding the European Union*, Macmillan, Basingstoke, p. 198.
104. Kevin Featherstone (1999), 'The Political Dynamics of Economic and Monetary Union', in Laura Cram, Desmond Dinan and Neill Nugent (eds), *Development in the European Union*, Macmillan, Basingstoke, p. 325.
105. Henry Kissinger (1982), *Years of Upheaval*, Weidenfeld & Nicolson, London p. 146.
106. Peter J. Katzenstein (1997), 'United Germany in an Integrated Europe' in Peter J. Katzenstein (ed.), *Tamed Power*, Cornell University Press, Ithaca and London, p. 31.
107. Kevin Featherstone (1999), *op. cit.*

5. The forging of a common foreign and security policy

INTRODUCTION

By implication, the concept of a European common foreign and security policy is inherent in that of political unification; it dates back at least to the Brussels Treaty of March 1948 creating the Western European Union, a mere two months or so before the Hague Congress which called for a united, democratic Europe.[1] However, whereas economic integration proceeded at a brisk pace in a fairly linear direction, the gestation of a common foreign and security policy was beleaguered by a succession of failures, the European Defence Community (EDC) in 1954 and the Fouchet Plan in 1962, then, from the 1970s, by a slow development under the title of 'Political Cooperation' outside the European Community institutional framework.[2]

That is hardly surprising. At first sight, economic integration is a matter of 'low politics',[3] whose opacity derives from its highly technical nature and incremental development, thus generating a certain degree of tolerance by ignorance, as it were. It could be – wrongly – dissociated from political integration i.e. a surrender of national sovereignty, as it was, for instance, in the British campaign for the 1975 referendum. However, some sixteen years later when it came to signing up to a single currency, the UK government clearly saw the political implications and therefore secured an opt-out clause. Conversely, foreign and security policy is traditionally perceived as a matter of 'high politics', of a potentially dramatic nature, which engages the nation as much as the state through discourse, where the fate of sovereignty is played according to the rules of a zero sum game, and where publicised decisions or vacillations are subjected to instantaneous popular (or populist) commentary.

Economic integration has serious political implications (as illustrated by Chancellor Kohl's dogged campaign to drive the EURO through public hostility) but is entirely governed by Community rules and procedures enshrined in or derived from the treaties. Foreign and security policy, which also encompasses economic decisions in relation to, for instance, economic sanctions and military procurement, is nevertheless governed by a hybrid system of Community and intergovernmental decision-making, and leaves large expanses of policy within the exclusive scope of member states' governments. The Community framework could be seen as a crutch or as a yoke, but in the case of foreign and security policy, it is too weak to be either. The European Union in the new millennium remains an economic giant and a political dwarf.

The European Union is perforce composed of member states whose international weight and status differ enormously. Through its individual member states it is well represented in a 'rich tapestry of organizations'[4] like the G8, OSCE, OECD, the Council of Europe, and the Security Council of the UN. That is the conundrum with which the European Union has to live: the very international clout of some of its member states can and does act as a brake in the coalition-building which maintains a momentum towards a genuinely *common* foreign and security policy. Within the European Union, member states can either act as separate entities, or create bilateral or multilateral partnerships, or carry out joint actions under the European Union treaties. These various scenarios are or have been played in the past few years, thus confirming the protean nature of Europe. The Franco-German partnership, which has so famously contributed to the development of the European Union, has not been particularly successful in promoting a common foreign and security policy, both for structural and circumstantial reasons.

Fundamental cleavages between France and Germany affect their respective priorities in foreign policy. Both geography and history have dictated that Germany should look east, while France should look south. The very structure of the state, centralised in France and federal in Germany, encourages tight and hierarchical policy lines west of the Rhine, diffuse and occasionally contradictory policy lines east of it. The French statist tradition favours national champions, which ill accords with the German tradition of economic liberalism as applied, for instance, to armaments cooperation. Last but not least, France is profoundly eurocentric, i.e. considers that Europe naturally constitutes an autonomous entity with the potential to become a main pole in the global system, while Germany is profoundly atlanticist, i.e. considers that Europe is by necessity part of a larger entity which includes North America, at least in terms of security.

Foreign policy options are also influenced by external factors outside the control of national governments or European institutions. The last few years have witnessed such major upheavals as the emergence of democracies in Central and Eastern Europe; serious financial and economic crises in the Far East; political and military conflicts in the Balkans, the Middle East and Africa; the aggressive and erratic progress of globalisation; and a US *de facto* monopoly of superpower status and behaviour, all of which to a greater or lesser degree have had an impact on the European Union and its member states.

The reunification of Germany and the revival of the Central and East European democracies changed the power relationship between France and Germany. Up to the 1990s, France had benefited from three main assets: she was a member of the group of victorious powers who presided over the fate of Germany (and more lastingly over the fate of Berlin), she had secured a permanent seat in the UN Security Council, and she was a nuclear power. This enabled her to assert her political pre-eminence in the European Community, to which Germany acquiesced. In spite of her economic power, Germany strove for security and stability above all, and was content to let France take or appear to take most initiatives. The situation, however, changed with German reunification. Paradoxically, reunification handicapped Germany by unwittingly but inevitably reviving the spectre of a German Europe, and by generating an enormous economic and administrative burden in the reconstruction of the "new Länder". Nevertheless, through her sheer territorial, demographic and economic weight, Germany now appeared as the indisputable major partner, and the awareness of this new status would at once restore her self-confidence and induce her to be more assertive in advancing her foreign policy aims. If Franco-German cooperation was to endure, it would have to act within these new parameters.

A striking feature of Europe's Common Foreign and Security Policy (CFSP) is that it is evolving by default, as it were. Whereas economic integration has fairly well defined contours, there is no equivalent political integration. And yet, the European Union is trying to acquire a political dimension, as demonstrated, however clumsily, by the Treaties of Maastricht and Amsterdam. Security is included as a means of safeguarding economic achievements and as a means of developing a Community diplomacy.[5] Throughout the development of the European Community, there have been gropings towards some form of unified decision-making authority, but tensions about the choice between intergovernmental or more integrated solutions have been compounded by divergences on which organisation should ultimately ensure the security of Europe. In order to give an overview of the various processes, the chapter is divided into four main thematic sections analytically separating events which may have happened coincidentally: Franco-German relations in the development of the concept of foreign policy; the fate of Franco-German divergences on European security; case studies on the problems of implementation of a foreign and security policy; and armaments cooperation.

VAGARIES OF FRANCO-GERMAN RELATIONS IN THE DEVELOPMENT OF A EUROPEAN FOREIGN POLICY

From the Post-war Years to the Collapse of the Soviet Bloc

Zeus gave Europa three sons and notoriety through deception and rape. Modern Europe also came of age as a result of violence: the Second World War and the Cold War. The preamble to the Brussels Pact, signed by the UK, France and the Benelux countries in March 1948 stated among the signatories' aims '*To afford assistance* to each other, in accordance with the charter of the United Nations, in maintaining international peace and security and in resisting any policy of aggression', this immediately followed by '*To take such steps* as may be necessary in the event of a renewal by Germany of a policy of aggression'.[6] Germany then had not recovered her statehood and was still perceived, at least by France, as a potential aggressor, together with the Soviet Union. But within a few weeks, a series of cascading dramatic events would radically transform opinions and policies: from June 1948 the Berlin Blockade and Airlift, the following winter Mao Tse Tung's victorious march to Peking, in April 1949 the signing of the North Atlantic Treaty, in May the birth of the German Federal Republic and the creation of the Council of Europe, in October the advent of the German Democratic Republic, and finally in June 1950 the Korean War. Just as the worsening of the Greek civil war had intensified European (above all, British) pressure on the US to commit their military might to the defence of Europe, the Korean War precipitated a panic demand by Washington that European military forces, including those of Germany, be mobilised. The spectre of a new *Wehrmacht* arising a mere five years after VE Day, horrified citizens of Western Europe, including the German Social Democratic Party. Only some five months had elapsed since the Schuman Declaration of 9 May 1950, when René Pléven, the then French President of the Council (i.e. Prime Minister), presented his 'Plan' to the National Assembly on 23 October 1950, stating that its aim was to avoid the 'creation of a German army..., the setting up of German divisions, of a German ministry of defence'.[7] The solution proffered was the creation of a European Defence Community, broadly modelled on the Schuman Plan (both were in fact the brainchildren of Jean Monnet), which would integrate military forces from the signatories of the treaty. After a tortuous path, which included the refusal by the United Kingdom to participate in the project, the addition of a European Political Community to exercise democratic control over the European army, and a continuous reluctance by successive French governments to introduce the necessary ratification debate in the French National Assembly while it raged within political parties and public opinion, the project was eventually defeated in that Assembly on 30 August 1954. The coincidence of a lessening of tension between East and West and the rejection of an integrated European army, eased the way towards the restructuring of the Brussels Treaty Organisation into a Western European Union to include Germany. In that whole episode, Germany was a clear winner. On the same occasion she recovered her quasi sovereignty (except for Berlin and certain related questions, and except for a prohibition on production of atomic, bacteriological and chemical weapons, and certain armaments), and would join NATO in May 1955.

The failure of the EDC was not merely an unfortunate episode in the dynamics of European integration. Whatever the merits or demerits of the plan, whatever the motivations of those who voted for or against it, its rejection was interpreted as a rebuff for European unification and a manifestation of distrust of Germany (Adenauer was devastated).[8] The fate of the EDC shed a stark light on the limits of tolerance for supranationalism, demonstrated the impact of external factors on European politics, and defined the positions of the protagonists which would be maintained, either overtly or covertly, right up to the collapse of the Soviet Union and the reunification of Germany. This was the era of the bipolar world. What was the place of Western Europe in a bipolar world? Western Europe was at the edge of the fracture that disconnected Western and Eastern concepts of democracy and generated the build up of ever more terrifying weapons of mutual destruction for the members of NATO and those of the Warsaw Pact.

In contradiction to its stand on economic integration, where the original Six, joined later on by the United Kingdom and others, proceeded with determination and coherence from a customs union to a Single Market (eventually to a monetary union), which enabled them to become the first world trading power, the protagonist countries of Western Europe offered divergent interpretations of its position and the conditions best obtained to guarantee its security.

Between 1948 and 1955, Germany's recovery was spectacular. She went from the quasi starvation of the immediate post-war years to Erhard's 'economic miracle', and from constitutional non-existence to full participation as a virtually equal partner in European post-war organisations. Yet there remained a keen awareness of her fragility. Fragility of her security because of her exposed position as an immediate neighbour of the Soviet bloc. Fragility of her status as her Nazi past was still too close and her democratic institutions still untested. As a result, Germany would look for the protection of the most powerful sponsor, i.e. Washington, and would be prepared to accept a relationship of dependence with the United States in exchange for protection of her territory. In practice, this means that Germany, like the United Kingdom, considered that NATO, albeit under the military command of and with its weapons provided by the United States, fulfilled both necessary and sufficient conditions to safeguard the security of Western Europe. Germany would also tenaciously maintain a low profile in international politics, lest she be accused of releasing old nationalistic demons. This was particularly visible in her partnership with France.

While Germany was on upward curve, France seemed to be caught in a whirlpool of disasters. Her parliamentary majorities were so brittle that they collapsed almost on any new policy initiative, bringing down governments in their wake, or forcing them to look for expedients to help their own survival rather than sustain coherent policies. Her resources and international standing were further damaged by costly and unpopular colonial wars. Her foreign policy was shackled by the presence of an anti-Western Communist party and a conglomerate of Gaullist movements, both of whom were ultimately nationalist, but who were pulling in opposite directions. Nor did her membership of NATO appear to help her much. As a result of her rejection of the EDC, France had to accept Germany's rearmament and integration into NATO. Furthermore, NATO's presence in the Mediterranean provided no relief for French military adventures in Indochina or, more relevantly, Algeria: NATO's guarantees did not extend to France's overseas territories. The fiasco of the 1956 Suez expedition confirmed, in appalling fashion for the French who saw Egypt as a training and propaganda ground for the Algerian 'rebels', the discontinuity between American (Washington disapproved of the Franco-British invasion of Egypt and acted accordingly) and French interests. For the French, membership of NATO was becoming a burden – mobilising French military resources – with few palpable compensations. Relations with Great Britain and the United States were tense, while a number of tentative steps towards Franco-German cooperation on nuclear projects had brought Germany much nearer to France,[9] but without tangible results. By the time the IVth Republic self-destructed in May 1958, France's international standing was at its lowest since the defeat of May 1940. The weak IVth Republic could nevertheless count two major achievements in its balance sheet: the Treaty of Paris creating the European Coal and Steel Community and the Treaties of Rome creating EURATOM and the European Economic Community.

When de Gaulle came into power after the dramatic May 1958 events, there was fear that he might undo what had so painstakingly been achieved. De Gaulle, however, was not opposed to the building of Europe, quite the opposite. De Gaulle's European policy is the result of his vision of a 'European Europe' and his self-proclaimed pragmatism: 'the union of Europe should not mean the fusion of its peoples, but can and must result from their systematic rapprochement',[10] and the kind of union he had in mind found its concrete expression in the project for a political union known as the Fouchet

Plan. In his press conference of 5 September 1960 de Gaulle had stated that 'France considers that regular cooperation between the states of western Europe in the political economic, cultural and defence fields is not only desirable, but both possible and practical.' The official negotiations started with a summit conference in February 1961 and were terminated in failure in April 1962, owing to the opposition of the Netherlands and Belgium, and the vacillations of Italy. It might at first sight be considered as simply a quixotic attempt by de Gaulle to create a modern version of the 19th century 'Concert of Europe' under France's leadership. It contained, however, the seeds (one could almost say the genes) of our contemporary foreign and security policy. First of all, it rested on two basic principles: that of Franco-German solidarity, and that of intergovernmental cooperation not against, but side by side with the supranational method prevalent in the three European Communities.

Time and again in his *Memoirs of Hope*, de Gaulle pays homage to Adenauer's sense of reality and loyalty, mentioning *en passant* that up until mid-1962 they exchanged about forty letters, met fifteen times, and spent over one hundred hours in face-to-face talks.[11] This was a personal commitment by Adenauer, who encountered some degree of scepticism in his own Cabinet and political party, for example from ministers such as Erhard or von Brentano,[12] but for whom, as for de Gaulle, Franco-German partnership was the bedrock on which European unity must rest and prosper. As one commentator summed up their motivations: 'For de Gaulle, Germany was important primarily for the weight it could lend to France's international ambitions. For Adenauer, rapprochement with France was important above all to prevent Paris from obstructing Western unity or European integration.'[13]

In his press conference of 5 September 1960, de Gaulle had clearly stated what he meant by realities: 'Now, what are the realities, what are the pillars upon which Europe can be built? These are, in fact, the states – states that while undoubtedly differing widely one from the other – are the sole entities endowed with the right to command and to be obeyed.' For all the attempts of France's partners to introduce more visibly integrationist elements, the successive drafts of the Fouchet Plan reflected this primacy of the states. The institutions of the European Union would consist of a hierarchy of Council (consisting of Heads of State or Government acting by unanimity, with the proviso that 'the absence or abstention of one or of two members shall not prevent a decision from being taken'); a Committee of Foreign Ministers, a Committee of Ministers for Defence and for the Armed Forces, and a Committee of Ministers of Education or of Ministers responsible for international cultural relations, who would meet at regular intervals (twice yearly for the Council, four times a year for the ministerial Committees); an appointed Political Commission and a Secretary-General both appointed by the Council 'to assist the Council'; a European Parliament with a consultative role and a Court of Justice, both in common with the European Communities. The balance was heavily in favour of intergovernmental organs, the other institutions being devoid of decision-making powers. The original French wording had included economics amongst the aims of the Union, but this frightened the other delegations who saw in that an attempt to undermine the European Economic Union, so that the amended Article 2 stated: 'It shall be the aim of the Union to reconcile, coordinate and unify the policy of Member states in spheres of common interest: foreign policy, defence and cultural affairs.'[14] The stiffening of the French attitude and the misgivings of the Benelux partners (particularly the Netherlands who, in addition to their commitment to federalism, strongly supported the United Kingdom's attempt to join the Six, and generally disliked French hegemony in the EEC as much as France disliked American hegemony in NATO), reduced to nothing Italy's attempts to mediate, and the project came to nothing.

Coming after a stillborn European Defence Community, a stillborn political union seemed to confirm the hopelessness of trying to promote and institutionalise a European foreign and defence policy. Circumstances, however, differed. In 1954, the improved international climate on the one hand, and British refusal to participate on the other, had demotivated a divided French Parliament. Conversely between 1960 and 1962 international tension had increased around Berlin, the two superpowers were engaged in a race for nuclear and space supremacy, Britain was half-heartedly negotiating for membership of the European Community, and de Gaulle was giving France a strong constitutional structure and aiming to place her at the forefront of the international stage. In spite of all the rhetorical caution, the proposal to engage the Six in the construction of a common foreign and defence policy looked to her partners like a bid by France to undermine Atlantic solidarity, which might in the end compromise European security. That suspicion was further confirmed a *posteriori* when de Gaulle on 14 January 1963 broadcast France's veto on British membership of the European Communities, and on 7 March 1966 wrote to President Lyndon Johnson to announce that France was withdrawing from the military command of NATO.

Meanwhile, France and Germany signed on 22 January 1963 a friendship treaty incorporating bilaterally many of the features of the Fouchet Plan. This treaty seemed doomed to strictly cosmetic usage, but proved enduring and effective beyond the most optimistic speculations in sustaining the Franco-German rapprochement. That same year, Chancellor Adenauer finally retired after 14 years in power during which he had brought back Germany to almost full sovereignty (bar certain restrictions on armaments, and the status of Berlin etc.), democracy, economic prosperity, integration into the Atlantic Alliance and the European Community, and partnership with France. With the departure of Adenauer the great chapter of Franco-German reconciliation was concluded. The last years of de Gaulle's presidency would be marked by disagreements and mutual disappointments between France and Germany. Strains between the two countries had shown in 1964 during the finalisation of the Common Agricultural Policy. When in 1965 the Commission proposed a package that included financing of the CAP from the EEC's own resources, de Gaulle was unable to accept this further step towards supranationality, and France hoped to enrol Germany in resisting this proposal. France, who held the Presidency of the EEC at the time, felt badly let down by a Germany who, anxious to protect her farmers, failed at the last minute, and contrary to French expectations, to support France in the negotiation of June 1965 over the mode of financing the CAP. This created the worst crisis to date, with France withdrawing for a full six months from the EEC institutions. In his ground-breaking analysis of the crisis[15] John Newhouse argued convincingly that behind the crisis on agriculture loomed a deeper discord over the Multilateral Force project launched by the United States and supported by Germany. Adenauer's successor, Chancellor Erhard, having failed to ingratiate himself with de Gaulle by refusing offers of cooperation on building a European atomic force which would have mostly entailed financing by Germany, further infuriated the General by actively canvassing for the MLF project, to which France was very hostile (and the United Kingdom distinctly lukewarm, incidentally). It seemed to de Gaulle that when it came to defence, Erhard was prepared to sacrifice the Franco-German alliance for the sake of the Washington shield. The French Prime Minister Pompidou warned in December 1964 that: 'If the multilateral force were to lead to the creation of a German-American military alliance, we would not consider this as being fully consistent with the relations we have with the Federal Republic which are based on the Franco-German treaty. Nor would they be consistent with our concept of the defence of Europe, nor with the ideas we have of a European defence policy…'.[16] Lacking support from most European partners, the MLF project eventually fizzled out, but not without leaving a trail of resentment and mistrust on either side of the Rhine. It had glaringly revealed the contradictory defence priorities of France and Germany: France wanting to develop a European defence policy (possibly based on her own 'force de frappe', however lagging behind it might be), while Germany clung on to the immediately much more attractive protection of NATO's, i.e. in practice American nuclear, armoury. This contradiction was to remain an irritant between the two countries throughout the era of the bi-polar world. It also clouded various attempts at cooperation in the field of armaments production, as Germany found herself pulled by France to undertake a number of joint projects like the Transall military transport aircraft, which was indeed built, but found practically no outside buyers because it was more expensive than the American Hercules. Germany also found it expedient to repay American and British military expenditure on her soil by purchasing US and British armaments, with the consequence that opportunities for Franco-German procurement cooperation were much reduced. This was further jeopardised by France giving priority to the building up of her nuclear force, which absorbed nearly 70% of her military expenditure.[17] All in all, throughout the 1960s, there was little prospect of a European procurement policy based on Franco-German initiatives: France's pull away from, and Germany's dependence on, NATO created political, technical and financial obstacles to anything more ambitious than isolated and limited joint manufacture projects.

Even though Chancellor Kiesinger, who succeeded Erhard in late 1966, and his team were anxious to maintain good relations with France and to continue to implement the Franco-German treaty, they found little echo in France. The new Foreign Minister of the German Grand Coalition, Willy Brandt, would soon start paving the way for an *Ostpolitik* that would eventually lead to normalisation of relations with the German Democratic Republic and with Poland. Meanwhile, a disillusioned de Gaulle also turned his attention to a more distant Eastern Europe, only to see his dream of a Europe 'independent' of the 'two hegemonies' shattered by the Soviet invasion of Czechoslovakia in August 1968. He even attempted to repair relations with Great Britain in February 1969 by 'thinking aloud' about a Franco-Anglo-Italo-German political directorate for Europe in front of the bemused British ambassador, the substance of which, when reported to London, failed to seduce Albion, but created an uproar in Germany and above all among France's smaller European partners when London indiscreetly passed it on. Some ten weeks on, on 28 April 1969, de Gaulle resigned after a referendum on constitutional issues had gone against his proposals. His ambition to build a European Europe had not been fulfilled, but the Franco-German treaty was, in a pedestrian, non-obtrusive way, firming up the reconciliation which the Adenauer-de Gaulle tandem had spectacularly bequeathed to their respective nations and to the new Europe.

Adenauer and de Gaulle, both authoritarian democrats, had rebuilt their countries on sound constitutional foundations, and presided over their economic revival. But the material prosperity of the 1960s was not an exalting value for the young who, in France shaken by the Algerian war, in Germany by a Vietnam war fought under the banner of the 'free world', were rebelling against bourgeois capitalism. In France, the students persuaded ten million workers to strike, while in Germany the children of bourgeois democrats plotted to destroy 'the old order by creating the *Rote Armee*

Fraktion and engaging in acts of terrorism. The two Republics overcame the revolutionary jolts, but with a sense of unease compounded by their helpless witnessing of another invasion of Czechoslovakia by foreign troops. The wave of protest in Western Europe was matched by the destabilisation of Eastern Europe, and, aggravating the climate of uncertainty, a petulant Middle East raised the spectre of a serious oil crisis.

It was against the background of social unease that, in June and October 1969 respectively, Pompidou succeeded de Gaulle, and Brandt was elected Chancellor. Neither of them would serve very long, Pompidou dying in April 1974 and Brandt resigning in May of the same year. Nor did they take to each other, one being conservative and pragmatic, the other socialist and romantic. Nevertheless they worked together. On Pompidou's initiative, the Six held a summit meeting in the Hague on 1–2 December 1969, during which Brandt and Pompidou vied for oratorical supremacy, and Pompidou coined the tryptich 'completion, deepening, enlargement' (see Chapter 6). Not only was the green light given to enlargement to include the United Kingdom, Denmark, Ireland and Norway, not only was the financing of the Common Agricultural Policy finally settled on the principle of 'Own Resources', but Pompidou also put foreign policy back on the agenda. What he had in mind was not a revival of the elaborate structure worked out in the Fouchet Plan, but regular meetings of the member-states' foreign ministers 'in order to try to harmonise our foreign policies and in any event to inform ourselves better of our respective policies.'[18]

A working party of senior officials from the foreign ministries of the Six, including Jacques de Beaumarchais for France, and Berndt von Staden for Germany, was duly convened under the chairmanship of Etienne Davignon of Belgium, who held the presidency of the EEC at the time. A discussion paper prepared by the *Auswärtiges Amt* was circulated[19] and a final report was adopted by a Conference of Foreign Ministers in October 1970. The machinery of European Political Cooperation was to be as light and flexible as possible, consisting essentially of quarterly meetings of the foreign ministers, backed by monthly meetings of political directors of the foreign ministers called the Political Committee, which might also include on an *ad hoc* basis other senior officials specialised in relevant foreign policy areas. The meetings of the Political Committee in turn were to be prepared by senior officials working as the Group of Correspondents. The question of a secretariat had to be left open when a rift occurred between France, who wanted the secretariat to be located in Paris, and her partners, who preferred Brussels. Meanwhile each presidency would service European Political Co-operation in turn. Foresight was demonstrated in the initiation of an elaborate communications network named Coreu (short for 'Correspondents Européens') linking up the foreign ministries of the member states, and including their embassies in crucial locations. Thus was European Political Co-operation given its official existence, with the same membership but outside the institutional framework of the European Communities. Details of procedure were refined over the next few years, but throughout the principle of strict intergovernmentalism was adhered to, and democratic control was limited to sending an annual report to the European Parliament. This principle was very much in accordance with French preferences; the Germans, like the Dutch, would naturally have preferred a more federalist approach, but prudently acquiesced to the arrangements for fear of stopping the process altogether.

As the machinery was put into place, plenty of issues found their way into the agenda, the two outstanding ones being the setting up of the Conference on Security and Cooperation in Europe (CSCE) (1971–75) in which the Nine spoke and negotiated with remarkable unity, and the problems of the Middle East, sparked by the Yom Kippur War of 1973. The CSCE marked a high point in European Political Co-operation; not only was the concept of one representative for all the member-states of the European Communities accepted once and for all, and subsequently maintained in the 1977 Belgrade meeting and the 1982 Madrid meeting within the CSCE framework, but it provided a possible framework for a future European security policy in that it included France (still maintaining her distance from NATO). The CSCE demonstrated the effectiveness of Europe speaking with one voice, the Middle East the difficulty of reconciling such opposite views as those of the pro-Israeli Dutch (and Germans) and the pro-Arab French. Moreover, in practice, despite French intransigence in the matter, it would not always be easy to separate European 'political' cooperation from the European 'economic' Community agenda.[20] Foreign policy had become increasingly involved in trade and economic relations, and it was for instance impossible to adopt a Middle East policy which would ignore the issues of arms sales or oil imports. The Geneva-Helsinki negotiations, meant to institutionalise improvements between the Western and the Eastern blocs, included economic measures which necessarily demanded an input from the Commission. With the death of Pompidou, the distinction between the economic and political features of issues was less rigidly observed.

One of the first moves of the newly elected President Giscard d'Estaing was to promote the idea – originally considered by Pompidou – of regular meetings of heads of state and government. Pompidou's original intention had been that there should be *informal* meetings of heads of state and government, who could then engage in 'fire chat' types of communication. At that level, it was a misconception. However, the idea of informality was picked up by Germany which, during its Presidency of 1974, invited the Foreign Ministers to a meeting at Schloss Gymnich. This meeting successfully resolved a conflict within the Nine in which France had challenged her partners to stand up to the United States on the Middle East oil crisis. As a result, the 'Gymnich formula' became, and has remained, standard practice for some of the Foreign Ministers' meetings. As for the heads of state and government, in Paris in December 1974, under French Presidency and at President Giscard d'Estaing's invitation, they formed themselves into what was officially named the European Council. Although there was no blueprint of its functions, it quickly became a bridging institution between the Communities and the Political Cooperation machinery. Gradually the Commission became selectively involved in the European Council meetings.

By the 1970s, therefore, Political Co-operation was well established. It was primarily a means of consultation, occasionally producing resolutions such as the June 1980 Venice Declaration of the European Council recognising the right to security of Israel and the legitimate rights of the Palestinians, or giving support to closer cooperation with new democracies like Portugal in 1975, or condemning apartheid in South Africa in 1977. It meant, at the very least, that all member states were better informed about each other's foreign policy aims and stances. It did not prevent, however, countries like France from recognising Angola ahead of her European partners in 1976, or intervening in Katanga 'in the name of Europe' in 1977. Furthermore, Giscard d'Estaing initiated a meeting between himself and Brezhnev in Warsaw in May 1980, after the invasion of Afghanistan, without a mandate of the Nine, yet again speaking 'in the name of Europe'. Giscard had previously, on 5 February, issued a joint declaration on Afghanistan with Chancellor Schmidt, but none was issued on behalf of European Political Cooperation for lack of consensus.[21] France indeed acted at three levels which sometimes overlapped. She tended to act on her own on instances where her particular areas of interest, like Africa, were concerned. She acted on the whole in close cooperation with Germany when dealing with East-West relations, as in response to the Soviet invasion of Afghanistan. She acted within the context, and as a protagonist of Political Cooperation on issues like Atlantic relations, European security and détente, and the Middle East.

In all these instances Germany, who wielded economic power and had successfully conducted her own *Ostpolitik* in the early 1970s, was anxious not to awaken any suspicions of playing power politics, and therefore found Political Cooperation a useful means of participating in global policy in an inconspicuous and unthreatening manner.

In spite of some institutional innovations like the creation of the European Council or the turning to the election of the European Parliament by universal suffrage (as prescribed by the Treaty of Rome), and some policy initiatives like the setting up of the European Monetary system, and in spite of the excellent personal relationship between President Giscard d'Estaing and Chancellor Helmut Schmidt, in spite (or perhaps because) of enlargement to nine member states, European integration was going through a mood of despondency. As the French commentator and former member of the Commission Jean François Deniau remarked: 'Europe, when it speaks with one voice, has little to say and, anyhow, sounds *dépassée*'.[22]

A number of attempts to invigorate political unification were either commissioned, the Tindemanns Report of 1976 and the London Report of 1981, or jointly undertaken, like the Genscher-Colombo Plan of 1981. The first one was quietly shelved. The second one was the outcome of Lord Carrington's reflections on the inadequacies of EPC, made glaringly obvious at the time of the Soviet invasion of Afghanistan. It was meant to improve intra-EPC coordination by enhancing the role of the EC presidency and strengthening, for instance, the Troika mechanism and breathe life into the concept of European security. The third initiative, the Genscher-Colombo Plan which actually took up some of the ideas contained in the Fouchet Plan, like setting up ministerial councils for culture and defence, was reduced to the status of a Solemn Declaration agreed at the Stuttgart European council of June 1983, and failed to be fully implemented. This episode, incidentally, seemed to confirm the widespread opinion that no initiative taken without getting the French on board had much chance of success.[23]

By the mid-1980s the situation had radically altered. With the Greek accession, the Nine were now Ten, with the prospect of soon becoming Twelve. The European Community had loyally supported the United Kingdom's war effort in the Falklands. Poland was in turmoil as a result of the 'Solidarnosc' movement being outlawed and martial law declared. France had a socialist president, Mitterrand, and Germany had a Christian-Democrat Chancellor, Helmut Kohl. Speaking in the Bundestag on 20 January 1983 to mark the twentieth anniversary of the Franco-German treaty, Mitterrand, to the delight of the new German chancellor Helmut Kohl and that of former Chancellor Helmut Schmidt if not of his party, had passionately pleaded with the German parliamentarians to support the US 'twin-track initiative' (negotiation and action) designed to discourage the Soviet stationing of SS20 missiles against NATO countries. Two months later, Mitterrand took what was perhaps the most momentous decision of his presidency when, facing serious financial stresses, he opted for a policy of economic austerity and financial orthodoxy, i.e. a policy of 'franc fort' and compliance with EEC trade rules, against the wishes of the more radical elements of his government (see Chapter 4). Those were but a few of the events that marked the climate of economic recession within a 'mini-cold' war outside the European Community at the time.

Throughout this period of tension between the United States and the Soviet Union, the Ten, either singly or within EPC, while being firm with the Soviet Union, nevertheless tried to maintain an open dialogue. Even Mrs Thatcher had refused to comply with American demands on further trade restrictions with the Soviet Union. Germany, the obvious first victim of a potential nuclear conflict, was apprehensive of any further deterioration of East-West relations. The foreign minister, Hans-Dietrich Genscher, had persuaded his partners in EPC to issue a declaration in early 1984 inviting the Soviet Union to work towards détente and hinting at developing cooperation with Eastern Europe.

In 1984 also, as France held the Presidency of the European Community, Mitterrand felt confident enough to try and clear the rut in which it seemed to be stuck. The Fontainebleau European Council granted Mrs Thatcher the rebate on Britain's contribution to the budget she was demanding, agreed to finalise the entry of Spain and Portugal into the Community, and commissioned James Dooge of Ireland to chair a working-group on the drafting of a new treaty and Adonino of Italy to chair a Committee for a People's Europe. If the latter's report met almost the same forlorn fate as the hapless Tindemans Report of some ten years earlier, the Dooge Report did lead directly to the Intergovernmental Conference which negotiated the Single European Act. The French member of the Dooge Committee was Maurice Faure, a former minister, and more significantly a signatory of the Rome Treaty, who therefore had the double credentials of being pro-integrationist and an old political friend of Mitterrand (though not of the same, but of an allied party). The main working paper, on which discussions were based, was indeed produced by Maurice Faure, and must have had the informal assent of Mitterrand. The German representative, a senior official of the *Auswärtiges Amt*, enjoyed no such relationship with Chancellor Kohl,[24] and this was reflected in the minor key, especially so soon after the inglorious outcome of the Genscher-Colombo Plan, in which German positions were expressed.

The Genscher-Colombo Plan had nevertheless had the merit of keeping political union firmly on the agenda, and that was reflected in the Single European Act. The drafting of the document which took place under the Italian and Luxemburg presidencies, signed in February 1986, and coming into force in 1987, was mostly based on a Franco-German draft. It established in its very Article 1 the principle of linkage: 'The European Communities and European Political Cooperation shall have as their objective to contribute together to making concrete progress towards European unity'.[25] That statement also foreshadowed the distinction between 'pillars' that would be developed in the next Intergovernmental Conference in 1991, maintaining the distinction between the Community rules which governed economic integration and the intergovernmental character of foreign policy development. As well as institutionalising the European Council, without however defining its tasks, it gave 'Political Cooperation in the sphere of foreign policy' the formal and legal character of being enshrined in a treaty (concluded between 'High Contracting Parties', a language not used for the rest of the treaty), defining its aims, structure and procedures.

European Political Cooperation was also given a permanent secretariat (replacing the Troika secretariat) in Brussels to assist the presidency with exclusively administrative functions. EPC still had only vague working principles and weak instruments: Art. 30.1 merely gave an obligation to '*endeavour* to formulate and implement a European foreign policy', and undertakings were limited to mutual information and consultation; actions by national governments should not impair cohesiveness; decisions were to be taken by unanimity. The whole text of Title III looks like a precarious balancing act between cautious and vague terms ('endeavour', 'as effectively as possible', 'desirability', 'point of reference', 'avoid any action or position which impairs...' 'refrain from impeding', etc.) and dynamic implications ('common principles and objectives ... gradually developed and defined', 'ready to coordinate their positions more closely'). The introduction of the concept of security, albeit qualified by 'political and economic aspects' and 'technological and industrial conditions' into para. 6 of Art. 30 echoed some of the doomed ambitions of the Fouchet Plan; reference to the Western European Union and the Atlantic Alliance reflected the ambivalent character of the commitment to European security.

In the preface to his *Réflexions sur la politique extérieure de la France* published in 1986, Mitterrand wrote: 'We are short of Europe as we are short of air in the métro', and undoubtedly the Single European Act brought a less fresh Europe than could have been anticipated, particularly that 'political Europe' which the French President wanted to see built. It could be that a common foreign and security policy came relatively low on his priorities at the time.[26] Nevertheless, the Franco-German tandem had once more put European integration on the rails, pushing for the emergence of a European Political Cooperation endowed with legal personality. Even Denmark's referendum was positive and enabled the Single European Act to be ratified and implemented. Predictably enough, economic integration was proceeding at a lion's pace, and political integration proceeding at a snail's pace.

Institutional Evolution from the Single European Act to the Amsterdam Treaty

In April 1990, that is, some time between the fall of the Berlin Wall in November 1989 and the opening of the Intergovernmental Conference in

December 1990, Kohl and Mitterrand addressed a joint letter to the President of Ireland (which then held the European Presidency) to advocate the completion of economic and monetary union and of political union. The motivations behind this initiative were primarily the prospect of German reunification and the fear of destabilisation in Central and Eastern Europe. As already pointed out in Chapter 4 the prospect of German reunification had generated a degree of unease in France and Mitterrand's first reflex had been to fly to Kiev to meet Gorbachev, then to obtain from Kohl some assurance about the permanence of the *Oder-Neisse* frontier. For Mitterrand, the *sine qua non* condition for a sustained Franco-German alliance was the active joint pursuit of European unification, by both economic and political means.

The last paragraph of Title III of the Single European Act called for a re-examination possibly followed by a revision of that Title five years onwards. The changing international environment and the legal requirements of the SEA combined to create the necessary conditions for convening a new intergovernmental conference. The setting up of a true common foreign and security policy figured prominently on the agenda of the Commission (which produced a memorandum on the topic in October 1990) and of some member states like France and Germany in particular, though not on that of Britain who preferred the existing informal negotiating mode hitherto prevalent. Even between France and Germany there were differences of interpretation on the scope of a security policy – with implications for a potential common defence policy – (see below). The overt declarations of solidarity between the two countries covered a certain amount of fuzziness within the French notion of political union, which was less federalist than what the Germans hoped for. In practice, the detailed and precise conditions for economic and monetary union were duly set out in the Treaty on European Union, but no such detail or precision was afforded in the chapter on common foreign and security policy, usually referred to as the second Pillar of the European Union.

Article J of the Treaty on European Union unambiguously states that 'A common foreign and security policy is hereby established', an advance on the 'endeavour' of the SEA. The objectives of the common foreign and security policy are clearly set out in Art. J.1. Moreover, this CFSP is to be conducted no longer by 'The High Contracting Parties' but by the Member States who act within the Council. Not only does the Council define common positions (Art. J.2), but, following guidance from the European Council, the Council can decide to proceed with joint actions (Art. J.3). The scope of CFSP extends to 'the eventual framing of a common defence policy' (Art. J.4.1) and the Western European Union, 'which is an integral part of the development of the Union' shall 'elaborate and implement decisions and actions of the union which have defence implications' (Art. J.4.2). Although decision-making still operates under intergovernmental rules, the European Parliament is to be consulted by the Presidency on relevant matters (Art. J.7) and the Commission is now 'fully associated with the work carried out in the common foreign and security policy field' (Art. J.9). Moreover, a new Art. 228a is added which gives the Commission the right of initiative for Council joint actions 'to reduce or interrupt ... economic relations with one or more third countries', a timid but rational step towards bridging Pillars 1 and 2.

Germany would have preferred common foreign and security policy to be governed by less strict intergovernmental principles, and to give the European Parliament a greater role in foreign policy decision-making procedure, in line with her overall federalist outlook.[27] But, like the Netherlands Presidency which had produced a paper where the distinction between pillars was somewhat blurred, and that had proved unacceptable, Germany had to forgo these objectives. France, as usual struggling to reconcile the irreconcilable, i.e. trying to create an effective common policy (which would rein in any German tendency towards domination) without compromising her sovereignty, had finally adopted a solution mid-way between British intergovernmentalism and German federalism, for instance by accepting that the Secretariat for CFSP should be attached to the Council of Ministers rather than to the European Council.[28] On the whole, France was happy merely to reinforce the framework within which European Political Cooperation had developed.[29] The very French concept of a 'European power' was thus seriously weakenend. That Mitterrand's personal preference for federalism was not shared by French public opinion was demonstrated by the razor thin majority that approved the Treaty on European Union in the referendum of September 1992. It reinforced the uneasy feeling that European Union was no longer the self-evident panacea which Mitterrand had poetically embraced when he proclaimed that 'France is your homeland, and Europe is your future.'

With the election of Chirac in June 1995 and the death of Mitterrand in January 1996, the departure from the European scene of the Mitterrand-Kohl tandem had more than a symbolic significance. Their working principles were those of continuous consultation, in and between meetings, so that each had acquired a profound knowledge not just of the other's perceptions and modes of reasoning, but of the problems, strengths and weaknesses of the other's country as well. That did not prevent divergences and difficulties between the two countries, but it created a climate in which those divergences could be narrowed down and difficulties ironed out. The great strength of that particular partnership was precisely the ability of Kohl and Mitterrand to overcome national considerations.[30] The election of Jacques Chirac as Mitterrand's successor put paid to this intimacy, and created serious wobbles in the relationship. Difficulties also arose from a lack of personal empathy at lower levels, such as the well known tension between Defence Minister Volker Rühe and his French counterpart Charles Millon, to the point that the Germans were tempted to by-pass the French Ministry of Defence altogether and deal directly with the Elysée.[31] The validity of the alliance contract was vigorously maintained, but there seemed to be added an awful lot of small print.

The times were not particularly auspicious when the preparations for the 1996 Intergovernmental Conference started. In terms of foreign policy, the contribution of the European Union to the disentanglement of the Bosnian imbroglio (see below) had come down to French and British strategic and financial participation. France was hampered by her reluctance to accept the primacy of NATO over the WEU in providing a guarantee for the survival of Bosnia. Germany had been prevented from participating in military actions both psychologically because of World War II memories and constitutionally by a provision of the Basic Law forbidding military intervention in areas beyond the protection of the actual NATO-covered territory. This provision was abolished by a decision of the German Constitutional Court of 12 July 1994, which allows such military actions with mere authorisation from the *Bundestag*. This means that Germany could take part in SFOR which was set up in order to implement the Dayton agreement. Furthermore, Germany was running into serious financial difficulties mostly due to the cost of rebuilding the New Länder.

Looking forward to the forthcoming Intergovernmental Conference, Foreign Minister Klaus Kinkel had stated a rather ambitious set of objectives, which were supposed to guarantee 'effectiveness, coherence, continuity, solidarity and visibility' for the common foreign and security policy.[32] The main items to be covered were:

- the creation of a planning unit to define the common interest of the EU;
- the appointment of a secretary general to head this unit;
- the extension of decision-making majority voting, leaving unanimity for 'rare exceptions';
- the progressive integration of WEU into the EU;
- the development of a common armaments policy;
- a flexibility clause in decision-making.

By contrast, the French agenda was remarkably modest and seemed to be mostly concerned with creating the post of 'Mr PESC',[33] who would represent the European Union and 'speak for Europe', as it were, in international fora, who would be appointed and controlled by the European Council, and whose essential brief would be 'to improve foreign policy coordination between the member-states when European crises arose'.[34]

Differences between France and Germany persisted. In October 1996, a Franco-German seminar presided over by Michel Barnier and Werner Hoyer, respectively European affairs ministers of France and Germany, failed to reach agreement on how the European Common and Foreign Policy should evolve, particularly the vexed question concerning the extension of the qualified majority vote, and the two ministries withdrew their proposals. In an effort to generate a better understanding of their mutual positions, the Centre d'Analyse et de Prévision of the Quai d'Orsay and the Planungsstab of the *Auswärtiges Amt* produced in the winter of 1996–97 a joint document analysing the divergences between the two countries. Recognising the indifference and disenchantment of public opinion and the decreasing intensity of Franco-German exchanges, it advocated, for example, more public opinion debates, more joint actions, such as a common strategy for the IGC leading to Amsterdam, a joint trip of the French President and the German Chancellor to Washington, a thorough review of the cooperation networks, intensive exchanges of very senior civil servants, substitution of 'representations' for embassies, media mobilisation to improve mutual images of politicians, stationing of troops in each other's countries, etc.[35] Those measures, however, were either cosmetic or long term. They could not be properly implemented in time to secure harmonious and bold initiatives during the final stages of the Amsterdam negotiations.

Those negotiations coincided with the worst tension between France and Germany since the 1960s. Within the European Community, unified Germany appeared to add political clout to her economic dominance. The European Germany that both Mitterrand and Kohl had envisaged was jutting out into France's patch: already some two years earlier the Schäuble-Lamers Paper of September 1994 on potential development towards further political integration[36] had stolen the limelight; nor had the belated French Prime Minister Balladur's response[37] been a match in substance or impact. In foreign policy, the prospect of Eastern enlargement would inexorably increase Germany's political clout at the expense of France's. Moreover, Germany's intensive investment in Russia was pre-empting the influence that France had painstakingly striven to secure over the Soviet Union. Overall, in addition to mutual misgivings about the conditions pertaining to the setting up of the single currency, there prevailed a climate of general distrust (about the future of Airbus, about NATO, about nuclear deterrence, about relations with the US).

In the course of the negotiations, perhaps surprisingly, the French appeared better placed than the Germans to accept partial surrender of sovereignty in most areas except foreign and security policy, where the French preference for consensus was maintained. Conversely, Chancellor Kohl, who found himself subjected to intense pressure from the Länder, especially from such annoying figures as the CDU Biedenkopf of Saxony and CSU Stoiber of Bavaria, did a U-turn on institutional reform, resisting its progress on behalf of 'Germany's vital interests',[38] at precisely the same time as France appeared to go some way towards meeting traditional German federalist preferences. Significantly Germany produced jointly with Austria and Belgium a declaration on subsidiarity, obviously designed to protect the prerogatives of their regional entities. Nationalistic stances having blatantly taken over from concern for the development of European integration, an explosion between the French and the Germans was only avoided thanks to the mediation of the Luxemburger Jean-Claude Juncker.[39] At the time of the European Council of 16-17 June 1997 which concluded the negotiations, President Chirac was still smarting from the electoral defeat which put Jospin and the 'Plural left' in power, while Chancellor Kohl's position some fifteen months ahead of a general election looked singularly fragile. The two partners appeared to have switched roles traditionally held in the drama of negotiations, and that left the partnership in a sorry state.

As a result of all these tensions, previous proposals were watered down. The profile of High Representative for the common foreign and security policy and Secretary-General of the Council, 'Mr PESC', was drastically lowered. Cautious words ('progressive framing' … 'which might lead to' (Art. 17, ex Art J.7) were used when referring to a common defence policy. Decisions were to continue to be taken 'by the Council acting unanimously' (Art. 23, ex Art. J.13). There was, however, a new provision for 'constructive abstention' which meant that an abstaining member state would not necessarily stop an action voted by the other member states (Art. 23, ex Art. J.13). Shy of substantial reforms, the Amsterdam Treaty nevertheless reinforces the cohesion of European foreign policy by giving legal legitimacy to the concept of common strategies which are to be decided by the highest authority, the European Council (Art. 13, ex Art. J.3), and by creating in a Declaration to the final Act added to title V a 'policy planning and early warning unit'. The Amsterdam Treaty having come into force only on 1 May 1999, it remains to be seen how these provisions will be interpreted and implemented. The first 'Mr PESC', High Representative Javier Solana, the Spanish former Secretary-General of NATO, was duly appointed in the summer of 1999, and will have to coordinate his work with that of Chris Patten, the new Commissioner for External Affairs, and of the successive Presidents of the European Union. This could be seen as reinforcing the cohesion of the Union if the Commission and the Council are seen to work hand-in-hand and efficiently, or as heightening the danger of fragmentation and inefficiency, if to the points of view of fifteen member states must be added the disharmony of three competing executive entities.

Having hardly stepped into the Quai d'Orsay at the closing of the Intergovernmental Conference, the Foreign Affairs Minister of the new Jospin Government, Hubert Védrine, set out to repair the damage done in the previous two years. He had been special adviser to Mitterrand and had been well aware of the change in the nature of the Franco-German relationship in the recent past. He announced at the close of a Franco-German meeting in Bonn on 3 July that a number of measures would be taken 'to make Franco-German cooperation between our ministries more automatic'. Those measures, the promotion of joint ministerial initiatives, the strengthening of ties between corresponding departments in the German and French foreign ministries, and the improvement of working methods,[40] were very much in line with the recommendations made in the joint paper that had been issued by the two ministries some six months earlier. The German Foreign Minister, Klaus Kinkel, added his goodwill note in mid-August, insisting that there was 'no contact fault' between the two governments. A few days later, on 28 August, Chancellor Kohl and Prime Minister Jospin met informally in Bonn under slightly better auspices, as Germany was by now somewhat reassured about the European credentials of the new French government. Furthermore, the 70th bilateral summit of 19 September 1997, held for the first time ever in Eastern Germany, in Weimar, and which included both Chirac and Jospin, proved to be as consensual as the previous one three months earlier, in Poitiers, had been dysfunctional. Although questions of foreign policy were hardly mentioned, except for enlargement and military cooperation, the terrain now lent itself to a better understanding of each other's positions.

Following the victory of the French socialists in the election of June 1997, 1998 saw a similar upheaval in German politics. After sixteen years in power, Helmut Kohl made way for the socialist Gerhard Schröder, not particularly noted for his sympathies with France or, for that matter, with Europe. In any case, the year had been marked essentially by the ironing out of differences on the finalisation of monetary union (see Chapter 4). Foreign and security policy was not very high on the agenda and the Amsterdam Treaty would have to be ratified before major changes could occur.

THE SECURITY ASPECT OF A EUROPEAN COMMON FOREIGN POLICY: LANDMARKS AND PROBLEMS

Background to the Post-Maastricht Developments

The impact and memories of two distinctive but related successions of traumas have consistently governed French and German attitudes towards European security. In the case of Germany, the ideological and military imperialism of nazism, her virtual annihilation in 1945 followed by the carving of the country into four occupation zones, and the falling of the Iron Curtain, which divided her into two adversary states on either side of it. In the case of France, the collapse of her army and government in 1940, her absence from the Yalta Conference (revealing the shallowness of her status of 'victor' in 1945), her dependence on American dollars to survive the decade following the war, and the last gasps of her overseas ambitions in Dien Bien Phu, Suez and most painfully of all, Algeria.

For Germany, the member of the European Community most directly exposed in the Cold War confrontation, at first without an army of her own, and then without her own nuclear deterrent, the United States' protection was the unquestionable guarantor of her survival, and occupation forces quickly turned into wooed knights-at-arms whose dominion was not only welcome, but seen as the guarantee of America's commitment to the security of Europe. Germany was allowed to join the Atlantic Alliance in 1955, and her view of Europe was and remained to the end of the Cold War one of partnership with the USA, in other words an Atlanticist Europe. Germany carried this principle further than any of her European NATO partners in 1964 when she endorsed the American proposal to create a multilateral nuclear force (MLF), going as far as suggesting the setting up of a 'bilateral' MLF when the original proposal was seen to have eventually failed.[41]

Conversely, France did not perceive the Cold War in quite the same dramatic fashion. An original signatory of the North Atlantic Treaty, she never recanted her commitment to the Alliance, but she was both unsure of the durability of the American commitment, and concerned at the built-in subservience of the other members to the USA whose interests and therefore decisions might not coincide with those of their European partners. What, according to de Gaulle, France aimed for was a 'European Europe' i.e. a Europe free of any American tutelage. The most spectacular manifestation of this aspiration had been de Gaulle's decision to withdraw from the integrated military command of NATO, a situation that prevails to this day, various steps towards reintegration notwithstanding.

We therefore find France and Germany not merely diverging, but having diametrically opposed views of what, within the Atlantic Alliance, the relationship with the US should be: for France minimalist, for Germany maximalist. The collapse of the Soviet bloc in theory heralded an era of new understanding and good will between East and West and therefore reduced the pressure that a threat creates within an alliance; that, to some extent, lessened the distance between the two standpoints, but so far the gap has not been bridged.

The issue is somewhat obscured, rather than clarified, by recurrent attempts to create a European security system which de Gaulle would have recognised as 'European'. After the failure of the European Defence Community, the actors of the day providentially remembered the Brussels Pact signed by France, the United Kingdom and the Benelux countries in 1948 and turned into the Western European Union in 1954, and invited the Federal Republic of Germany to join it in October 1954. In practice, the Western European Union had only virtual reality, as it were, for the next three decades, as the Atlantic Alliance provided the institutional and strategic framework deemed sufficient to guarantee Western security. Additionally, the Conference on Security and Cooperation in Europe, by the Helsinki Agreement of August 1975, brought together members of NATO and of the Warsaw Pact plus a number of non-aligned or neutral countries (thirty-five signatories altogether, including the Holy See and San Marino!). Thus there were in principle established channels of peaceful communication and cooperation between the two sides of the Iron Curtain.[42] In the early 1980s, a 'mini-cold war' triggered by the invasion of Afghanistan and the imposition of martial law in Poland, darkened the international sky, and the need for a clarification and rationalisation of relations between NATO and WEU, strengthening the role of the European pillar, was felt more keenly. As a result, a Protocol signed in Rome in October 1984 reactivated the institutions, and enlarged the scope of the WEU, emphasising in particular 'Europe's contribution to the strengthening of the Atlantic alliance'.[43] In the Treaty on European Union of 1992, defence was duly included, and WEU was given a role as 'an integral part of the development of the Union'. Title V of the Treaty on European Union specifically states among the objectives of the CFSP 'to strengthen the security of the Union and its Member States in all ways', and by its Article J.4 the WEU is requested 'to elaborate and implement decisions and actions of the Union which have defence implications'. A Declaration of the WEU Members of the European Union, attached to the treaty, further emphasises the close links and cooperation with the Atlantic Alliance. That remained a far cry from the European system that the French would have preferred to set up, at that stage loyally supported by the Germans.[44] But the general vagueness of the terms used reflected the disparity of aims of the WEU member-states together with the need to engage in a kind of positive procrastination allowing a firming-up of policies in the future. It was part of the response to a new awareness that different threats would have to be identified, that the Cold War structures would have to adapt to a post-Cold War challenge, and that various security organisations would have to proceed with a new sharing out of tasks and competences. As the then Prime Minister Pierre Bérégovoy stated in a speech to the Institute for Higher National Defence Studies about NATO's new strategic concept signed at the Rome meeting of November 1991: 'it recognises that institutions other than NATO ... have roles to play in defence and security in Europe ... This is therefore the shape of the flexible architecture today emerging in Europe and enabling the European Community to be an integral part of an entity with a continental dimension, without one institution becoming the other's rival.'[45]

Franco-German Attempts at Convergence up to the Cologne European Council

The negotiations leading up to the Treaty on European Union demonstrated further that, at crucial moments, France and Germany rallied to present common proposals on European defence, and it was the United Kingdom, supported by Greece and Portugal, which blocked the establishment of an autonomous 'European defence'.

On the vexed question of European dependence on the United States to guarantee European security, two main factors had greatly contributed to a rapprochement between the two partners. On the one hand, ever since the end of the 1970s, France's doctrine of independence had been softened by an understated but real policy of closer participation in NATO 'events', i.e. consultations, meetings, and military exercises. Symbolically, the French Prime Minister Pierre Mauroy attended the annual NATO summit in 1982, and France hosted the next one in 1983.[46] On the other hand, the collapse of the Soviet bloc and the reunification of Germany accelerated her willingness to tighten up the Franco-German dimension of European security. In 1963 the Bundestag had demanded the insertion in the Franco-German Treaty of a preamble balancing Franco-German cooperation with the maintenance of the transatlantic relationship. Without relenting on the necessity to maintain a strong American commitment, Germany gradually came to accept that there was a case for beefing up a specifically European defence pillar. Chancellor Kohl was happy to sponsor the creation in January 1988 of a Franco-German defence and security council, and, in October 1990, of a Franco-German Brigade, which was to develop into a Eurocorps comprising as well forces from Belgium, Luxembourg and Spain. Some SPD members were unhappy about the Eurocorps, seeing it as an attempt by the French to pull Germany away from NATO, and the reception in America was mixed, although Chairman of the Joint Chiefs of Staff Colin Powell considered it 'politically and militarily well equipped to deal with interregional crises, humanitarian means and peacekeeping.'[47]

In June 1993, virtually the same wording was used when the WEU member states adopted the Petersberg Declaration which added to the WEU's defence role the possibility of using military units for 'humanitarian and rescue tasks, peace-keeping tasks, tasks of combat forces in crisis management, including peacemaking'.[48] Thus was defined a set of aims for a potential European defence policy which had been left totally vague in the Maastricht Treaty.

At the NATO Summit meeting of January 1994 in Brussels, the way was opened to develop a 'European Security and Defence Identity' and to provide members of NATO or WEU with the necessary 'separable but not separate military capabilities' for carrying out operations under 'Combined Joint Task Forces'.[49] This was a very important point for European members of NATO, particularly for the French, for it enabled members of the Alliance to use NATO's operational tools without the direct involvement of the United States. It also signalled a change of attitude of France vis-a-vis NATO: whereas until then France had resisted the 'politicisation' of NATO, i.e. NATO acting beyond the terms of Art. 5 of the Washington Treaty, at the Brussels Summit France endorsed the project of a Partnership for Peace and the eventual eastward enlargement of the Alliance. She was moreover prepared to accept that NATO might fulfil collective security missions on behalf of the UN or CSCE, as proved crucial in the setting up of UNPROFOR to guarantee the security of Croatia.[50] This more sympathetic attitude to NATO was partly due to a change of personnel in the French Government, when the general election of March 1993 had produced a trouncing of the socialist government, immediately replaced by a moderately conservative team headed by Edouard Balladur, with the Europhiles' Alain Juppé as minister for Foreign Affairs, Alain Lamassoure as junior minister for European Affairs, and François Léotard as defence minister, still under the Presidency of the arch-pro-European François Mitterrand. Informed by the vexations and helplessness of the European Union and its leading member states in the Yugoslav mire (see below), Balladur devised a plan for 'Pact for Stability and Security in Europe', which he presented to the European Council in Copenhagen in June 1993, and which was adopted by the following European Council in Brussels in December 1993. Actually, that plan accorded well with Mitterrand's often reiterated own worry over the potential 'balkanisation' of Europe. This rapprochement between France and Germany was accorded spectacular celebration when, on 14 July 1994, the Eurocorps, including elements of the *Bundeswehr*, took part in the military display down the Champs-Elysées, and that same afternoon Chancellor Kohl was invited to the traditional garden party offered by the French President.

Germany had made a positive gesture towards France by supporting the creation and the development of the Eurocorps, thus giving a signal that she would be a reliable partner in the prospective building up of a European defence system. France in return appeared to overcome her distaste for both the Americans' hegemonic position in the Atlantic Alliance and the some- what hasty eastward march of NATO, thus demonstrating to her German partner that she was prepared to go a long way to support what was primarily a German security interest.

This tentative convergence of Franco-German attitudes towards European security was however brutally interrupted after the election of Jacques Chirac to the Presidency of the French Republic in May 1995. In spite of his previous reassuring words, such as 'Franco-German cooperation is irreplaceable; our two countries must deepen their mutual understanding and build together a common project for Europe',[51] presidential candidate Jacques Chirac had appeared as a bit of a bogeyman to German politicians who remembered all too well his aggressive defence of French farmers' interests as Minister for Agriculture in the late 1960s and his notorious 'Cochin Appeal'[52] during the first European Parliament electoral campaign of 1979, when he had warned against a German invasion of France by economic means! Nor did the appointment of Alain Juppé as Prime Minister totally assuage German fears.

In the summer of 1995, the newly elected President Chirac confirmed Germany's misgivings when he decided to enact the decision, announced during his electoral campaign, to resume French nuclear tests in the Pacific. That was a very rash decision indeed, clearly taken without consulting European partners, thus demonstrating a betrayal of the Franco-German consultation mechanism, and working against the very idea of a genuine European defence system. President Chirac's proposal to put the French nuclear deterrent at the disposal of Europe not only failed to attract his German partners, but showed gross insensitivity to the prevalent German reticence towards nuclear armaments. German public opinion interpreted the obstinacy and haste with which the series of tests were carried out in the summer of 1995 as signs of French arrogance,[53] and failure to recognise that Germany was no longer the compliant junior partner of pre-reunification days.

Questions could then legitimately be raised about the reality of Franco-German cooperation in European security matters, and a further blow was dealt by France in early 1996. In spite of protestations by President Chirac in the first week of the New Year that Franco-German concertation was going to be given new impetus, he remained very vague as to what measures would be taken, and an informal meeting in Paris with Chancellor Kohl, presumably to clear the air, apparently lasted rather less than a quarter of an hour.[54] On the contrary, President Chirac yet again ruffled German feelings by declaring in February his intention to abolish conscription and to set up a professional army, again without any prior consultation with or warning to the German government. However well founded that decision might have been from a strategic French point of view, it was offensive towards Germany both in form and in substance. In form, because it was a cavalier way of treating one's 'declared closest ally', and the consequent withdrawal of French troops from German territory (17 000 out of a total of 20 000) could have a highly symbolic significance. In substance, because it undermined the very structure of the Eurocorps – the creation of which had itself been a German concession to French desiderata and seemed to indicate that France would want to build the necessary military capabilities for intervening in overseas conflicts independently of NATO. Moreover, it could be seen as a retrograde step in the development of a common foreign and security policy for the European Union, in contradiction with France's own stated policy goals, on the very eve of the opening of the 1996 Intergovernmental Conference.[55] As an anonymous collaborator of Chancellor Kohl ruefully noted: 'When Chirac decided to carry out nuclear tests on Mururoa, Kohl signalled his approval, whereas the enormous majority of the German population disapproved of the decision. Kohl had thus taken an enormous political risk, thinking that it would generate an atmosphere of mutual trust between Chirac and himself. But that was not to be … when France decided to abolish conscription and to reform her army, Chirac did not breathe a word of warning to Kohl.'[56]

This sorry state of affairs – compounded by Germany's uncompromising demands for French compliance on the final stages of setting up the single currency – did not augur well for Franco-German cooperation in two important fora: the NATO summit meeting in Berlin in June 1996, and the Intergovernmental Conference which officially opened on 29 March 1996.

The Berlin NATO meeting gave the green light to the rationalisation and reorganisation of military structures, clarified relations between the WEU and NATO, and refined the concept of Combined Joint Task Forces. The development of CJTFs, whose employment for specific tasks would have to be vetted both by the North Atlantic Council and the WEU Council, implied close cooperation between NATO and WEU, and raised the question of adapting NATO's command structure. Its immediate result was to raise the profile of WEU by giving it an active operational role. This could only meet with the approval of the French, for whom a reformed NATO was 'a first step towards fulfilment of France's ambition to equip Europe with the capacity to project military power and mount a wide range of operations by 2000'.[57] However, some French hopes were frustrated when, later on in the summer, France put forward the proposal that the Southern European flank of NATO should be put under European command. By asking that a European (preferably, but not necessarily a Frenchman) should head the Naples high command, the French were attempting to promote and enhance the European role in NATO. It met with the absolute opposition of the United States, who were unwilling to restrict their freedom of action in the eastern Mediterranean which the US fleet had traditionally played an active part in policing. Germany, conscious of the positive consequences for Europe of a greater

French commitment in NATO, at first supported this French proposal, but weakened in the face of American opposition, and the French had to give in. On 12 June 1997, Washington declared the matter closed.

The anticipated full reintegration of France into the NATO structures was therefore put into cold storage. On 2 July 1997, a few days before the NATO summit meeting in Madrid, a Communiqué issued by the Ministry of Foreign Affairs stated bluntly: 'In the present state of the negotiations, and while noting that progress has been made, particularly on the assertion of a European defence identity, France considers that the conditions it laid down for a re-examination of its relations with NATO's military structures have not been satisfied.'[58]

This episode gave a striking illustration of Germany's continuing dilemma of pursuing a policy of steadfast support for a US-led NATO (the guarantor of German territorial integrity throughout the Cold War), while at the same time promoting European political and security integration jointly with a France aspiring to a world role for Europe alongside rather than within the orbit of American leadership.

As for France, aware of the limits of her influence within the Atlantic Alliance, and faced with the prospect of an eastward enlargement of NATO, she tried to redefine her security policy on three premises: that the Atlantic alliance would indeed reform according to the Berlin summit conclusions; that it was imperative to pursue the development of a genuinely European defence system; and that the Organisation for Security and Cooperation in Europe, which alone incorporated the whole of Europe including Russia, must be reinforced. Meanwhile, bridges with Germany were in sore need of rebuilding.

In practice, relations between France and Germany were not quite as bad as the misunderstandings and misconceptions about defence or the EURO made them appear. It may well be that in both countries public opinion had reacted strongly, in Germany, to Chirac's initiatives, in France to Germany's rigid attitude towards the EURO and what looked like a shift of interest away from Western Europe in favour of Eastern Europe. There remained, however, serious trumps in the European camp. Chirac, who had supported the 'yes' vote in the 1992 referendum, was far more pro-European than his party; he was also personally amenable to better relations with NATO, and approved of its eastward enlargement (going as far as supporting the membership not just of the Czech Republic, Hungary, and Poland, but also of Romania and Bulgaria); Kohl, whose 'nationalistic' stance in the Amsterdam IGC was mostly due to his electoral preoccupations, had supported France on projected reforms of NATO. Their commitment both to a single currency and to a 'European defence identity', however vague the concept, was not in question.

That is why the relevant ministries and offices before Amsterdam, had worked hard to make a success of the Nuremberg meeting of 9 December 1996, which produced the much vaunted 'common strategic concept'. The document stated that:

> ... the Franco-German Defence and Security Council has decided to give a new impetus to Franco-German cooperation on security and defence, looking at it from both a European and Atlantic perspective. To this end, our two countries are determined to press on with developing a European security and defence identity in the Alliance as part of the latter's reform and to place the transtlantic partnership with the North American States on a new solid foundation. The European and Atlantic institutions are destined to be enlarged. Both our countries will play an active part in defining the terms of the involvement of the new member States and the various partners, as appropriate in each case, in the carrying out of the alliance's collective defence and crisis management tasks conducted under the aegis of the international community of nations.

The text then enumerated and developed the principles of the four components of the concept:

- the definition of common objectives for our security and defence policies;
- common analysis of our countries' security environment and framework;
- a common approach on the strategy and missions of the armed forces;
- common guidelines on military cooperation, including the assembly of common military capabilities, and on armaments policy.[59]

As Lucas Delattre and Daniel Vernet commented in *Le Monde,* this Nuremberg statement resolved a number of sensitive issues: it put an end to a number of Gaullist dogmas by placing Franco-German cooperation within the European and Atlantic Alliance framework, it clarified the status of Franco-German relations by placing France and Germany on an equal footing; it acquiesced, albeit softly softly, in the doctrine of nuclear deterrence in the context of a European defence policy; it also implied that neither capital would take military initiatives, either in Europe or beyond, without *a priori* consultation of its partner.[60]

The Nuremberg concept was successful in that it put an end to the mood of rancour and suspicion that had worsened in the recent months and drew up a comprehensive and realistic blueprint for cooperation in matters of European security. However, it remained open to different interpretations. From the German point of view, it recognised the primacy of NATO, including in the field of nuclear deterrence. From the French perspective, it emphasised the Europeanisation of NATO.[61] Nevertheless, even if France considered security policy in part as a rank reinforcing mission, whereas Germany continued to consider it as a protection mission, it signalled the beginning of a convergence towards the better balancing of American-European relations. It also meant that France now seriously meant to put nuclear deterrence in the context of a European defence policy, and that Germany went beyond concerns of strictly territorial protection and took on aspects of peace-keeping and preservation of human rights.

Meanwhile, the debate on the European Security and Defence Identity and the role of defence within the European Union continued. While France had recognised the impossibility of dissociating the WEU from the Atlantic Alliance, Germany recognised that the European Council had a role to play in decisions on a European defence policy. In the autumn of 1998, the new Chancellor, Gerhard Schröder, was unlikely to have very different ideas from that of his predecessor on the relationship between WEU and NATO. During the Austrian Presidency of the EU, in October 1998, the Defence Ministers of the Fifteen met informally at Parschacht and again in Vienna in November to discuss the implications of the Amsterdam Treaty. For the first time, the position of the UK was now shifting closer to that of France and Germany towards accepting the integration of WEU into the EU, while at the same time George Robertson maintained that 'NATO remains the linchpin of European security'. This radical change of attitude was probably due to British concern and frustration over the European Union's inability and the United States' refusal to act in the Kosovo crisis which was threatening to turn into another 'Bosnia-type' disaster, and also by the United Kingdom's fear of isolation after having postponed any decision on Economic and Monetary Union.

On 4 December, the Prime Ministers of the UK and of France met at Saint-Malo, and Tony Blair granted for the first time ever that the European Union must have a European defence policy of its own within the framework of the Common Foreign and Security Policy. According to the communiqué, the two Prime Ministers agreed that the European Union must have the necessary operational capabilities to decide and act according to the commitments towards NATO. In other words, there should be an agreed division, not duplication, of work and costs. This may have been read by some as not much more than 'a New Year's resolution ... with good intentions (but) ... minimal substance',[62] but it was a radical departure in the UK's position, now accepting that the WEU would eventually be absorbed into the EU, at last putting flesh on the bones of the Amsterdam Treaty. It also signalled to the European partners that initiatives on defence matters would include the United Kingdom.

The stakes were open once more as to the future relationship between the EU, WEU and NATO. The Washington meeting of NATO convened in April 1999 to celebrate the fiftieth anniversary of the organisation had little cause to celebrate. The NATO intervention in Kosovo was very fraught and open to criticism, and the mood was not for any significant changes. The Washington summit confirmed that the stronger European role would be seen as contributing to the vitality of the Alliance, and that there was no conflict between a development of the CFSP within the European Union and the common security policy within the framework of the Atlantic Alliance. Details of NATO assets to be made at the disposal of EU-led operations were in principle agreed upon.

The changes would come not from NATO, but from the EU. To prepare for the next European Council under German Presidency, the fifteen Foreign Affairs Ministers met informally in Reinhartshausen on 13–14 March 1999, and formally in Council on 17 May. Finally, on 30 May, Chirac and Schröder met in Toulouse and issued a joint declaration, whereby they were determined to strengthen the military role of the European Union and to build up the Eurocorps into a Rapid Reaction Force. They reaffirmed their determination to integrate WEU into the EU, and to use the Cologne European Council of 3–4 June to that effect. France and Germany were once more coming together to start a new initiative, this time with the support of the United Kingdom.

Contrary to previous documents, Annex III of the Cologne Communiqué gives specific details on the orientation and means of a potential European policy. The European Union is to have appropriate capabilities to assume its tasks of conflict prevention and crisis management, particularly in the field of intelligence, strategic transport, command and control. European defence industries have to be restructured. The emphasis of the communiqué was very much on endowing the European Union with a capacity for autonomous action and all necessary operational capabilities to ensure the success of this action. Decision-making in crisis management within the scope of the Petersberg tasks must be made effective, and the EU must be provided with a capacity for analysis of situations, sources of intelligence, and a capability for relevant strategic planning.[63]

We now have a blueprint for a maximalist interpretation and implementation of the Amsterdam Treaty provisions on CFSP. Interestingly, the ultimate federator has once again proved to be a set of external parameters: the crisis in Kosovo and the detachment of the United States in the autumn of 1998, which appeared to have finally persuaded Britain's government to give serious consideration to the European Security and Defence Identity, i.e. to an autonomous European defence system. Once that blockage was removed, the famous Franco-German engine was turning again. It might yet misfire. A multiplicity of questions will arise, starting with resources at a time of stringent budgetary orthodoxy, which has incidentally plagued Franco-German relations on armaments cooperation in the last decade. The United States devote 3% of their GNP to defence, the Fifteen barely reach 2%.[64] How serious is the French standing offer to put her nuclear deterrent at the disposal of Europe, and how relevant? What will be the role of the neutrals in decision-making *à quinze* in the field of defence? What are the limits of autonomy within the framework of the Atlantic Alliance – a problem partially resolved by the Petersberg tasks format but hardly tested in practice?

How will the three new Central European members of NATO fit into the PESC pattern between now and the time when they become members of the European Union? Above all, how will all national security interests be absorbed into one European security concept? Will France, for instance, restrict the scope of her aims in Africa, or separate the issues with the attendant problem of drain on resources which she has previously complained of? Taken one at a time, these questions are fairly familiar and must have generated a number of scenarios in the think tanks of most member states. But now the moment of truth has come. It took thirty years to bring monetary union to fruition, albeit without the participation of all member states. It may well take as long again to build up a European defence system, and the process started almost as long ago. It is inconceivable without the full cooperation of France and Germany, but it also needs the commitment of the other nuclear and major military power, the United Kingdom, and the acquiescence of the benevolent hegemon in the Atlantic Alliance, the United States. Because of the interconnection of the various security systems and the complexity of command and decision-making structures, it is even more complex than monetary union. One of the conundrums which contributed to the failure of the European Defence Community, almost half a century ago, was the decision-making vacuum due to the non-existence of a supreme political authority. The consequence of decisions taken at the Cologne European Council could well be the return of federalism, not constitutional, but functional, by the back door.

FRANCO-GERMAN POSITIONS ON SOME KEY POLICY ISSUES: IRAQ, BOSNIA, KOSOVO

The year 1991 was momentous in the western international system, which was put to the test by three crises: the Gulf War, the dissolution of the Soviet Union, and the dissolution of the Yugoslav Federation. Whereas Western states had no part to play apart from speculating on the consequences of the developments that took place in Russia from August to December, they found themselves immediately dragged into the two other conflicts, in the first one militarily, in the second one diplomatically. The response of the European Community (the Twelve, and eventually the Fifteen) differed in the two cases, which constitutionally allowed different initiatives. The responses of France and Germany, members of the European Community, of WEU, of NATO and of the UN, were radically different from each other because of their different policy aims and traditions, and each of the crises generated a momentum which influenced responses to the next.

The Gulf War

The invasion of Kuwait by Iraq took place on 2 August 1990, that is almost five months before the Intergovernmental Conference officially opened, and two months and a day before German reunification (monetary unification had been achieved a month earlier). The war itself started on 17 January 1991, over a year before the Treaty on European Union was signed. What this reminder means in practice is that there was no formal or real European Foreign and Security Policy at the time, although Art. 30 of the Single European Act stated that the High Contracting Parties (in other words, the member states, but significantly this term was eschewed in the whole Title III) 'shall endeavour jointly to formulate and implement a European foreign policy.' There was indeed no question of the European Communities engaging as such in the war, as they possessed no legal instruments, no armies, no formal diplomacy. The only specifically European engagement in that Middle-Eastern conflict was the role played by the Western European Union which co-ordinated patrols by the European navies in the Persian Gulf.[65]

On the other hand, considering that the invasion of Kuwait was the invasion of a member state of the United Nations Organisation by another, France would from the outset play a very active role as permanent member of the Security Council which, on the very day of the invasion, voted Resolution 660 condemning Iraq, while Germany, constrained by her Constitution, would take a back seat. According to Mitterrand's then adviser Hubert Védrine[66] 'if France did not participate, she would be morally, militarily and diplomatically discredited on the European and Euro-Atlantic fronts where, at the very same time, her creditworthiness and her future role were at stake.' In other words, Mitterrand's strategy was based not primarily on upholding French interests in the Middle East – though that obviously played some part – but on maintaining France's place in Europe and in the Atlantic Alliance.

It had been, so far, a difficult year for Franco-German relations. In spite of Mitterrand's retrospective concern that he be not judged as opposed to or even worried by the prospect of German reunification (this is the central topic of his last book, *de l'Allemagne, de la France*, a kind of manifesto for

Franco-German partnership), or the optimistic conclusion of an article by the then French external trade minister Jean-Marie Rausch reaffirming that 'German reunification will help develop even further Franco-German economic relations, and to build up Europe with Germany',[67] reunification inevitably altered the balance of power between the two partners. To participate fully in an operation which could figure as one aspect of her overall Arab policy was one way in which France could remind the world in general and Germany in particular that her standing in the world was that of a major actor, if not power. Moreover, France wanted to demonstrate that she was a reliable ally within the Atlantic Alliance.[68] France in fact acted on two levels: Mitterrand played the diplomatic card right to the eve of the military conflict, by trying to mediate with Saddam Hussein (presumably on the grounds that France had been a *de facto* ally of Iraq, passing on nuclear know-how some two decades earlier, and supplying arms during the Iraq-Iran war), but fully supported the military intervention once the operation Desert Storm was launched.

France's military engagement in the Iraqi conflict started as early as September 1990 as a result of hostage-taking by the Iraqis in the French Embassy in Kuwait with the sending of 4 200 troops to Saudi Arabia as Operation Daguet[69] as well as dispatching the aircraft-carrier *Clémenceau* to the proximity of the Gulf. It continued as a partner of the United States and Britain during Desert Storm, setting in action a total of 12 000 ground troops, 150 light and heavy tanks and 130 combat and transport helicopters.

Meanwhile, Germany was keeping distant from military operations, although she contributed to the financing of the operation to the tune of DM 18 billion, i.e. 10% of the total.[70] In fact, the conflict in the Gulf was potentially dangerous for Germany at the time of reunification in that the Soviet Union, one of the partners in the Two plus Four Conference, had entertained friendly relations with Iraq, and might react strongly to any demonstration of German solidarity with the Western response to the invasion of Kuwait.[71] Moreover, the conflict was clearly taking place outside the European security area and was not threatening German security. Because of historical considerations, the idea of military intervention outside German territory was not only repugnant to German public opinion, but perceived as contrary to a provision of the Basic Law. Conversely, the German government was loath to appear uninterested in maintaining loyalty towards NATO and West European allies. Germany also had to take into consideration the fact that her ally Israel was under direct threat from Iraq. Hence the solution adopted of sending no troops but making a substantial financial contribution. Ironically, this decision was in glaring contrast with that of the European Council, who at a meeting on 7 September 1990, announced that they would make no financial contribution to the United States' operations in the Gulf.[72]

The official German policy is somewhat different from what was perceived at the time. Germany actually deployed some military forces not on the battlefield, but in the Mediterranean as part of NATO's protection operations, and in Turkey which is a member of NATO. Volunteers also contributed to the policing of Iraq's northern border once the Gulf War proper was over.

In that conflict, both France and Germany acted, in their own ways, as a result of a Security Council resolution, and as members of NATO and WEU (of which France held the Presidency at the time). But they could not act as executives of European Political Cooperation whose only instruments were resolutions, and economic sanctions through the European Economic Community, which is precisely what EPC used against Iraq on the very day of the Kuwaiti invasion. Within a few days, an embargo on oil imports from Kuwait and Iraq, and a suspension of the application of the Generalised System of Preferences[73] demonstrated that it was not lack of will, but lack of military capability, which limited EPC's effectiveness. Franco-German cooperation as such had hardly played a part because the basic foreign policy parameters in this particular conflict were too disparate. Some characteristics were quite striking: the Germans' actions went beyond the government rhetoric; conversely, the French, and especially Mitterrand, were seen as extremely active, particularly between August and January, but the French military participation did not quite come up to expectations. That lesson would not be lost on the French, by the way, in their future negotiations in WEU and NATO, and in the perception that France needed a complete overhaul of her forces' structure.

The Dissolution of Yugoslavia – Bosnia

Whereas the Gulf War had not directly threatened the security of the member states of the European Community, the conflict in Yugoslavia did. The most immediate threat was that of destabilisation, first in the Balkans where Italy and Greece had common frontiers with the Federation, and then in Eastern Europe where neighbouring countries to Germany might be involved. Another threat was the possible reaction of Russia, who has an obvious interest in protecting Slav populations, and who was smarting from the humiliation of the implosion of the Warsaw Pact. Thirdly, as was painfully demonstrated in the course of the conflict, EC countries ran the risk of having to shelter thousands of refugees, which would put an additional burden on their budgets, increase the risk of violent reactions in socially deprived areas and give political fodder to extreme rightwing nationalist movements, especially in France and Germany. The European Community as such was literally disarmed in the face of the conflict, her only weapon being moral outrage supported by economic sanctions. The Conference on Security and Cooperation in Europe, which might have been able to use its advantage of including Russia and Eastern European countries, was even less endowed than the EC, having neither mandate nor proper instruments for intervening in the conflict. It would therefore fall by default to the United Nations, NATO and a weak WEU to devise and impose a solution. In practice, the main players would be the countries that eventually formed the Contact Group: the United States, Russia, Britain, France, Italy and Germany.

While the Dutch Presidency during the 1991 Intergovernmental Conference was struggling to work out a compromise that would reconcile the 'sovereignist' British and French views with the German federalists, the Yugoslav drama put these divergent powers to the test. The European Community became involved – under the Luxemburg Presidency – when in the spring of 1991 Slovenia and Croatia addressed to the Twelve a request for recognition, so that the issue had to be at least mentioned in the Luxemburg European Council of 23 June 1991. Two days later, Slovenia and Croatia proclaimed their independence, and fighting ensued throughout the rest of the year, notwithstanding the EC's Troika's several attempts to defuse the issue.

In order to explain the divergences between France and Germany on the best way to handle the constitutional question, it is not enough to say that history put the French on the side of the Serbs and the Germans on the side of the Croats. The Germans supported Croatian independence *because* they have a million Croats on their territory. The French took a pro-Serb stand *because* they were worried about the destabilisation of Yugoslavia. Considerations of political philosophy would also incline the French towards supporting a unitary state, and the Germans towards supporting regional entities. France would also tend to support the established legal order, whereas Germany would be more sensitive to the reality of ethnic aspirations.

From the start of the conflict, France played an active part, not least by lending in 1991 the President of the Constitutional Council, and former Minister of Justice Robert Badinter, to head an international Advisory Commission to enquire and counsel on the wishes of the various Yugoslav republics on the legal suitability of the Yugoslav republics' applications for EC recognition for independence.[74] The recommendations of the Badinter Commission might just have saved the Yugoslav Federation, but Germany, under pressure from the *Bundestag*, and German public opinion, was impatient to support Slovenia's and Croatia's claims to independence which was opposed by France, Britain and the United States. Before the Badinter Commission's conclusions could be properly assessed by the member states, Bonn announced on 23 December that it would shortly recognise Slovenia and Croatia. The other member states reluctantly followed suit, official EC recognition being proclaimed on 15 January 1992, but it created an unhealthy climate of resentment and recrimination against Germany's perceived petulance. Henceforth Germany would maintain a fairly discreet stance in order to preserve good relations with her Western allies and with Russia.

As the conflict developed and various peace plans failed, Germany was increasingly drawn into military airborne operations in support of UN Security Council sanctions against recalcitrant Yugoslavia, such as enforcing a UN exclusion zone over Bosnia. A provision of the German Basic Law, forbidding military intervention in areas beyond NATO territory, was eventually abolished by the decision of the German Constitutional Court of 12 July 1994. The new provision allowing such military actions provided they were authorised by the *Bundestag* and approved by the UN. This meant that Germany could take part in IFOR (Implementation Force) which was set up in order to implement the Dayton Agreement of 1995.

However angry at Germany's hasty recognition of Croatia and Slovenia, France, like her other EC partners, chose not to protest but to follow suit in the name of EC cohesion, and in order to avoid a conflict with Germany at the very time when the government would need public opinion support for the ratification of the Maastricht Treaty. France officially switched support from Serbia to the Bosnian Muslims at the Lisbon European Council of June 1992, immediately after which Mitterrand paid a surprise visit to besieged Sarajevo.

By the time the Contact Group was formed in April 1994 to coordinate the policies of the six countries concerned, the situation in Bosnia had assumed catastrophic proportions, after the failure of the Vance-Owen Plan which would have created a decentralised Bosnian State. The setting up of the Contact Group paved the way for an active American involvement, and produced at last a more united perspective on policy decisions. It managed the end of hostilities between Croats and Bosnian Muslims. The initiative for diplomatic moves slid from Europe – the former Swedish Prime Minister Carl Bildt appointed as the new EU mediator – to the United States, with endemic Russian irritations eventually smoothed over. The Dayton Accords, for the most part based on former European proposals, but negotiated with vigour and determination by US Richard Holbrooke's team, were signed in Paris on 14 December 1995. They put an end to the war in Bosnia and laid conditions for the protection of human rights, provisions for elections (entrusted to the OSCE), administration of Bosnia (the EU was to take over the running of the town of Mostar) and the reconstruction of Bosnia, a task which fell to the EU.

Devoid of military capability, the EU, after the very damaging disagreements between Germany and her partners in 1991, slowly developed a fair degree of coherence in its policies. Whereas results were disappointing, learning points were gained. At various stages, political and technical coordination with the UN, with OSCE and with NATO was successfully achieved. Moreover, the idea of a European defence pillar of NATO for which WEU would be the obvious choice grew in strength. This was precisely what the French, working alongside NATO, strove for. They had decided in May 1995 to commit 10 000 troops to UNPROFOR (the UN Protection Force in Bosnia) as part of an Anglo-Franco-Dutch Rapid Reaction Force. Throughout the conflict France had advocated the use of force as a means of ending the diplomatic imbroglio, but that had been repeatedly resisted by her allies. Once implementation of the Dayton Accords was put into place, France, who had deployed 9 000 troops at the time of the setting up of the Rapid Reaction Force, committed 3 500 men in IFOR.[75] The difficulties and honourable failure which the EC/EU had experienced throughout the conflict persuaded France that without a reform of procedures, the prospect of an autonomous European defence policy was remote.

Kosovo

While Bosnia recovered at least an appearance of normalcy in its administration under joint NATO-OSCE-EU conditions, a new if not totally unforeseen threat was looming over Kosovo. Its Albanian population had been deprived of its autonomous status by President Milosevic in 1989. Outrageously rigged elections on 21 September to 5 October 1997 had produced a massively pro-Serb majority, and a Kosovan Liberation Army (KLA or UKC) had started waging a guerrilla war, further destabilising the region. Both France and Germany were so concerned at the deteriorating situation that Foreign Ministers Klaus Kinkel and Hubert Védrine sent a joint letter to President Milosevic in November 1997, asking him to start negotiations with a view to restoring Kosovo's autonomy, but to no avail. In March 1998 the Contact Group drew up a text designed to put pressure on Belgrade. This text was approved by a Conference of EU member states and applicant countries, 26 in total, at a European Conference held in London under United Kingdom Presidency on 12 March. In a further attempt to obtain some response, Kinkel and Védrine made a joint visit to Zagreb and Belgrade on 19 March 1998, which produced no results.

On 22 March 1998, an election within the Albanian community produced a victory for the moderate leader Ibrahim Rugova. In April 1998, negotiations between the Federal Yugoslav Republic and the Albanian leadership failed, and the summer of 1998 saw an increase of hostilities.[76] Throughout the autumn, as atrocities worsened and over 200 000 Kosovar Albanians had been displaced, the United States attempted shuttle diplomacy to reach a settlement with the Yugoslav Republic. Plans and counter-plans were exchanged, but never accepted. At Christmas 1998 and in January 1999 more evidence of massacres emerged. On 15 January a massacre of 45 Albanians in the village of Racak was denounced by the OSCE Kosovo Verification Mission as 'a crime against humanity', whereas Serbian authorities claimed the victims were members of the KLA. This atrocity set in train a number of measures from NATO members and France, including naval and air force concentration movements in Italy and the Adriatic, signalling that NATO and the Contact Group were prepared to use force if President Milosevic failed to respond positively to diplomatic pressure. At that point, on 27 January, US Secretary of State Mrs Albright and Russian Foreign Minister Ivanov met, and the United States declared that henceforth a combination of diplomatic pressure and threat of use of force would be applied on the Yugoslavian Republic. The following day, Secretary-General Javier Solana declared that NATO would support a 'political settlement under the mediation of the Contact Group', and that military involvement in support of the demands of the international community might not be excluded. Following various unsuccessful moves by the Contact Group, approved by the UN Security Council, to obtain from the FRY an agreement designed to stop the hostilities and ensure the autonomy of Kosovo, a one-page 'non-negotiable' document was presented to the Federal Republic and the KLA.

The Contact Group summoned the FRY and the KLA to a conference in Rambouillet. The choice of the venue was not accidental. France had deliberately put forward the invitation in order to underline that the Europeans were not to accept minor roles as they had had to do at Dayton. The Conference opened on 6 February, formally co-chaired by Foreign Ministers Robin Cook and Hubert Védrine, but in practice negotiations were conducted for the Contact Group by the American, German (representing the EU) and Russian delegates. Oddly and ominously, the Kosovar delegation was not led by President Rugova, but by a KLA member. The ten basic principles presented to the two parties underlined the necessity to obtain a peace settlement, included the provision of a mechanism for a final settlement at the end of three years, territorial integrity of the Federal Republic and neighbouring countries, free elections and the protection of the rights of all national communities. Implementation would be supervised by the OSCE and a NATO military presence in Kosovo, KFOR, would ensure compliance. Opposition came first from the Kosovar delegation which insisted on a status of independence, then by Milosevic who objected to the occupation of Kosovo by NATO troops, but would have settled for an international force that would include elements from the EU and Russia. The conference was deadlocked. Talks resumed in Paris on 15 March, but again the talks failed, partly due to divisions within the Contact Group, objections coming mostly from Russia, partly because the Serb delegation found it impossible to accept the package in its entirety.

The response was immediate and brutal. Without waiting for an official mandate from the UN Security Council, NATO forces were engaged from 24 March in aerial bombardment of the Federal Republic and Kosovo, with the aim of annihilating the Serb air defence system. Within a week, a second phase of the operations included the destruction of military capabilities from Belgrade to the southern border of Kosovo. Apart from Serb casualties which probably numbered several thousands, the bombardments triggered off new revenge atrocities in Kosovo and the forced exodus of hundreds of thousands of Kosovars, mostly to Albania and Macedonia, and to a lesser extent to Montenegro and even Bosnia.

The French government wholly supported the operation, and provided the second largest strike force after the US, with 3 000 troops in Macedonia, 800 in Albania, over 60 aircraft, the aircraft-carrier *Foch* with 2 500 men, tanks, etc.[77] However, a violent debate among prominent intellectual figures raged in the pages of the French press, on the effectiveness and moral justification of the bombardments. France was prepared to undertake ground operations if Britain decided in favour.

In Germany, Chancellor Schröder also supported the operation, and engaged German troops (for the first time since World War II), but met internal opposition from the Greens who are part of the government coalition. German public opinion was also divided on the effectiveness and moral justification of the bombardments, and that was also echoed in the German press. Germany provided over 4 000 troops in Macedonia and Albania, and 14 Tornado aircraft flying in non-combat intelligence missions. Germany was not prepared to undertake a ground offensive. Officially sponsored by the Atlantic Council, the air offensive was managed in practice by the governments of the four main NATO powers, i.e. the US, the UK, France and Germany.

By the middle of May, escalation to a phase 3 which would have covered the whole territory of the Federal Republic was being unofficially undertaken. Meanwhile, Russia was conducting her own diplomatic campaign to find a political settlement of the conflict, and the Russian representative Viktor Chernomyrdin was joined on 14 May by the Finnish President Martti Ahtisaari. On 5 June, Belgrade accepted the proposals put forward by the pair, and NATO operations ceased on the basis of a ten point peace document, which included the posting of KFOR troops in Kosovo to a maximum of 53 000 with contingents from the six Contact Group countries. It is significant that, since the autumn, KFOR is headed by the German general Klaus Reinhardt who succeeded the British General Michael Jackson.

However justified reservations on the moral ground, the crisis over Kosovo was managed successfully in a way that the Bosnian crisis was not. France reined in her pro-Serb reflexes, overruled opponents of the bombardments, and operated efficiently within the NATO team. In a parallel manner, Germany overcame her aversion for military engagements and gave loyal support to the operations in the face of opposition from the Greens and some elements in the other parties, including the SPD. The EU as such only played a supporting role, but there is no doubt that the ostentatious and sometimes brutal lead assumed by the United States in Kosovo as previously in Bosnia, reinforced both German and French, and probably also British convictions, that it was now time for the Europeans to take their own defence into their own hands. The Cologne European Council took place one day before the cessation of hostilities in Kosovo.

ARMAMENTS COOPERATION

The history of European armaments cooperation is dominated by two factors: first, when the North Atlantic Alliance Treaty was signed in April 1949, a very weak Europe was looking for the protection of a militarily and economically very strong United States, and *de facto* gratefully accepted that the bulk of the hardware and the final decisions would come from the United States. Second, when Germany was admitted to NATO in May 1955, she was still considered as potentially unreliable, and she accepted a clause barring her from producing or using atomic, bacteriological and chemical weapons.

Throughout the history of NATO and the European Community, there has been a stark contrast between the might of American weapons industry and the quasi-monopolistic position of American armaments in NATO military operations, and the fragmentation and under-utilisation of European weaponry in those operations. For their survival and prosperity, European armaments industries which, incidentally, are commercially in competition with each other, have relied heavily on overseas markets. Furthermore, European production is least developed in the areas of highest technology, such as surveillance and intelligence.

This phenomenon has not escaped European decision-makers, but the process of modernisation, rationalisation and unification of European armaments is slow and arduous, partly because of the diverse structures of national industries – from the totally privatised British and Dutch to the majority government-controlled French.

The 'abc' prohibition of Germany has led her to adopt a low international profile in terms of defence, but also to develop conventional armaments fully. In the turbulent last decade of this century, Germany continued to play a minor part in conflicts where NATO was engaged, even though both her constant stance as a strictly civilian power and the reunification of the country have enhanced her status both as responsible and at least equal in rank with the two former world powers France and Great Britain.

In terms of Franco-German armaments cooperation, the same cleavage as for security has hitherto prevailed: France is very keen to develop a European armaments industry. From the French point of view, arms cooperation would not only boost exports (weaponry represents about 5% of total French exports, but only 1% of Germany's), but would also create a West European pole which, under French leadership, could play a strong international role independently of the United States.[78] By contrast, Germany, which all too often has been asked to bear the lion's share of the costs of joint projects, is much more prepared to let American dominance prevail.

As early as the 1960s, France developed a keen interest in a space programme, and was instrumental in the setting up of a European Space Agency in 1975, with headquarters in Paris, which brought together the European Space Research Organisation (ESRO) and the European Organisation for the Development of Space Vehicle Launchers (ELDO). Its main achievement has been the permanent development of the commercially successful Ariane Project. But it also has military ambitions, embodied in the Hermes space shuttle project and the Colombus orbital station project, which were agreed upon in 1987. By the early 1990s, the cost of these projects was estimated at around $10 billion, and Germany, who was facing heavy budgetary constraints because of reunification, asked for a spreading out of costs in time. This has actually been the sad story of other projects in armaments cooperation, and in particular the Helios-II satellite programme.

Problems of Cooperation: the Example of the Helios Satellite Programme

France who, outside the command structure of NATO, had been painfully aware of having to rely on US intelligence, suggested to Germany in 1983 that the two countries set up a joint programme to build a military observation satellite. The Germans, who were keen to observe military developments among Warsaw Pact countries and also had to rely on the good-will of the United States, welcomed the French suggestion. The French already had a satellite project, the *Satellite Militaire de Reconnaissance Optique* (SAMRO) on their drawing boards. What they wanted from the Germans was cooperation on production, but not on design, and a minority share of production, at that. This was unacceptable to the Germans, who withdraw from the programme a year later. The French eventually persuaded the Spanish and the Italians to join the project, which was renamed Helios.[79] Now Helios-I, the observation satellite, has been in operation since 1995 and was used during the mid-1990s USA-Iraq crisis. But it is not an all-weather satellite.

The French therefore approached the Germans again, and in May 1996 Chirac and Kohl agreed on the creation of a new infra-red and optical observation system consisting of 3 satellites, to be called Helios II. It would become operational in 2001 and would be constructed by France (Matra and Aerospatiale). Assuming that Germany would be willing to carry 25% of the costs, Spain and Italy would also join the programme (probably bearing 15% and 5% respectively, as was done for Helios-I). Concurrently, there were plans for Germany to build yet another all-weather electromagnetic satellite system, to be operational by 2005, for which France would contribute 30% of the costs and Italy 20%. However, budget constraints, and cuts in military expenditure, contributed to a change of plans in Germany, who now intended to transfer credits allotted to Helios-II to Horus. This was a blow for France who would either have to give up Helios-II or bear the extra costs.[80]

This example illustrates some of the problems inherent in armaments cooperation, where projects are extremely expensive. The first one is to consult the potential partners to check on similarity of aims and availability of resources. The second one is to have sound assessment of costs, and a margin of flexibility. The third one is to have clear agreements on who does what, in terms of design and production. The fourth one is to have the capability to carry the project to fruition. Interestingly, at a Franco-German meeting of parliamentarians in Aachen in January 1997, the German Ambassador to NATO stated, that 'out of forty-five satellite channels used to observe Bosnian territory, only two were not American', and those two (which are NATO's) gave poorer images than the American.[81] Again, for operations in Kosovo, only US satellites could provide proper observation, and their limitations in cloudy conditions reduced the possibilities of sorties on frequent occasions. Partly as a result of this, France and Germany decided at the Toulouse Franco-German meeting of May 1999 to relaunch the Helios-II programme.

The Helios satellite programme is by no means the only project in the field of European Armaments cooperation. Schemes under the management of the Organisation for Military Armaments Cooperation, created in May 1996, has a long list of projects, including the Tiger helicopter project, a NATO helicopter NH90, a troop transport vehicle, long-range missiles, an Apache cruise missile, an ATF transport aircraft, with participation variously from France, Germany, Britain, Italy, the Netherlands, Belgium, and Spain. The potential is therefore enormous, but problems inherent in cooperation are unlikely to disappear, and competition from the United States, which benefits from long experience, homogeneous industrial structures, and well established markets, is ferocious. An integrated and competitive European armaments industry remains a long way off.

CONCLUSION

Compared with the previous two decades, the European Community in the last two decades has made two giant steps: the single market and monetary union. The latter one in particular signals the erosion of the concept of sovereignty. Completion of the single market was mostly due to the paradoxical alliance of Margaret Thatcher and Jacques Delors, because, as it happened, Thatcher saw the single market as a means of liberalising trade, whereas Delors saw the single market as a means of furthering European integration: it was not a question of partnership but of one using the other's means to achieve their own objective. When it came to monetary union, the approach was completely different: the partnership of Kohl and Mitterrand was as voluntarist as that of Thatcher and Delors had been coincidental. It was the final gesture of two statesmen whose common passion was to use the formidable joint weight of their two countries to ensure the future of 'Carolingian Europe' (and indeed the present 'Euroland' excluded the peripheral member states Greece – though only until 2001 – Denmark, Sweden and the United Kingdom). In certain ways, monetary union is a way of pursuing the political union of Europe in an underhand, or at least roundabout, manner. What has not yet advanced very far is foreign and security policy, partly because the loss of sovereignty in that area would be much more conspicuous, partly because not all member-states have the same, or even compatible foreign policy agendas, partly because there does not appear to be much of an external federator. Already the American suspension of détente under Reagan, but even more clearly recent events in the Middle East and in the Balkans have, however, demonstrated that foreign policy cleavages between the United States and most West European states are very real. Whereas France blows hot and cold on the prospect of rejoining NATO, the West European Union seems at last to be extricating itself from the dilemma of being the European arm of NATO or the defence arm of the European Union by the acceptance that there is no incompatibility in being both. In terms of defence. The Saint-Malo meeting between Blair and Chirac marked a turning point by removing the ambiguity about Britain's commitment to European Defence. But the real departure was signalled at the Cologne European Council, committing the European Union to a real defence policy, something that even Kohl had shrunk from. The most striking new element in defence policy is the United Kingdom's commitment to the European

Security and Defence identity. Perhaps, after all, as far as this area is concerned, the Franco-German tandem remains a necessary, but no longer sufficient condition for forging a CFSP proper?

NOTES

1. For a historical survey of these events, see Pierre Gerbet (1987), 'The origins; early attempts and the emergence of the Six (1945–52), in Roy Pryce (ed.), *The Dynamics of European Union*, Croom Helm, London, 35–48.
2. Simon J. Nuttall (1992), *European Political Co-operation*, Clarendon Press, Oxford, Chapter 2.
3. The concept of 'high and low politics' was first developed by Stanley Hoffmann in 'Obstinate or Obsolete: the fate of the nation-state and the case of Western Europe', *Daedalus*, **95**, Summer 1966, 862–915.
4. This is the title of a chapter in Brigid Laffan (1992) *Integration and Co-operation in Europe*, Routledge for UACES, London and New York.
5. Jacques Walch (1998), 'Défense dans le monde' in *Défense Nationale*, May.
6. Extracts from the Brussels Treaty quoted in Lawrence Freedman (ed.) (1990), *Europe Transformed, Documents on the End of the Cold War*, St Martin's Press, New York, p. 11.
7. Quoted by Alfred Grosser (1989), *Affaires Extérieures, La politique de la France 1944–1989*, Flammarion, Paris, Chapter 4.
8. Pierre Maillard (1990), *De Gaulle et l'Allemagne*, Plon, Paris, p. 139.
9. Grosser, *op. cit.*, Chapter 5.
10. Charles de Gaulle (1970), *Mémoires d'Espoir Le Renouveau 1958–1962*, Plon, Paris, p. 181.
11. *Ibid.*, p. 191.
12. Pierre Gerbet, 'In search of political union: the Fouchet Plan negotiations (1960–62)', in Roy Pryce (ed.), *op. cit.*, pp. 109–10.
13. Stephen A. Kocs (1995), *Autonomy or Power? The Franco-German Relationship and Europe's Strategic Choices, 1955–1995*, Praeger, Westport CT and London, p. 47.
14. European Parliament Political Committee (1964), *Towards Political Union – A selection of documents with a foreword by Mr. Emilio Battista*, General Directorate of parliamentary documentation and information.
15. John Newhouse (1967), *Collision in Brussels, the Common Market Crisis of 30 June 1965*, Faber & Faber, London.
16. Quoted in John Newhouse, *op. cit.*, p. 40.
17. For a detailed account of the attempts at Franco-German collaboration in the field of armaments, see Stephen A. Kocs *op. cit.*, Chapter 3, 69–91.
18. Quoted by Simon J. Nuttall.(1992), *European Political Co-operation*, Clarendon Press, Oxford, p. 49.
19. Simon J. Nuttall, *op. cit.*, 51–2.
20. A particular episode of this distinction being carried out *ad absurdum*, acquired notoriety: on 23 July 1973, the Foreign Ministers of the Nine met in Copenhagen in the morning to discuss matters of political cooperation, then that same afternoon flew to Brussels to meet as General Affairs Council.

21. Simon J. Nuttall, *op. cit.*, pp. 155–6.
22. Jean-François Deniau (1977), *L'Europe Interdite*, p. 150, quoted by Stanley Hoffmann (1995), *The European Sisyphus, Essays on Europe, 1964–1994*, Westview, Boulder, Colorado p. 183.
23. Giovanni Bonvicini (1987), 'The Genscher-Colombo Plan and the Solemn Declaration on the European Union (1981–1983)', in Roy Pryce (ed.), *op. cit.*, pp. 183–6.
24. Bonvicini, *op. cit.*, pp. 221–4.
25. Single European Act, Title One, Article 1, First Paragraph, Office for Official Publications of the European Communities, 1987.
26. Cf. Françoise de La Serre (1996), 'The impact of François Mitterrand', in Christopher Hill (ed.), *The Actors in Europe's Foreign Policy*, Routledge, London.
27. Reinhardt Rummel, 'Germany's role in the CFSP: Normalität or Sonderweg?', in Christopher Hill (ed.), *op. cit.*, pp. 50–51.
28. Geoffrey Edwards and Simon Nuttall, 'Common Foreign and Security Policy', in Andrew Duff, John Pinder and Roy Pryce (eds) (1994), *Maastricht and Beyond*, Routledge, London, pp. 93–4.
29. Françoise de la Serre, 'France', in Duff, Pinder and Pryce, *op. cit.*, pp. 32–3.
30. Hubert Védrine (1996), *Le Nouvel Observateur*, 18–24 January.
31. *Le Figaro*, 9 December 1996.
32. Klaus Kinkel (1996), 'L'agenda européen à l'horizon 2000', *Politique Etrangère*, March.
33. French acronym for 'Politique Etrangère et de Sécurité Commune'.
34. Speech by President Chirac to French Ambassadors, August 1995.
35. *Le Monde*, 22 May 1997.
36. *Überlegungen zur europäischen Politik*, CDU-CSU Fraktion des Deutschen Bundestages, 1 September 1994.
37. *Le Monde*, 30 November 1994.
38. Mard Deger, 'Français et Allemands en quête d'un terrain d'entente', *La Tribune*, 13 June 1997. See also Hans Stark (ed.) (1998), *Les relations franco-allemandes: état et perspectives*, Introduction, p. 9.
39. *Courrier International*, 30 July 1997, reprinting an article from *Der Spiegel*.
40. 'Strengthening Franco-German cooperation on foreign policy', Statement issued by the Ministry of Foreign Affairs, *SAC/97/159*. Ambassade de France in London.
41. For details, see John Newhouse (1967), *op. cit.*, Chapter 2.
42. Lawrence Freedman, *op. cit.*, pp. 85–102.
43. Lawrence Freedman, *op. cit.*, p. 103.
44. For details of the negotiations leading to the Maastricht treaty, cf. Colette Mazucelli (1997), *France and Germany at Maastricht, Politics and Negotiations to Create the European Union*, Garland Publishing Inc, London and New York, Chapters V and VI, 135–206.
45. Pierre Beregovoy, Speech at the opening of the 45th Session of the IHEDN, 3 September 1992, French Embassy, *Speeches and statements*, Sp.St/LON/194/92, 7 October 1992.
46. Douglas Porch (1987), 'French Defense and the Gaullist Legacy', in Lewis Gann (ed.), *The Defense of Western Europe*, Croom Helm, London, p. 208.
47. Philip Gordon (1995), *France, Germany and the Western Alliance*, Westview Press, Boulder, Colorado, p. 42.
48. *Europe Documents*, No 1787.

49. Andreas Kintis (1998), 'NATO-WEU: an Enduring Relationship', *European Affairs Review*, **3**, 537–62.

50. Frédéric Bozo (1995), 'La France et l'Alliance: les limites du rapprochement', *Politique Etrangère*, April, p. 866.

51. Jacques Chirac (1994), 'Une volonté pour l'Europe', *Le Monde*, 16 December.

52. A satirical nickname for Chirac's declaration, evoking the famous appeal to resistance against the German invader by de Gaulle in London on 18 June 1940.

53. Dominique Moïsi (1995), 'De Mitterrand à Chirac', *Politique Etrangère*, April, pp. 849–55.

54. Pascal Riché (1996), 'Vous avez dit effort concerté?', *Libération*, 7 January.

55. Cf. Karl Feldmayer, in an article of the *Frankfurter Allgemeine Zeitung* quoted in *Le Monde*, 3–4 March 1996.

56. Quoted in *Le Canard Enchaîné*, 'Chirac frappé par un mauvais tour de Rhin', 21 August 1996.

57. *Financial Times*, 4 June 1996, quoted by Andreas Kintis, *op. cit.*, p. 551.

58. Communiqué issued by the ministry of Foreign Affairs spokesman on behalf of the French authorities, French Embassy, London, SAC/97/150-NATO.

59. Franco-German common security and defence concept, Nuremberg 9 December 1996, made public in Paris on 30 January 1997, French Embassy, London, SAC/97/32.

60. Lucas Delattre and Daniel Vernet (1997), 'La France et l'Allemagne préparent une défense concertée', *Le Monde*, 25 January.

61. Hans Stark (1998), *Les relations franco-allemandes: état et perspectives*, Ifri, Paris, p. 19.

62. Leading article, *The Guardian*, 7 December 1998.

63. Presidency Conclusions, Cologne 3–4 1999, Annex III.

64. *Le Monde*, 6–7 June 1999.

65. Pierre Servent (1991), *Le Monde*, 10 December.

66. Védrine, *op. cit.*, p. 527.

67. Jean-Marie Rausch (1990), *Le Monde*, 14 December.

68. François Heisbourg (1992), 'France and the Gulf Crisis', in N. Gnesotto and J. Roper (eds), *Western Europe and the Gulf*, Institute for Security Studies, Paris, p. 20.

69. Védrine, *op cit.*, p. 529.

70. Philip H. Gordon (1995), *France, Germany and the Western Alliance*, Westview Press, Boulder, Colorado, p. 37.

71. Karl Kaiser and Klaus Becher (1992), 'Germany and the Iraq conflict', in Gnesotto and Roper, *op. cit.*, pp. 41–432.

72. *Ibid.*, p. 43.

73. Nuttall, *op. cit.*, p. 264.

74. For information on the Yugoslav conflict, we are mostly relying on the excellent study by James Gow (1997), *Triumph of the Lack of Will*, Hurst & Co, London, especially Chapters 7 and 10.

75. 'Former Yugoslavia', Communiqué issued by the Ministry of Foreign Affairs on behalf of the French authorities, Paris, 14 December 1997, French Embassy, London, SAC/97/290.

76. Marc Weller (1999), 'The Rambouillet conference', *International Affairs*, **75** (2), April, 211–51.

77. Information on military commitments comes from a table in *The Guardian*, 19 May 1999.

78. Joachim Rohde (1998), 'French-German arms cooperation: Issues and perspectives', in Stark, *op. cit.*, p. 76.
79. Kocs, *op. cit.*, pp. 172–4.
80. Jacques Isnard (1996), 'Discorde entre Paris et Bonn sur le satellite-espion Helios-2', *Le Monde*, 15 October.
81. Lucas Delattre (1997), *Le Monde*, 28 January.

6. The enlargement of the European Union

INTRODUCTION

Next to the EMU project, the forthcoming fifth enlargement to include Central and East European countries (CEEC) as well as Cyprus, Malta and Turkey constitutes the single most significant event since the Treaty of Rome; but at the same time, the inclusion of economically backward new member states will stretch the Union's institutional and financial capabilities, forcing contentious decisions on EU financing, regional aid and the Common Agricultural Policy.

Periodic enlargements of the EU have been a consistent and ongoing event in the European integration process since the entry into force of the Treaty of Rome in 1958. The commitment to admit new members is based on the then EEC's principle of openness to 'any European nation' (Art. 237 in the Treaty of Rome) meeting its criteria in terms of democracy and the principles of law and on the TEU's preamble defining the 'ending of the division of the European continent' as one of the new Union's fundamental aims. Enlarging the Union is therefore a state of normality and, indeed, the Community has successfully coped with four previous relatively unproblematic enlargements which, with the exception of the Mediterranean countries, had been highly developed economies run by stable democracies with established political institutions. In sharp contrast however, the forthcoming expansion of the Union is unprecedented both quantitatively, in terms of size and qualitatively, in terms of implications on EU institutions and policies. The challenges are formidable as the Union is unable to draw from its history in this case, but at the same time the opportunity to help stabilise Eastern Europe and to integrate it into Europe politically, economically and culturally has been described as 'breathtaking'.[1]

Quantitatively, there is the sheer scale of eastward enlargement, posing problems which make this fifth enlargement unique. Never before did the Union have to deal with more than three members at the same time. In terms of quality, the expected incorporation of Eastern European countries into the Union affects its structure and cohesion producing a lasting change in its character and in the balance of interests between its existing members. Although the Union has experience in admitting countries which have emerged from dictatorship, it never had to deal with countries burdened with the political and economic legacy of communism. There are major disparities between the EU and the applicants: structurally, economically and socially, all of which require massive financial investments in these countries which will have a significant impact on the EU's budgetary framework. Whereas in all previous enlargements, the burden of adjustment was mainly borne by the new members, the EU's fifth enlargement demands sacrifices of varying degrees from several of its members.

The inclusion of countries with relatively large rural populations and agricultural contributions to GNP heightens the pressures on existing member states at a time when financial constraints have left little margin for economic manoeuvring. Thus the political and economic effect of the accession of five central and eastern European states as well as Cyprus in the early part of the 21st century and the prospect of a second wave of eastward enlargement, soon after, will put an enormous pressure on the EU and require it to adapt to this challenge in two ways: first institutionally, by streamlining decision-making and secondly, by a revision of existing policies originally designed for a Community of six member states. This is clearly reflected in the Commission's study on the challenges of enlargement[2] and was reiterated in 1997, when the Commission proposed that a new IGC 'be convened as soon as possible after 2000 to produce a thorough reform.[3]

Looking back over the past 10 years it seems clear that Eastern enlargement is welcome intellectually by all member states: ever since the fall of the Berlin Wall the Community has resolved to play a major role in the stabilisation of the new democratic region. By the early 1990s pressures from these countries and from some of the member states led to economic and technical assistance on behalf of the EC, afforded through the PHARE programme and the establishment of the European Bank for Reconstruction and Development (EBRD) in 1990, the TEMPUS programme – assistance in educational development – and through the signing of trade cooperation agreements. These efforts were further developed by the 'European Agreements' concluded with the new democracies between 1991–3 providing for an asymmetrical transition to free trade and a political dialogue. The statement by the European Council in Copenhagen in June 1993 that any country that so wished could join the Union so long as it satisfied certain criteria (i.e. Copenhagen criteria) constituted a turning point, although no date was set. It was here that the European Agreements which were essentially Association Agreements were linked to accession. Thus the Copenhagen European Council marked a political reorientation and was the beginning of the Community's new *Ostpolitik*.

Further progress was made at the Essen summit in December 1994 which created a comprehensive pre-accession strategy for preparing the applicants for membership, at Corfu in the spring of 1995 and at Madrid in December 1995. It was here that the leaders of the 15 member states stipulated that within six months of the conclusion of the IGC accession negotiations should be launched. The European Council also called on the Commission to draw up a 'composite paper on enlargement' including a financial framework for the Union beyond the existing one, i.e. beyond 1999.

As requested by the European Council during the Madrid summit in December 1995 the Commission in June 1997 duly submitted its paper, 'Agenda 2000 – For a stronger and Wider Europe', which included the long-awaited Commission opinions on all CEEC applicants as well as setting out the challenges posed by this enlargement. The Commission recommended that negotiations should be opened with five of the CEEC countries (Hungary, Poland, the Czech Republic, Estonia and Slovenia), but that full accession of the other five (Bulgaria, Romania, Slovakia, Latvia and Lithuania) should be postponed. The European Council accepted the Commission's recommendation at its December 1997 Luxembourg meeting and put forward the idea to hold a European Conference as a way of bringing together all applicant countries with the 15 existing EU member states.

The first European Conference convened in London on 11 March 1998 and was attended by 10 applicants from Central and Eastern Europe and Cyprus. Although there are currently 13 applications lodged with the EU, from the 10 CEEC countries, as well as Cyprus, Malta and Turkey, negotiations opened on 31 March 1998 with the '5 + 1' (i.e. Poland, Hungary, the Czech Republic, Estonia, Slovenia plus Cyprus), marking at the same time the end of the association process. As stated above, the European Commission had recommended that negotiations be opened with these countries, but even these six might not necessarily join at the same time and might accede with significant transitional periods and derogations, particularly since it had become clear that the Berlin summit (March 1999) had only been partly successful in tackling reform.[5] As the European Conference in March 1998 had already made clear, the EU is trying to avoid a process of selective enlargement and thus a new division in Europe. However, the Commission will apply the 'principle of differentiation', i.e. each applicant will move ahead at its own pace after meeting the Copenhagen criteria, since some countries face problems in bringing agricultural or environmental standards and social policies into line with those of the EU. The Commissioner for enlargement of the new Prodi team declared that 'negotiations should proceed on the basis of merit, not on the basis of compassion'.[6] Negotiations with the second wave of applicants (Latvia, Lithuania, Bulgaria, Romania, Slovakia and Malta) started in 2000.

This chapter examines some of the key issues of eastern enlargement against the background of Franco-German relations and their influence on the enlargement process. Not all aspects of the forthcoming enlargement are considered here, partly because this study concludes at a time when some issues, e.g. institutional reform, have not been settled. Although significant reforms in decision-making were agreed, both in the TEU and in the Treaty of Amsterdam, neither resolved the question of the size of the Commission nor the weighting of votes granted to member states in relation to their population. Moreover, as the EU expands, pressure increases to subject more areas of legislation to majority voting and to make the Union more democratically accountable through the powers of the EP. These issues (i.e. leftovers) were addressed by the present IGC which started on 14 February 2000 and concluded in December 2000 in Nice.

The policy areas analysed in this chapter, i.e. the reform of the CAP and, by implication, budgetary implications of eastward expansion, are of major significance for the Union and the enlargement process in themselves. Moreover, they have also been classical conflict areas between France and Germany. No progress in the enlargement debate would have been possible without prior Franco-German agreement on these issues. Had no compromise been reached on these issues, the entire enlargement process might have been derailed.

This chapter is divided into three parts. The first establishes basic French and German positions in both past and current enlargement processes; the second defines the issue areas as mentioned above; the third is a more detailed analysis of the negotiations to the run-up of the Berlin summit in March 1999 when these issues, i.e. the financial framework and CAP reform, were finally agreed. While this chapter cannot give a complete analysis of the enlargement issue, it is hoped that it highlights some of its wider implications for both the European Union at large and also for the Franco-German axis. Agricultural and budgetary issues are not the only and, arguably, most important issues; there are more intangible geo-strategic aspects as a result of a new balance of power. France sees Germany as a 'core issue in French policy towards Eastern and Central Europe, and a French-led *Ostpolitik* is a way to counterbalance Germany. An eastward enlargement without French involvement would reinforce Germany's position in the EU'.[7] While on the one hand eastward enlargement would dilute the domination of the Franco-German axis which might be welcome by those states (old and new) which have lived in the shadow of more powerful neighbours, the inclusion of some central European states into the Union will provide new allies for Germany, a development which would have 'unpredictable implications for the Franco-German axis'.[8]

I   FRANCE, GERMANY AND ENLARGEMENT: SIMILARITIES AND DIFFERENCES

As in other policy areas, France and Germany have been the motor behind each enlargement, although for different reasons and although their respective enlargement rhetoric has tended to subside and recede under the pressure of national priorities and domestic needs. Indeed, de Gaulle's veto of British membership in January 1963 had dashed any hopes of enlarging the EEC from its original six member states, at least for the time being. This unilateral decision came as a profound shock to Germany, which was 'sad, appalled, almost desperate'.[9] De Gaulle's second veto in November 1967 and even the election of Georges Pompidou as de Gaulle's successor maintained for some months the uncertainty about France's stance on enlargement. But, as has been noted[10] Chancellor Adenauer did not want to put at risk the new post-war Franco-German rapprochement.

In Germany there had been important changes as well. The new social-democratic government under Chancellor Brandt put great emphasis on progress in the enlargement question. Time was opportune for further progress as there were changes in the European political climate as well: the departure of both de Gaulle and Hallstein (the Commisison President during the period of the 'empty chair') from the European scene helped to smooth relations between Bonn and Paris. The new Brandt/Scheel government emphasised the special importance of the imminent conference in The Hague which coincided with the enunciation of Brandt's *Ostpolitik* and the support of the French government was a *sine qua non* for this new venture.

During the *Bundestag* debate following the declaration, it became clear that two issues had priority for the FRG: first, a move towards complete economic and monetary union and, second, progress in the enlargement question.[11] Brandt contacted Pompidou directly to ascertain whether there was a genuine chance of progress by taking steps towards the enlargement of the Community.[12] During the subsequent private talk between Brandt and Pompidou on the eve of the first day of the conference, the French President wanted reassurance from the FRG that Franco-German cooperation would not suffer as a result of enlargement and, more particularly, that the financing of agriculture, of crucial importance to French national interests, would be safeguarded. In return, Pompidou gave the green light to enlargement by incorporating it into the famous triptych 'completion, deepening and enlargement'. Pompidou's pronouncement thus put an end to de Gaulle's strictures and marked a sea change. Moreover, it encapsulated in a striking formula what was to become France's doctrine on enlargement, i.e. that it should go hand in hand with deepening. The problem is that deepening is a rather vague term, which may mean different things at different times. At the time of this first enlargement deepening referred more to policies than institutions.[13]

When Greece, Spain and Portugal, each emerging from a dictatorial regime, applied in turn for membership in 1975, the positive response in principle accorded to them by the European Community had political, not economic motivations. Giscard d'Estaing, then President of France, lyrically recalled Greece as the cradle of Europe and democracy, and although displaying no particular enthusiasm for enlargement, it was French support that enabled a doubtful Commission opinion to be overturned.[14] In the case of Spain and Portugal, France's reservations were of an economic, not of a political nature. The French southern farmers were very worried by prospective competition on Mediterranean agricultural products and showed their concern by mounting demonstrations. Moreover, France was concerned by the additional budgetary burden this enlargement would create. Giscard d'Estaing therefore, rather successfully, mounted a slowing down operation in 1980, claiming that 'it is necessary that the Community should give priority to completing the first enlargement before it can be in a position to undertake a second'.[15] Thus Giscard d'Estaing, although having agreed to Greece's membership, blocked that of Spain and Portugal. It would take a new Presidency, that of François Mitterrand, to ease matters by letting the Spanish and Portuguese applications through. Significantly, the entry of those two countries into the European Community was formalised less than two months before the signature of the SEA, which undoubtedly further deepened European integration.

In Germany, by contrast, there has been a general consensus on the fundamental desirability of the EC's second enlargement. Because this underlying motive was so strong, there had hardly been any public discussion on this issue, nor had the entry question of the Mediterranean countries been a subject of dispute between the ruling parties and the opposition. The surprising aspect of this decision was, however, that it was clearly an emotive response triggered by Germany's interest in stabilising the three democratic regimes, but the commitment to support enlargement was neither based on a critical cost-benefit analysis nor was it the result of a systematic foreign policy.[16] While Art. 237 of the Rome Treaty explicitly stated that every European state may apply for membership, the requirement for all contracting parties to ratify accession suggests that there was no question of an unconditional right to membership. This had already been made abundantly clear by de Gaulle in the 1960s, although this has been the only case when a single member state has prevented the enlargement of the EEC/EU. Nevertheless, it appears that for politico-strategic reasons German support for the new entrants had to be cloaked in legalistic terms, perhaps to deflect possible objections after a thorough cost-benefit analysis had been carried out.

When the fourth enlargement, that of the Scandinavian countries and Austria was under discussion, Mitterrand, true to the French tradition, had maintained that a 'wider Community demands stronger institutions'.[17] At the Birmingham European Council, 11–12 December 1992, the Twelve agreed to start negotiations for the membership of Austria, Finland, Norway and Sweden. The Maastricht Treaty had been duly signed and although it failed to eliminate the 'democratic deficit', it nevertheless marked a further advance in integration, both in terms of institutional reform and policies. At the Copenhagen European Council of 21–22 June 1993, France agreed with her partners that the negotiations for accession should be concluded before 1 January 1995. Although France had misgivings about the boost to the concept of a free-trade area that would be given by this particular round of applications, it did not object. Asked about the risk raised by the pro-free-trade leanings of the applicant countries Mitterrand remarked somewhat ruefully: 'Indeed, but Europe itself is pro-free-trade, and, regrettably, excessively so'.[18]

The challenge of the present process of enlargement against the background of Franco-German relations is crucial as it touches upon several interrelated areas which dominate the present 'European debate'. The position of each member state differs according to its geographical position and historical tradition. While each member state will benefit from the implications of eastern enlargement, the stabilisation of central and eastern Europe is of vital interest for the FRG in particular. Expansion of the Union into Eastern Europe constitutes both a formidable challenge and a great opportunity, not least for Germany.

The German Position on Eastern Enlargement

There appears to be a general consensus among academics and observers that Germany has the most to gain from enlargement:[19] sources of German interest in the expansion of the Union are unique among EU member states deriving from location, traditional economic and political ties and history. Indeed, it has even been argued that this is a 'German led enlargement'.[20] There are several reasons for German interest in enlargement: first, it will make Germany the geographical centre of the EU. Second, the inclusion of such a vast area embracing 100 million consumers will provide a new export market for Germany. (She is already responsible for some 50% of the EU's eastern trade.[21]) Third, the incorporation into the EU of Germany's hinterland will also expand Germany's own security belt. Finally, there are psychological reasons: sheer gratitude to countries like Hungary who were instrumental in eliminating the Iron Curtain by opening its borders with Austria in 1989.[22]

Germany itself sees enlargement as a 'strategic imperative',[23] a position which has its roots in an ideologically based concept of a free Europe and a democratic social order. German policy-makers are particularly sensitive to any elements which might endanger the principle of parliamentary democracy and free enterprise. Integration of these countries into the political system of the EU would exclude a possible backlash to authoritarian regimes. By consolidating their young democracies and taking advantage of the natural connection of this area stretching beyond the Urals and the Balkans, the EU will be fostering its political stability and strengthening the Union's voice at international level. The cumulative effect of a Community of 25 or more will have considerable quantitative and qualitative advantages with its productive wealth outpacing any other region. The almost imperial dimension of an enlarged Community will work in Europe's favour in a variety of international fora. There is one further aspect which might have considerable influence on Germany's approach to the new entrants. The desire of these countries for international recognition and their need to strengthen the new democratic institutions are very similar to the circumstances in which the FRG found herself during the early post-war years. Having shared these experiences, one can appreciate that Germany must feel a special affinity toward the new entrants and a deep understanding for their needs.

Chancellor Kohl, as early as 1990, gave backing to the countries' membership, in particular to Poland. This undertaking was written in the bilateral treaties the German government signed not only with Poland but also with Hungary and Czech Republic between 1991 and 1992,[24] a commitment repeated on several occasions since. At the opening of enlargement negotiations in March 1998, the then German Foreign Minister Kinkel (FDP) said that the expansion of the EU was a 'historical' obligation and logical continuation of the European integration process. 'There is no alternative to enlargement.'[25]

Bonn's position at that time was clearly an emotive response triggered by Germany's interest in stabilising the East, an attitude which is strikingly similar to the one expressed during the Mediterranean enlargement round. However, in the case of the Mediterranean enlargement, it was only after the political decision had been made and public assurances had been given to that effect to the three applicants, that the German bureaucratic machinery began to evaluate the costs and benefits of integrating three new members. By contrast, German attitudes towards the forthcoming enlargement are far more cautious: policy-makers seemed to have been more aware of the likely economic and political costs involved. In fact, as early as the Essen summit of December 1994 – which created a comprehensive pre-accession strategy for preparing the applicants for membership[26] – Kohl articulated some caution by warning not to encourage 'false expectations' as to the time-scale of accession. A year earlier, albeit unofficially, at the Madrid summit in December 1995, Chancellor Kohl tried to put a brake on the EU leaders' resolution to begin the preparatory phase of accession six months after the end of the IGC by limiting this promise to Germany's favourites: Poland, Hungary and the Czech Republic. Already at that time Germany was anxious to reduce the impact of enlargement in terms of CAP reform and budgetary costs, while these three countries were the most important in terms of stabilisation of German borders. In the event, Kohl's suggestion for an *avant-garde* enlargement did not carry the day.[27]

Germany's position is not clear-cut. While enlargement has significant advantages for the FRG, there are also a number of constraints. The shift of the EU's geo-strategic gravity to the East has made Germany very vulnerable at the eastern edge of the EU and as such exposed the country to political and economic instability. Although officially the wisdom of enlargement is politically a taboo – none of the politically relevant groups would dare to question it – the apparent discrepancy between the political rhetoric of German policy-makers and their actual behaviour at the negotiating table made for considerable ambivalence in Germany's overall approach to enlargement and a number of contradictions particularly during the latter part of the 1990s in an otherwise consistent political German strategy: Bonn pressed for speedy enlargement, but refused to consider releasing additional funding. This meant that Germany's policies were riddled with contradictions as the country became hesitant to undertake necessary policy reforms and, in direct contradiction to her pro-enlargement position, demanded a cut in its net contribution to the EU budget.

The French Position on Eastern Enlargement

In parallel to the German situation, French interests in eastern enlargement are also closely linked to historical reasons and to be understood against the background of the end of the Cold War. According to the French Minister for European Affairs, M. Pierre Moscovici, 'the enlargement process is, first of all, a political response to the events of 1989–91 which triggered ... an acceleration of history ...'.[28] French interests in eastern enlargement are linked to broader security and geopolitical issues which include NATO expansion and relations with Russia. The latter is viewed by France as 'an essential partner in any European security settlement'.[29] At the same time the present enlargement question touches significantly on both Franco-German leadership in the EU and the traditional French strategy to 'bind in Germany' which, in the past when it had been a matter of controlling a divided and semi-sovereign country, had given France the upper hand in Franco-German relations. The mistrust of Germany's *Ostpolitik* is a recurring theme as can be seen by Mitterrand's attitude to German Unification. Both in 1969 and in 1989 France was fearful of the economic and political flexibility afforded by *Ostpolitik* and German unification and anxious that Germany might drift into neutralism or choose a *Sonderweg*. Since German preoccupation with its past has gradually faded over time, it has also removed a source of French influence.

The recent German push towards the east and the shift in the EU gravity towards 'Mitteleuropa' has worried Paris at two levels. On the one hand France is concerned about the continued influence of the Franco-German axis on European events and, on the other, it fears that the new balance of power in Europe might relegate France to the fringes of the European arena. It is not acceptable to France to leave Germany in a position of control in what is a changing political constellation. Eastern enlargement would, just as the EFTA accession had done, benefit Germany and not France and might challenge the geo-political Franco-German power asymmetry in Europe. This .situation might explain France's ambiguity towards enlargement which is defensive, reflected by attempts to resist or at least postpone eastern enlargement. In fact, during the negotiations of association agreements with Hungary, the Czech Republic and Poland, Germany grew impatient over French unwillingness to grant concessions. It was only after German threats that it would 'go it alone' if necessary, that France was persuaded to change its mind.[30]

On the other hand, however, France displays a more prudent and classic French strategy: it has created a linkage between admission of new members and deepening the integration process. Like Germany, France suffers from a 'role conflict'[31] i.e. widening versus deepening. Like in Germany, France has couched pledges for EU support for the CEEC, in normative language, always asserting the special responsibility the Union has for the eastern countries or pointing to the 'historic significance' of the forthcoming expansion of the EU and French commitment to this process recalling de Gaulle's vision of a 'Europe from the Atlantic to the Urals'. This situation then creates a dilemma, not only between widening and deepening but also between the desire for enlargement or the acceptance of its inevitability and domestic interests.[32] It has been argued[33] that as a result of French concern over a shift of the EU's centre of gravity towards the east, Kohl, in 1990, abandoned plans to make 'widening' a priority of Germany's 1994 EU presidency.

Since France cannot within reason openly resist the German 'enlargement drive', it can however slow down the process and at the same time attempt to strengthen the EU's Mediterranean policy as a counterweight to eastern enlargement: France has already been successful at the Cannes summit in

June 1995 when it traded acceptance of more economic aid to the east for an improved package for the Maghreb. The Mediterranean south has more relevance to France than to Germany. People from the east in search of a better life look to Germany, migrants from the south seek refuge in France. 'The East is to Germany what the South is to France'.[34]

However, having said this, France has long-standing cultural ties with some of the central European countries, especially Romania and, to a lesser degree, Bulgaria. The will of both France and Germany to act together became evident when France became part of the 'Weimar Triangle'. In August 1991 the foreign ministers of France, Germany and Poland met to discuss the mounting conflict in Yugoslavia, although the former two were divided over the issue. As Chapter 5 has shown, the FRG, historically supportive of the two break-away states Slovenia and Croatia, became an irritant to France who has been historically more pro-Serbian, but more specifically resented the way Germany broke rank with France and threatened to recognise unilaterally these two states, one of which, Slovenia, is a candidate for EU membership.[35] In the event there was a trade-off: Germany pressed the cause of the Visegrad countries, above all Poland, France that of Romania and Bulgaria.

Thus, since French attitudes towards enlargement have to be positive in the context of the ending of the Cold War, the enlargement issue is not a question of *if*, but rather one of *how* and *when*. Yet utmost caution characterises the French approach which is defensive, aimed at protecting the viability of the existing Union. French sensitivity towards anything that might threaten the existence of the integration system was already apparent during negotiations with Britain: France's resistance to British membership clearly affected its determination to protect its own privileged position in the Community. Although this concern did not resurface in connection with the Iberian accession, the question of power politics has resurfaced once again in the context of eastern enlargement.[36]

In terms of influence and trade France cannot compete with Germany. But whatever French reservations, ideologically or economically, the immediate issue for France, as indeed it was for Germany under Chancellor Kohl, was the question of reforming a crucial policy area: the CAP. Already in the early 1990s France had pointed out that the admission of eastern European countries would double the costs of the CAP.[37] This key area led to a serious confrontation between France and Germany and almost threatened the successful conclusion of the Berlin summit and thus, by implication, the enlargement process.

II THE IMPACT OF ENLARGEMENT: THE ISSUES

The Financial Framework

The sheer scale of eastward enlargement means that the EU is confronted with challenges of unprecedented magnitude: with a combined population of 106 million and an area of 1.1 million square km, the CEEC represent 29% of the population and 33% of the area of the EU, but would add only 4% to EU GNP. In fact, the average per capita GDP in the 10 CEEC countries is only one eighth of the average EU level. Many of the applicants have backward and inefficient industries, are environmental polluters, with inadequate transport, energy and telecommunication networks, have weak administrative structures and no or little experience of a free market economy. On joining the EU, new members will become eligible for substantial financial aid from the EU, from its agricultural, structural and cohesion funds which account for some 80% of the EU's budget.[38] Consequently, the key to finding an acceptable solution to the challenges raised by CEEC accession is a deal on the future of the common budget. The Madrid European Council in December 1995 had requested the Commission to prepare a comprehensive proposal on future financing and reform of policies which would enable the EU to move into the new Millennium. The Commission duly submitted its findings in its afore-mentioned report of July 1997 'Agenda 2000'. The document deals with several interrelated aspects of the future of the Community, but it is the analysis of the estimated costs of enlargement and proposals for reforming the CAP and the Structural Funds, i.e. the overall financial perspective that is of most interest for our purposes. The EU's finances are raised from a variety of revenues: agricultural and sugar levies, customs duties, VAT and GNP contributions.[39] However, the sources of these fundings do not make for an 'equitable' contribution. Countries have different import patterns in terms of volume and type of produce imported, and national differences in levels of government expenditure and savings will affect the size of VAT base. Importantly, however, EU budgetary expenditure is dominated by the CAP (51%) and structural policies (32%). The latter does have a redistribution element within the budget: its size has expanded and has concentrated on poorer member states. However, leaving this apart, there is no relationship between GNP per capita and EU budgetary receipts.

In the past, enlargements were usually accompanied by expansion of the budget. By contrast, the Commission, in its paper Agenda 2000, assumes that the current limit on the budget of 1.27% of EU GNP will not be increased. Under the Commission's growth assumption, the total EU budget for 2000–2006 would be ECU 75 bn of which 10% was earmarked for the new entrants. This calculation was based on assumptions that the first round of accession will not occur before 2002 and will also be accompanied by long transitional arrangements, in which case the increase in expenditure would be within the specified limit. Thus the Commission in the run-up to the negotiations of the post-Delors II financial perspective which covered the period 1992–99, proposed that the budget for 2000–2006 should keep the 1999 expenditure ceiling of 1.27% of EU GNP, but allowing for increases in step with economic expansion. In order to release funding necessary to finance enlargement, the Commission recommended that the Structural Funds and above all the CAP would have to be reformed. The main issue raised by enlargement is therefore not the budget as such or its increase, but the redistribution of funds. Since the new members will all be net beneficiaries, the burden will fall mainly on current net contributors to the budget in terms of higher transfer or on current net beneficiaries in terms of a reduction in subsidies. Whatever the focus of negotiations, the financial implications of enlargement were bound to lead to conflicts between existing member states.

Structural aid comprises the European Regional Development Fund, the European Social Fund, the European Agricultural Guidance and Guarantee Fund and Investment for Fisheries Guidance. Before the mid-1970s regional policy was fragmented and mostly confined to the European Agricultural Guidance and Guarantee Fund. Successive enlargements highlighted the need for a more substantial regional policy. In the SEA regional policy was given a legal base (Title V Economic and Social Cohesion). Subsequently, the Community agreed on a financial package (Delors I) covering the finances of the EU for the period of 1985–92. By doubling the resources for structural funding, economic and social cohesion became the second largest expenditure item, next to the CAP. The TEU expanded on this and set up the Cohesion Fund, directed to the 'poor' member states i.e. the Mediterranean countries and Ireland. Also a second financial perspective, Delors II was agreed (1992–99) quadrupling Structural Funds (compared with 1987 level).

Enlargement will increase the number of poorer countries which would qualify as major beneficiaries. This was seen as necessary to prepare the ground for further enlargement as the CEEC countries would be most likely to fall under the category of the needy regions. In essence, the Commission proposed to reduce the proportion of EU population covered by the Structural Funds from the current 51% to between 35 and 40%. Eligibility for the funds should go to the most needy regions, which means that a number of existing member states' regions would see their eligibility phased out. Structural funding is based on a few major objectives. For Objective I status for example, the most sensitive area, regions must have a GNP less than 75% of the EU average calculated over the last three years, while resources from the Cohesion Fund are directed towards member states with less than 90% of the EU's average GNP. The Mediterranean countries' per capita GDP has risen from 66 per cent of the EU average to 74 per cent over the last 10 years; while Ireland is already over the 100 per cent mark. These countries would see their benefit eroded. Germany, too, because most of the new Länder in the East would also lose their Objective I status after enlargement. Northern Ireland, Lisbon, the Spanish region of Valencia, the French island of Corsica and the Irish Republic look vulnerable. So do the Franco-Belgian border regions of Valenciennois and Hainault which crept into the category in 1993. These states are not helped by CAP reform either as they are not big producers of those products most heavily subsidised. The Commission also wants to streamline 'Objective II' covering areas of industrial and rural decline: regions with high unemployment qualify under this objective. The Commission proposed that transition periods for the newly rich regions should be offered. In addition it suggested responsibility should be shared with national governments for selecting areas which qualify for Objective II on a 50:50 basis.

The Commission's proposal proved to be extremely controversial. In contrast to previous negotiations on financial perspectives, the 1999 negotiations were dominated by demands from the EU's biggest net contributors (i.e. Germany and the Netherlands) for a more equitable system. In a climate of fiscal austerity, the richer member states were not only resisting any increase of the current budgetary ceiling as a percentage of EU GNP, but indeed some member states demanded a reduction in their current net contribution. To compound these problems, the net recipients of structural and cohesion funding, led by Spain (the largest beneficiary of the Cohesion Fund) and in collusion with EU farmers, led by France, resisted attempts to redistribute benefits to the advantage of new entrants.

The prospect of eastward enlargement to include countries which will be net recipients from the EU budgets, highlights the crucial role Germany plays as major contributor to the common budget: in 1996 her net contribution was 10.2 bn ECU to the EU budget[40] rising to nearly 11bn ECU in 1998. While these contributions are not high in terms of Germany's total expenditure, rising net contributions to the budget have become an acute problem in the context of the costs of German Unification, high unemployment, slower growth and further enlargement to include countries with lower economic performance. The first and second Delors budget plan of 1988 and 1992 were largely funded by Germany: in 1988 Kohl agreed to an increase of regional aid to help Southern countries to adjust to the competitive pressures of the Single Market; in 1992 he met Spanish demands for a cohesion fund to help the country to meet the EMU convergence criteria. Germany's position in the enlargement debate is therefore crucial. Anxious that the financial costs of further enlargement and the Commission's 1997 reform programme should not be at Germany's expense, the government threatened to veto the entire Agenda 2000 package.[41]

Contrary to comments made both in the national and international press which expressed surprise at this seemingly unexpected preoccupation with financial issues,[42] Germany's concern over its contribution to the Community budget and agricultural expenditure, both of which are inextricably intertwined, is by no means new. Indeed, it is possible to trace Germany's reluctance to finance the common budget back to the 1965 negotiations on the (abortive) attempt to introduce 'Own Resources'.[43] The 1970s increased Germany's preoccupation with financial aspects of EC membership.[44] Bonn's well-publicised criticism of the Community's agricultural expenditure reached a climax in the later 1970s when it strongly resented its role as a milch cow of the Community.[45] Already in 1975 the then Chancellor Helmut Schmidt had described the CAP as a 'mammoth misguidance of economic resources'.[46] Protests over accelerating costs reached a climax during the summer of 1980 concerning a cash rebate to Britain. Schmidt, during a programme on German television, declared that future contributions to and payments from the EC budget would have to have a ceiling, a declaration which caused shock since it smacked of the *juste retour* principle.

Henceforth budgetary problems became a key consideration in German attitudes, both toward the Community at large but also in relation to periodic enlargements. In the mid-1980s for example, Chancellor Kohl skilfully linked his agreement on an increase of 'Own Resources' to the (German) desired accession of Spain and Portugal. This was spelled out very clearly by Foreign Minister Genscher to the German *Bundestag*: 'We are realistic enough to say that the Spanish and Portuguese accession is not possible without an increase in "Own Resources", but we are also firm enough to say that only if these two states become members of the Community will we be prepared for an increase in "Own Resources"'.[47] Schröder's attempt to reduce Germany's role as the biggest net contributor not only confirms a policy initiated by Kohl, but is the last attempt in a long series of many initiatives beginning with Schmidt to improve Germany's position.

But what had been acceptable under Waigel and Kohl (one was allowed to play the 'bad cop' in the search of Bonn's wasted resources, the other was unassailable because he had a 'strategic view of the value of the Franco-German partnership'), is not acceptable under Schröder and his team. France complained bitterly that the new German government used its Presidency to get 'their money back' which was regarded in Paris as distasteful, even Thatcherite.[48] And when it became clear that the settlement of the financial framework depended on savings in the farm sector, the CAP surfaced once again as the most explosive conflict in Franco-German relations.

Enlargement and the CAP

Stabilisation of farm expenses is a key element in a broader shake-up of EU finances. The CAP is still predominantly a price policy, financed mainly from Union resources. The CAP mechanism has tended to transfer income from the non-farming sector to producers of agricultural goods, this is in effect a financial transfer from consumers to farmers. Moreover because of divergent output of CAP products in different countries, the policy not only involves transfer between individuals but also between member states. This implies that the importing countries are net contributors to the Community budget. The impact of the EU budget on individual members resulted in many intra-Community crises one of which led to British demands for a more equitable redistribution of the EU burdens and benefits. Ever since, the two issues have been tangled up: the CAP problem has culminated in a budgetary problem, since it exposed the intra-Union transfers brought about by the CAP and the dominance of agricultural spending within the EU budget.

Agriculture is important in most of the applicant countries, accounting for between 3.3% of GDP in the Czech Republic to 20% of GDP in Rumania, and contributes an overall average of 7.8% of GDP and 26.7% of employment compared with the EU average of 2.5% and 5.7% respectively. The 11 applicant countries will be adding a staggering 10 million farmers to the current EU's 8.2 million.[49] In this aspect, eastward enlargement is not unique, the absorption of vulnerable industries, such as agriculture, and likely claims on structural funds and the budget have usually dominated previous enlargement negotiations, but never before to such a degree.

As a result, interest has centred on the adjustment of the new entrants' agricultural policies to EU requirements. In particular, concern has focused on the internal effect of the relatively high CAP price support system and border controls. Although the MacSharry reform has been a turning point in terms of agricultural support, prices are still significantly higher than in the CEECs.[50] The CEEC products are well suited to those most heavily subsidised by the CAP and the new countries would obviously be likely to capitalise on the CAP's generous market support scheme. It has been suggested that an increase of some 30–50% of the current CAP fund is necessary[51] and that, indeed, an unreformed CAP would lead to financial collapse.[52]

Furthermore, if these countries were to adopt the CAP in its present form, unacceptable surpluses, a notorious problem in the 1970s and 1980s, might emerge again, at a time when the EU is committed to eliminate export subsidies as part of the 1994 Uruguay Round Agreement on Agriculture and has agreed to reduce progressively measures which distort agricultural trade. Negotiations to this effect recommenced in the winter of 1999–2000 with a new round of multilateral trade talks under the World Trade Organisation (WTO). The Essen summit had viewed agricultural issues as a key element of the pre-accession strategy for the EU and had asked the Commission to prepare a report on alternative strategies for the development of relations in the field of agriculture. The Commission's Agricultural Strategy Paper, adopted in November 1995, was followed by the aforementioned Commission report Agenda 2000.

In this the Commission stressed the need for further reform and advocated a continuation of the trends introduced in 1992. The Commission plan envisaged cuts of up to 30% in guaranteed prices in the most important sectors: cereals, beef and dairy products. The European Council in December 1997 endorsed Agenda 2000 in principle and accepted that in terms of agriculture reform should continued on the lines of the 1992 MacSharry concept. But while the importance of price support has declined, market regimes are still guaranteed by minimum prices and farmers would be compensated with direct payments for price cuts.

The Commission's reform proposal on the CAP became the topic of heated negotiations at both the national level and European Council summits. For some countries the reform proposals did not go far enough, for others, e.g. France, they went too far. As a result of this controversy the Commission's precise legislative proposals for CAP reform completed in March 1998 were a slight amendment of its former reform proposal. The June 1998 summit in Cardiff finally agreed on an ambitious nine months' deadline for reform of the CAP and regional aid, thereby postponing potential disagreeable negotiations until after the September 1998 general election in Germany and putting at the same time great responsibility on the new German government which was to preside over the EU institutions for the first six months of 1999. Member states might have felt that in the event of the CDU and particularly its Bavarian sister party, the CSU, being replaced by a more left-wing coalition, the chances for a reform would be better. The CAP was therefore the key issue if enlargement were to go ahead, both, as a result of the importance of agriculture in the CEEC, but also because the CAP has always been an area of conflict, not only between countries who are agricultural producers and those who are the industrial exporters, but above all between France and Germany.

III   AGENDA 2000

The Franco-German Axis and Reforming the CAP: a Case-study

It is unfortunate that the budgetary issue of eastern enlargement is linked to the agricultural support, unfortunate that is for Franco-German relations, because historically it is this very area which has tested Franco-German relations to breaking point. From the beginning of the European integration in the 1950s agro-political issues have dominated Community affairs in general and Franco-German relations in particular. Disagreements on the formulation and application of the CAP have repeatedly shaken the Franco-German axis and indeed have threatened the very existence of the EC. This is not surprising, for the CAP being the major common policy was the focus of deliberation over the future of the EC in general. Importantly, for a long time the CAP has been the most highly developed form of common action where national governments have pooled virtually all decision-making competencies with scope for national policy-making heavily circumscribed.

The political and psychological thrust of the CAP, the great influence of farm lobbies on governments' policies in both countries, the strategic importance of farmers in French and German elections have made agricultural questions a key issue in Franco-German relations. In no policy area has it been harder to work out 'common positions' because in no other common sector have French and German policy preferences, structures and interests been so different. Whereas Germany historically has pursued a high price policy in an attempt to protect its dominantly small and medium-term family farm, France has been a net exporting country producing a variety of products both Southern and Northern for its export markets, giving France a *vocation exportatric* in this area. This meant that, since France had to compete in world markets, domestic farm prices were comparatively low until of course, with the operation of the CAP and under German pressure, France had to raise its price level bringing it more to that operating in Germany.

All major agricultural decision have centred on Franco-German conflicts, resolutions of which have had their core in Franco-German agreement: the 1961–2 marathon on the formulation of the CAP, the decision on the common price level in 1964–5, the conflicts over introduction and continuation of MCAs which periodically surfaced in the 1970s, and finally the two major CAP reforms in 1988 and 1992. In all cases resolution and agreement hinged on Franco-German mediating their conflicts. Why should agricultural reform as demanded in Agenda 2000 therefore be different? The Franco-German struggle over agricultural issues has remained part of the Franco-German conflict management scenario.

In the past, i.e. until the change of government in Germany in 1998, both countries had understood and, despite violent conflicts resurfacing periodically, accepted the other partner's vital interest (though for different reasons) in this sector. However, the arrival of a new government under Schröder reflected a lack of awareness, even ignorance, of the potentially explosive nature of agricultural issues for Franco-German relations, and its significance for the entire enlargement integration process.

With this background, it is little surprise that the greatest obstacle to an agreement on Agenda 2000 has been the reform of the CAP. Although the CAP had already been subjected to several reforms, they were all 'event-driven', i.e. past adaptation to the CAP regime had been agreed under pressure and had not been motivated by a genuine desire to make the policy more equitable or improve its efficiency. Thus the two most important reforms were undertaken under the threat of bankruptcy (February 1988) and international trade conflicts (May 1992). While none of the issues discussed at the Berlin summit was new, the forthcoming enlargement of the EU presents a new challenge where the differences between the two countries are greater than in almost any other area and where attempts to work out a common position have been repeatedly interrupted by major events, as well as political changes at the domestic level.

The Struggle Begins

Initially, the Bonn government, still headed by Chancellor Kohl and fired by its influential farm lobby, had rejected Agenda 2000, i.e the proposals for agricultural reform. During its party political conference in Bremen in May 1998, the CDU/CSU had confirmed its clear rejection of Agenda 2000. 'We reject the proposal in its present form. It is the aim of our agricultural policy to enable farmers to earn a high part of their income through the market.'[53] Following the Cardiff European Council summit, Kohl in his declaration to the *Bundestag* stressed that Agenda 2000 would not do justice in terms of German agriculture. He pointed out forcefully that it was not a matter of interests of a particular sector, but it was a question of solidarity with German agriculture which needs help and support.[54] In an attempt to find a solution, however, Waigel, the finance minister, suggested that farm incomes could be financed nationally and put under the jurisdiction of the Länder.[55]

The situation was a difficult one for Kohl. Waigel, who had been pressing for a cut in Germany's net contribution to the budget, was the leader of the Bavarian-based coalition party, the CSU, which was not only traditionally hostile to Europe but was reliant heavily on the rural farm vote. Bavaria has the greatest economic weight of the German Länder and has the strongest sense of regional identity. It has a large farming sector based on small and medium-sized family farms. 'We know better here in Bavaria how the work of our farmers should be rewarded' declared the Bavarian Minister President Edmund Stoiber.[56]

At the same time, it was not at all clear what the position of the SPD would be, if elected. While in opposition, the party had criticised the government's categoric rejection of Agenda 2000[57] and had called Kohl's demand for maintaining farm subventions 'an illusion'. The election in the fall of 1998, when a SPD-led coalition entered the government, was therefore important, not just from the German point of view. Whoever governed Germany would also preside over EU institutions in the first six months of 1999, when major decisions had to be met and the EU negotiating position in the forthcoming WTO round of negotiations on liberalisation of international agricultural trade had to be worked out.

The Austrian Presidency (July–December 1998) had narrowed down the terms of the Agenda 2000 debate, but virtually no progress had been made on agricultural reform. This meant that Germany, which had taken over from Austria in January 1999, was confronted with a difficult task: within three months it had to negotiate a compromise which would satisfy all 15 member states and which would not be at the expense of agricultural producers.

In the event, and quite contrary to earlier expectations, German attitudes under the new government were marked by continuity rather than change in terms of enlargement, particularly evident on two levels: first, the new Chancellor continued to stress the ideological importance, even necessity, of enlargement: 'It [the enlargement] is part and parcel of the responsibility we owe in the light of our history and our vision of a democratic Europe.'[58] Secondly, the new government continued the Kohl/Waigel opposition to Germany's large contribution to the common budget stating in fact that the 'time when crises could be solved with German money are over',[59] and warned that this matter would become one of the major priorities of the German Presidency. In his address to the *Bundestag* Schröder declared: 'We cannot and will not continue a policy which aims to buy the goodwill of our neighbours with net contributions, leaving us with an intolerable budgetary burden at home.'[60] He came under attack for his strong defence of German interests from his own junior coalition party, the Greens, who called his attempt to cut out 'a special role' for Germany (*Deutsche Sonderrolle*) 'insensitive and unproductive'.[61] Clearly, while this is a hidden attack on the former government, which according to Schröder had subjected Germany to a mere paymaster role in the Community, the new socialist government intended to demand a more equitable burden-sharing.

The only change was in relation to CAP reform. While the Kohl government had been heavily reliant on its Bavarian sister party, the CSU, for farm votes, Schröder felt less inclined to consider the agricultural sector (as all conservative German Chancellors before him did) as a voting reservoir.[62] Addressing the EP on 14 July 1998 he maintained that reform of agriculture was necessary.[63] Thus Schröder appeared somewhat immune to pressures from the farm lobby and insensitive, even ignorant, of the importance of this sector for France.

Negotiations intensified during the run-up to the German Presidency. The Chancellor and his foreign minister explored member states' positions in bilateral negotiations during countless visits to the 14 capitals. The Council and Commission worked closely together with high-level meetings nearly every week. Within Germany itself, the Secretary of State for Europe, Verheugen, became coordinator for the major policy-making fora where national German positions were defined and integrated with those of the other member states.

However, as will be seen later, the failure of the new government to grasp the importance of agriculture for France set Germany against other member states of the EU and, of course, particularly against France. A dispute on CAP reform had already flared up during the weeks preceding the Berlin summit. This was against the background of European diplomatic uncertainty following the replacement of the long-serving Chancellor Kohl, although it was generally agreed that the Franco-German axis had reached a low long before the departure of Kohl.[64]

The situation deteriorated as a result of the conflict over changes in financing the CAP. The Commission had suggested that 25% of CAP expenditure covering direct income support be switched back to member states, thus introducing the concept of 're-nationalisation' of the CAP.[65] For Germany these cuts would outweigh the extra expense of supporting the farm sector, while it would increase agricultural expenditure in countries such as France, Ireland and Greece. (The Commission had estimated that Germany would achieve a net gain of EURO 678.2 million p.a. by 2006, while France would be worse off by an estimated EURO 648 million p.a.).[66]

This idea seemed attractive to Germany: in 1997 she had transferred some 11 million ECU to the CAP fund Guarantee Section and had received less than 6 million ECU; France had transferred less than 6.5 million ECU, but had received 9.5 million ECU. The government under Kohl had hoped that co-financing might avoid a conflict with the farm lobby. It is interesting that the concept of co-financing still emphatically rejected in the early 1990s as it would 'undermine' the supranationality of the CAP and the Union,[67] had found acceptance by Bonn as a means of relieving Germany's net payer position. The concept of renationalisation was also accepted by the SPD. According to the chairman of the budget committee in the EP, Detlev Samland, the Commission proposals are 'going in the right direction. This is not a renationalisation of the EU Policy, because other sectors like structural and regional policies are partly financed directly by member-states.'[68]

France resented and rejected any proposal threatening one of the basic principles of the CAP, that of 'financial solidarity'. Asked whether France would eventually accept the 'renationalisation' of the CAP, M. Pierre Moscovici stated most forcefully the French position: 'Absolutely not. The CAP is one of the foundations of the original European argument of 1957 ... at the same time, we agreed to the setting-up of the Common Market from which the Germans have very greatly benefited, but we also got the establishment of the Common Agricultural Policy. We don't want any meddling with this founding pact. Any instilling of a dose of renationalisation is unacceptable to us. That's an absolute political pre-condition.'[69] Chirac had already made clear at the Vienna summit that the introduction of such a 'co-financing scheme' was out of the question. 'There are other and more sensible proposals.'[70]

France was in a difficult position, rendering her unable to make any concession on the CAP without incurring the wrath of the country's powerful lobby. CAP negotiations were accompanied by protests of angry farmers, not just in Brussels, Spain and Germany, but the most violent of these were on 8 February when 200 farmers from the Paris region ransacked the offices of the Green environment minister (who was seeking to introduce a tax on pollutants) provoking a rare rebuke from French Prime Minister Jospin.

Currently, farmers account for 4.2% of France's working population and generate only 2.4% of GDP, but like in Germany the lobby is powerful. Under the present 'co-habitation' between a socialist government and a right-wing President matters are complicated between the socialist Prime Minister and the President who as a former Gaullist minister for agriculture has staunchly defended farm interests. In particular, France resisted further drastic price reductions extending to products not yet tackled by the MacSharry Reform. In a special cabinet session on 17 February a common French position was hammered out rejecting the concept of co-financing and insisting that any agreement in agricultural reform would have to be linked to broader negotiations for the EU financing 2000–2006.[71]

The Berlin Package – a 'Messy' Compromise?

Germany, during the first Agricultural Council meeting under its Presidency on 18/19 January 1999, had revealed first concrete steps towards reform by proposing a top-down system of control on agricultural spending, i.e. holding farm spending to a ceiling lower than present guidelines.[72] Germany reiterated three demands which had to be met before Agenda 2000 could be agreed: first, a budget freeze, second the introduction of 'co-financing' in the agricultural sector, and third an extension to all EU members of the system which refunds the UK for over-payments. Foreign and finance ministers were instructed to maintain a firm grip on the farm talks prompted by fears that agricultural ministers might be swayed by their militant clientele. The German Chancellor also scheduled a 'mini' summit (Suchkonferenz) of EU leaders on 26 February in Petersberg/Bonn. According to a German diplomat Germany was 'going for broke: 'it's the end of March or nothing.'[73] In the event the February 'mini' summit ended in virtual failure when France rejected German CAP reform proposals as 'stupid'.[74] According to President

Chirac, who referred to agriculture as 'our strategic green weapon', the interests of farmers 'are the interests of France'.[75] The President requested that farm reform proposals be reworked, because they did not meet French demands. 'There will be no agreement on Agenda 2000 unless the French and German positions come closer', said the French Agricultural Minister Jean Glavany.[76]

As has been seen, rows over agriculture were by no means new, but as a senior European diplomat observes: 'What is new is that France finds itself in the dock with the Germans wanting their money back.'[77] It is unfortunate that the need to cut expenditure is greatest in the agricultural sector whose privileges are held sacrosanct both by President Chirac, himself a former agricultural minister representing the conservative Right, but also by Mr Jospin, who dared not trespass against historical privileges. On 4 March 1999 the French Minister for European Affairs, Pierre Moscovici, stated: 'This [the Berlin agreement] is really more than desirable, it is essential for the European Union ... It is also highly desirable from the point of view of Franco-German relations.'[78]

Although France played down the rift, Paris has been angered in private over what appeared to be a sudden break in diplomatic practices between Bonn and Paris. In the past, France maintained, neither Paris nor Bonn would press a policy opposed by the other partner. Common lines would be hammered out in advance to key meetings, this time however, France privately accused Germany of back-tracking on previous agreements.[79]

However, Germany was aware that, whatever happened, Agenda 2000 had to be agreed at the Berlin summit and that failure to do so would have 'grave consequences' for the continuation of the enlargement process. The new government realised that it could not 'afford' such a crisis.[80] Knowing that time was running out, Schröder suddenly budged to French demands. The switch in German attitudes was totally unexpected and baffled everyone since until then Germany had been behind fundamental change. One Commission official said: 'We had no forewarning. There was total confusion.'[81]

When questioned on a possible German U-turn and a major German concession on the question of co-financing, the new French minister for agriculture, Glavany, declared: 'The Germans have been showing France that they wanted cooperation and a constructive, trusting dialogue. We had a sort of crisis which broke out during an agricultural marathon when it was absolutely impossible to agree and when, indeed, Franco-German relations reached virtually rock bottom. Since then the Franco-German dialogue has returned to being positive, constructive. The fact that they are moving against co-financing – i.e. against re-nationalising part of the CAP, on which France had been very firm – makes the atmosphere more relaxed.'[82]

Nevertheless, French defence of agricultural interests resurfaced again dramatically at the summit itself, when even the 'compromise' package agreed only days before by the Farm Council was subjected to further 'compromise'. The German Presidency was forced to interrupt negotiations to formulate a new package acceptable to France: in the early hours of 25 March and after 20 hours of deliberations a deal was finally delivered. It included price cuts which would narrow the gap further between world market prices and those of the CAP, compensated only partly by direct payments to farmers, reform of the regional and cohesion policies, benefiting 'most needy regions', a financial framework to enable enlargement to take place, and reform of the budget to ensure a more equitable contribution by member states.

La Présidence Coûte Cher

The agreement of 25 March 1999 has been called 'the most comprehensive reform package in the history of the EU'.[83] For the first time the EU has subjected itself to a rigid stabilisation programme: the total budget will rise slightly from 89 590 million EUR in 2000 to 103 530 million EUR in 2006 and a reallocation and concentration of structural funding on specified regions will facilitate admission of new members. In a surprising move Schröder also recognised that 'the UK budget abatement will be maintained',[84] although some adjustments were made, i.e. contributions from other EU member states to the UK rebate would be charged to effect a fairer burden-sharing among other high net contributors and the poorer 'cohesion' countries e.g. Spain, Portugal, Greece and Ireland. Germany's net contribution (as well as that of the Netherlands, and Sweden) would 'see a reduction in their financing share to 25% of the normal share'.[85] Schröder had to concede however, that 'we Germans did not achieve everything we would have liked to achieve'.[86]

Agricultural costs were stabilised (rising from 40 950 million EUR in 2000 to 41 660 million EUR by 2006), but the European Council diluted the farm ministers' package by deciding to delay key cuts in minimum prices. In fact, on the morning of the 25 March 'CAP reform had evaporated with the morning dew'.[87] The milk reform was postponed until the 2006 marketing year, price cuts for cereals and beef were diluted (15% and 20% respectively), 'degressive' payments to farmers were avoided and the concept of co-financing was abandoned. Therefore, as had been the case with the MacSharry reform, the budgetary impact of the reforms is not as large as had been hoped and therefore the compromise may fail to achieve the ultimate objective of the Berlin summit, namely clearing the way for enlargement.

This is a far cry from what Fischler had called the 'most radical CAP reform'.[88] Nevertheless, the European Council Conclusions stated that 'efforts made notably in terms of reducing support prices, represent an essential contribution by the European Community in stabilising the world's agricultural markets. The European Council considers that the decisions adopted regarding the reform of the CAP within the framework of Agenda 2000 will constitute essential elements in defining the Commission's negotiating mandate for the future multilateral trade negotiations of the WTO.'[89]

Despite such rhetoric, the German Presidency has been subjected to severe and rare criticism.[90] The inexperience of the new government has produced the 'least effective Union presidency since ... an Italian administration ... in the first half of 1996'.[91] Although agreement has been struck, Schröder's lack of experience when it came to playing the Union game, meant that he failed to deliver the trade-offs vital to the running of the 15 member club. Schröder has been marked a loser; first, in terms of German interests and second, in terms of effecting radical reforms as demanded by Agenda 2000.[92] In particular Schröder was criticised for his dealings with France from which he should have got a better deal. Germany failed to demand a trade-off in exchange for dropping the co-financing concept.[93]

France, on the other hand, was satisfied in terms of the CAP: the principle of financial solidarity had been maintained. President Chirac was particularly pleased that the reform of the milk sector had been deferred until 2006 (a French requirement) and that intervention prices for cereals had been brought down – another strong French demand. The President observed that the Franco-German engine had never broken down during negotiations, but if it had, then 'there would certainly not have been agreement'. The enlargement was now 'a clearly reaffirmed objective'.[94] But, although France considered the German Presidency a success, since Germany's new leaders did follow 'in the footsteps of their predecessors' and 'have taken on board the principles and orientations of their predecessors',[95] Paris nevertheless felt slighted by Germany. The new government had ignored a long-standing Franco-German practice, namely never to walk into a Council meeting without a Franco-German deal. Thus one would agree with the *Financial Times* 'beware of any agreement ... that leaves everyone looking happy'.[96]

CONCLUSION

Like in many other areas, what begins as a Franco-German conflict turns into 'the Franco-German position'. It appears that Franco-German agreement on salient aspects of Agenda 2000 was the prerequisite for a successful outcome in Berlin in March 1999 and the overall acceptance of the Agenda 2000 package, which in itself was a necessary but not sufficient condition for enlargement to go ahead. However, in Schröder's desperate attempt to effect agreement at Berlin and importantly 'to lay the ghost of Kohl, to make himself a player of Europe',[97] the new German Chancellor has merely postponed complex decisions. This is a far cry from his policy statement to the *Bundestag* on 10 December 1998 when he said: 'our overriding goal is to create the necessary financial scope for the future enlargement of the European Union through stringent budgetary discipline and *effective reform in key spending areas.*'[98] Has the Berlin summit reflected this? Not quite: while agreement on the Commission's agenda was secured, signals were confused. The Chancellor's strategy was short-sighted and his U-turn would have been unnecessary with better preparations. In fact France, despite earlier praise, felt that 'the long night in Berlin' was the direct result of poor German statesmanship.[99]

When the new German government took over the EU Presidency and particularly when the Berlin summit approached in March 1999, it was keen to reach a compromise deal realising that a failure would lead to a postponement of the enlargement process. But it was only at the 11th hour that the German government decided to reconsider its negotiating position and thus secure agreement. It seems clear that, once faced with the realities of presiding over EU institutions and particularly with chairing the negotiations on Agenda 2000, Schröder began to understand the complexity of EU decision-making and the importance of 'package deals' as practised by previous German Chancellors. Thus the main objective, namely clearing the way to enlargement was not (fully) achieved. EU policy-makers and bureaucrats were thus resigned to have to 'return to the negotiation table' at a later date.[100]

Nevertheless, the German Presidency has, in partial accord with France, determined the direction of the enlargement process. Partly because the issue area was a classical and historical conflict area with the two countries being the chief protagonists, partly because French and German interests in the enlargement vary, the two countries have been unable to reach more than a modest compromise. Yet the fate of eastern expansion was not secured; urgent institutional reforms remained to be agreed at the IGC of 2000 in Nice.

NOTES

1. Gary Streeter (1998), 'The EU and the Challenge of Enlargement', *European Foreign Affairs Review*, **3**, 315.
2. Commission (1992), 'Europe and the Challenge of Enlargement', *Bulletin of the European Communities*, Supplement 3.

3. Commission (1997), 'Agenda 2000: For a Stronger and Wider Union', *Bulletin of the European Union*, Supplement 5.

4. These so-called Copenhagen criteria were political criteria (democracy, the rule of law and human rights and respect for and protection of minorities), economic criteria (the existence of a functioning market economy) and also a commitment to membership obligation which includes adherence to the aims of political, economic and monetary union.

5. Interview material, Permanent Representative to Brussels, German COREPER, 17 July 1999.

6. *Financial Times* (1999), 'Euro Zone Economy', 3 December, p. 6.

7. Victoria Curzon, Alice Laudan and Richard G. Whitman (eds) (1999), *The Enlargement of the European Union*, Routledge, London and New York, Introduction, p. 21.

8. *Ibid.*, p. 116.

9. F.R. Willis (1968), *France, Germany and the New Europe*, OUP, London, p. 305.

10. Sabine Lee (1999), 'Germany and the first Enlargement Negotiations 1961–1963', in Anne Deighton and Alan S. Milward (eds), *Widening, Deepening and Acceleration; The European Economic Community 1957–1963*, Nomos, Baden-Baden, p. 211.

11. Scheel vor dem 6. Bundestag, 29 Ocober 1969, Stenografischer Bericht, p. 89–91.

12. Willy Brandt (1976), *Begegnungen und Einsichten*, Droemer/Knauer, Munich, pp. 320–21.

13. See inter alia Roy Pryce (1973), *The Politics of the European Community*, Butterworth, pp. 24–7.

14. Stuart Croft *et al.* (1999), *The enlargement of Europe*, MUP Manchester and New York, p. 59.

15. Quoted by Derek W. Urwin (1991), *The Community of Europe*, Longman, London and New York, p. 209.

16. Beate Kohler (1980), 'Germany and the Enlargement of the European Community', in W.L. Kohl and G. Basevi (eds), *West Germany: A European and Global Power*, Heath & Co., Lexington.

17. François Mitterrand (1986), *Reflexions sur la politique exterieure de la France*, Fayard, Paris, p. 85.

18. Interview *Nouvel Observateur*, 6 May 1994, quoted by Hubert Vedrine (1996), *Les Mondes de François Mitterand*, Fayard, Paris, p. 570.

19. M. Baun (1997), 'Germany and EU Enlargement into Eastern Europe', Paper, ECSA Conference, Seattle, 29 May – 1 June.

20. G. Kolankiewicz (1994), 'Consensus and Competition in the Eastern Enlargement of the European Union', *International Affairs*, **70**, p. 490.

21. Baun, *op. cit.*, p. 7.

22. R. Freudenstein (1998), 'Poland, Germany and the EU', *International Affairs*, **74** (1).

23. *Bulletin*, **18**, 3 March 1997, p. 185.

24. See for example *Bulletin*, **68**, 18 June 1991, pp. 541–6, 4 March 1992, pp. 233–8.

25. *Süddeutsche Zeitung*, 31 March 1998.

26. *Bulletin*, **118**, 19 December 1994, pp. 1086–91.

27. Lykke Fries and Anna Murphy (1999), 'The European Union and Central and Eastern Europe: Governance and Boundaries', *Journal of Common Market Studies*, **37** (2), pp. 222–3.

28. M. Pierre Moscovici, interview, 'Tomorrow, a Thirty-Member Europe?', *Politique internationale*, 3 May 1999, reproduced by French Embassy in the UK, www. ambafrance. org.uk.

29. Patrick McCarthy (1999), 'France, Germany, The IGC and Eastern Enlargement', in Douglas

Webber, *The Franco-German relationship in the European Union*, Routledge, London and New York, p. 44.

30. Reinhard Stuth (1992), 'Deutschland's Rolle im sich wandelnden Europa', *Aussen-Politik*, **1**.

31. Henning Tewes (1998), 'Between Deepening and Widening: Role Conflict in Germany's Enlargement Policy', *West European Politics*, **21** (2), 118–33.

32. See for instance M. Pierre Moscovici, interview Note 28.

33. Christian Deubner (1995), *Deutsche Europa-Politik: Von Maastricht nach Kerneuropa?*, Nomos, Banden-Baden.

34. Rudolf Scharping (1994), *Aussen-Poltik*, **1**.

35. On this issue see Beverly Crawford (1996) 'Germany's Unilateral Recognition of Croatia and Slovenia: A Case of Defection from Multi-lateral Cooperation', *World Politics*, **48** (4), pp. 482–521.

36. Pedersen, *op. cit.*, p. 188.

37. McCarthy in Webber (1999), *op. cit.*, p. 46.

38. M. Hartmann (1996), 'Implications of EU Enlargement for the CAP', Paper, *Credit Conference*, Nottingham.

39. For a detailed discussion of the budget, see for instance B. Laffan (1997), *The Finances of the European Union*, Macmillan, Basingstoke.

40. Finanzbericht 1997, Bundesminister der Finanzen, p. 167.

41. *Süddeutsche Zeitung*, 10 July 1997, 20 March 1998, 23 March 1998, 24/5 March 1998, 27 May 1998, *Die Welt*, 23 March 1998.

42. See for instance *Financial Times*, 15 September 1997, p. 2 and *Süddeutsche Zeitung*, 11 December 1998.

43. See for example W.J. Feld (1981), *West Germany and the European Community*, Praeger, New York, p. 52

44. *Wirtschaftswoche*, No. 47, 19 November 1976, *Handelsblatt*, 20 May 1974, *Financial Times*, 15 March 1979.

45. K.O. Nass (1976), 'Der "Zahlmeister" als Schrittmacher?', *Europa-Archiv*, **10**, pp. 325–36, M. Leigh (1975), 'Germany's changing role in the EEC', *The World Today*, December, pp. 488–97.

46. *Herald (New York) Tribune*, European Edition, Paris, 15 September 1975.

47. *Das Parlament* (1983), 14/21 December, p. 10. *Bulletin*, 16 February 1984, p. 159.

48. *European Voice*, 22–28 April 1988, p 8.

49. C. Caspari (1996), 'Enlargement and CAP Reform', *EIU European Trend*, 1st quarter, p. 76.

50. European Commission (1995), 'Agricultural Situation and Prospects in the Central and Eastern European Countries', Brussels, Vol 2.

51. H. Grabbe K. Hughes (1997), 'Eastward Enlargement of the EU', RIIA, London, p. 44.

52. R. Freudenstein, *op. cit.*, p. 44.

53. *Die Welt*, 20 May 1998.

54. *Bulletin*, 2 June 1998, p. 581.

55. *Handelsblatt*, 5 August 1998.

56. *Münchner Merkur*, 21 January 1996.

57. *Süddeutsche Zeitung*, 20 March 1998.

58. G. Schröder, Policy Statement to the *Bundestag*, 10 December 1998, www.germany-info.org/govern/schröder.

59. *Süddeutsche Zeitung*, 9 December 1998.

60. Policy Statement to the *Bundestag*, 10 December 1998.
61. *Süddeutsche Zeitung*, 9 December 1998 and *Die Welt*, 14 December 1998.
62. *Financial Times*, 11 May 1998.
63. Printed by *Internationale Politik* (1998), **9**, pp. 118–22.
64. Interview material, German COREPER, Brussels, 16 July 1999.
65. Commission (1998), 'Financing the European Union: Commission Report on the Operation of the Own Resources System', Brussels, October 7, COM (98) 560 final, p. 35.
66. *Ibid.*
67. Interview material, German Chancellery, Bonn, 4 March 1992.
68. *Süddeutsche Zeitung*, 6 and 8 October 1998.
69. Interview given by M. Pierre Moscovici to *La Croix*, 24 February 1999, Paris.
70. *Süddeutsche Zeitung*, 14 December 1998.
71. *Financial Times*, 23 February 1999.
72. *Financial Times*, 25 January 1999.
73. *Financial Times*, 2/3 January 1999, p. 3.
74. *Süddeutsche Zeitung*, 24 February 1999, *Die Welt*, 8 March 1999.
75. *Die Welt*, 10 March 1999.
76. *Financial Times*, 2 March 1999.
77. *Financial Times*, 3 March 1999, p. 19
78. Interview Radio France, 4 March 1999, Bonn.
79. Interview material, French COREPER, 15 July 1999.
80. Günter Verheugen (1999), 'Deutschland and die EU Ratspräsidentschaft: Erwartungen und Realitäten', *Integration*, **22** (1), p. 3.
81. *Financial Times*, 9 March 1999.
82. Interview given by M. Jean Glavany Minister for Agriculture, RMC, 8 March 1999, Paris.
83. Ch. Jessen (1999), Agenda 2000: Das Reformpaket von Berlin, ein Erfolg für Gesamteuropa, *Integration*, **22** (3), p. 167.
84. *Financial Times*, 22 March 1999, p. 3.
85. *European Voice*, 24–30 June 1999, p. 9.
86. *Süddeutsche Zeitung*, 27 March 1999.
87. *European Voice*, 24–30 June 1999, p. 9.
88. *Die Welt*, 25 March 1999.
89. Presidency Conclusions European Council, Berlin, 24–25 March 1999, *Agence Europe*, 27 March 1999, Documents No 2131/2132, p. 5.
90. See for instance *Financial Times*, 29 March 1999, Editorial 'A Feeble Deal for Europe'. *Süddeutsche Zeitung*, 2 June 1999, 'Deutschland's Bescheidene Bilanz' and 'Scharfe Oppositionkritik an der Bonner Europa-Politik'.
91. *European Voice* (1999), **5** (25), p. 9.
92. *Frankfurter Rundschau*, 26 March 1999.
93. *European Voice* (1999), **5** (21), p. 8.
94. *Ibid.*, p. 6.
95. *Agence Europe* (1999), No. 7434, 27 March, p. 3.
96. *Financial Times*, 29 March 1999.
97. Quoted by *European Voice*, 22–28 April 1999, p. 8.
98. Policy Statement to the *Bundestag*, 10 December 1998, emphasis added, *op. cit.*

99. *Ibid.*
100. Interview German COREPER, Brussels, 16 July 1999 and interview French COREPER, Brussels, 15 July 1999.

PART III

The Outcome

7. Conclusion

> *Il y a les* époques *et il y a les* périodes.
> (Charles Péguy *Notre jeunesse*, 1910)

In this meditation around the Dreyfus Affair written in 1910, Péguy distinguishes between epochs, those times when spectacular events such as revolutions which have a deep impact on the world, and periods, those plateaux in history when routine, mostly peaceful and comfortable, sets in. The second half of the twentieth century, which has been the setting of this book, is framed in the Franco-German context by two epochs: the Schuman Plan which formalised the end of the 'hereditary enmity' of France and Germany and laid the foundations of an economic 'Carolingian' Europe, and the fall of the Berlin Wall which put an end to the ostracisation of half of Europe by the other half, and heralds the advent of a political Europe roughly coincidental with the traditional geographic representation of Europe. Predictably, the radical nature of the Schuman Plan was clearer to the 'Founding Fathers' Schuman, Adenauer, de Gasperi, Spaak, and of course Jean Monnet, than it was to the war-weary masses.[1] By contrast, the fall of the Berlin Wall was a 'happening' which virtually took place in every citizen's living-room.

The Schuman Plan was the first, and successful experiment of the Six in joint management of a project, generating a vision of the future: in order to have peace, we must build Europe. The Europe of which Schuman laid the foundation stone, reflected with great fidelity the credo of western liberalism: peace through prosperity. Its crowning achievement is Economic and Monetary Union, which in turn is likely to spill over into the areas of taxation and social provisions. The political repercussions of economic integration are also affecting such other spheres as judicial and home affairs, and foreign and security policy. In the year 2000, there is hardly any aspect of public life that remains untouched by European centripetal forces. In geopolitical terms too, the enduring effects of the Schuman Plan vision remain tangible. For all the spectacular friendships of de Gaulle and Adenauer, Schmidt and Giscard d'Estaing, Mitterrand and Kohl, or *a contrario* cool personal relations between Brandt and Pompidou or Chirac and Schröder, the Franco-German relationship is sealed by perceived necessity: it is helped by, but does not depend on personal friendships. Even at the worst times of the 1965 crisis or the conflicts of the mid-1990s around the 'Growth and Stability Pact', the two countries were anxious not to go over the brink, and compromises were eventually devised and approved. The Franco-German relationship itself is buttressed by a strong feeling of solidarity among the original Six,[2] which form the core of the 'Carolingian Europe' influenced in turn by the Christian-Democratic ideology and the 'Rhineland capitalism'[3] economic model with strong social protection connotations. Successive enlargements have demonstrated the attraction of this entity, which is constitutionally founded on the principles of democracy, human rights and economic liberalism tempered by social concerns. Every time there have been changes in Europe, from the Schuman Plan to the present day, whether in terms of substance or territory, these changes have proceeded according to the ratchet system: i.e. towards ever further integration, and towards ever increased membership.[4] The impact of the Schuman Plan has been profoundly to alter both the configuration and the politico-economic system of Western Europe.

Unlike 'all the King's horses and all the King's men' of the nursery rhyme, the fall of the Berlin Wall managed to put Germany together again in record time, less than eleven months! And now it is virtually the whole of Central and Eastern Europe, minus internecine-war torn Yugoslavia and poverty-stricken Albania, which has the declared ambition to join the European Union. The question is not just whether the applicant countries will be able to absorb and satisfy the huge demands of the *acquis communautaire*, but also whether the member states will be willing to make the necessary financial and trading sacrifices according to the very rules which they wish to impose on the applicants. As was demonstrated in Chapter 6 about the reform of the CAP as a pre-condition of enlargement, a failure by France and Germany to work out an agreed solution during the preparatory phase of a major negotiation leads to a chaotic negotiation and an unsatisfactory settlement from the point of view of the European Union. Thus, the prospect of enlargement is going to force a tighter cooperation between the member states, with a realisation that narrowly perceived national interests may have to be squeezed out of agendas under threat of deadlock or worse, disintegration. That is precisely what is at stake in the intergovernmental conference of 2000 which aims to reform institutions in order to make them workable with a membership almost double that of the present day. The regrouping of Europe around the same constitutional principles and rules of behaviour is thus having a profound impact on the existing European Union and, more specifically, on the policy priorities of both France and Germany.

As has been repeatedly maintained throughout this study, the self-perceptions and policy goals of the two countries remain that their cooperation is essential to the survival and prosperity of each of them. However, throughout the course of the last half-century, the progression of this voluntarist cooperation towards 'an ever closer union among the peoples of Europe'[5] has been anything but linear. There are landmarks of achievements, troughs of mistrust and divergences, bouts of nationalist intransigence. Can any pattern be discerned?

First of all, not for nothing have there been innumerable references to the Franco-German engine, the Franco-German motor of integration, the Franco-German tandem, the Franco-German axis, the Franco-German partnership, the Franco-German alliance, etc. Not only have France and Germany been singled out as the two major protagonists in the European drama, but they are usually paired up in a way that no other combination of states, except perhaps the Benelux countries (and then, with different connotations), is so consistently referred to. What, apart from geographical proximity, has brought these two states so close together?

To start with, a consciousness of failure having to be redeemed by virtuous ambitions. Still nowadays, when the grandchildren of the Nazi generation have reached maturity, Germany has to exhibit exemplary democratic behaviour to be accepted as a 'normal', let alone an 'ordinary' democracy, and can hardly conceive of a foreign policy outside the European framework. France, who within twenty years had lost a war, an empire and two republics, and is still haunted by the ghosts of the Vichy regime and the Algerian war, can only reassert her claim to planetary influence through the agency of a European Union which is not, after all, merely an enlarged Hexagon. Europe has been the rehabilitating factor of Germany, and the buttressing factor of France. And Europe demands, by default at the very least, that these two states work together for the sheer durability of the present European entity. That was the express objective of the Schuman Plan; it is the goal of Economic and Monetary Union; it is the ambition of the Eurocorps as constitutive element of a potential European Defence identity.

Even now, at a time when the events of 1989 have signalled the advent of the twenty first century, i.e. a different configuration of the international system, and when the words 'globalisation' and 'information society' are the accepted mantras, we remain witnesses of the difficulties experienced by 'nation states' to adapt to this new environment. Schröder's Germany may have willed away the clouds of history, but it does not quite manage to define its new virility, and Schröder himself swallowed his pride when confronted with French obstinacy over CAP reform at the Berlin European Council of 1999, thus preserving European wholesomeness, if not the credibility of his narrowly national ambitions. The French, who are among the staunchest defenders of national sovereignty within the European Union, in other words giving priority to intergovernmentalism against supranationalism, have had to swallow their words and advocate extension of qualified majority vote in the European institutions during the negotiations leading to the Amsterdam treaty. They then took on the invidious task of reforming the institutions to make them more workable prior to eastward enlargement.

Secondly, this prospect brings back the problems of political philosophy and of power politics. It is not only that institutional reform will inevitably entail a reassessment of the respective weights of member states, not just in the Council but in all the institutions of the Union. It is also that France and Germany have fundamentally different political traditions and principles. France is notorious for her Jacobin centralism favouring pyramidal structures and tighter hierarchical controls, and would for instance gladly grant the European Council much greater and better defined powers in foreign policy. Germany contrariwise, has traditionally had protean territorial identities, is compelled by history to prefer a federal, i.e. horizontal structure which in the past fifty years has served her democratic ideals superbly, and has loyally supported and increased the powers of the European Parliament. That is why, in spite of virtuous rhetoric on the matter, and a keen awareness that enlargement cannot proceed before reform has been agreed upon, hardly any real negotiations have been engaged so far. Even the Commission's 'Agenda 2000' found it safer to contend with financial perspectives and reform of the CAP, than to produce a blueprint on institutional reform, for fear of disturbing deep waters. There is a conspiracy of inactivity among the member states and the European institutions, which can overtly be justified by the momentous achievement of monetary union and the formidable task of negotiating the eastward enlargement, and which the intergovernmental conference at Nice has attempted to stir.

The reforms achieved by the Amsterdam and Nice Treaty are not negligible. The three-pillar structure has been shaken, and a new concept of 'enhanced co-operation', proposed and formulated by the Franco-German team, has been incorporated into the treaty (TEU Art.11, ex Art.5a). This latter principle should allow those member states who want to proceed with further integration to do so within the present institutional framework, without affecting those member states reluctant to surrender any more of their sovereignty. Its application, however, is hemmed in by arcane procedural clauses which may dampen and even discourage the enthusiasm and energy of the most integrationist governments, and could perversely be turned into a 'new version of the Luxembourg compromise'.[6]

The European Community, now the European Union, has not stood still since the fall of the Berlin Wall. Three gigantic projects towards further integration have been undertaken and sealed in the Maastricht and Amsterdam Treaties for two of them and in the decisions of the European Council for the third: the three projects at the heart of this study. Of the three, Economic and Monetary Union has now been established and is being implemented. It is expected to provide the participating member states with the means of achieving greater prosperity through the creation of a single monetary space and the preservation of monetary stability. The very fact that Greece has joined, on 1 January 2001, with the likeliness of being followed by Denmark and later Sweden, demonstrates the vitality of the project, despite the negative impact of armed conflicts on the European Union's periphery, embarrassing financial scandals, and the worrying potential onslaught on European democracy by the extreme Right.

The second project, a common foreign and security policy, is being realised piecemeal, with some degree of institutionalisation, and an ambitious prospect of a European defence policy, at present symbolised by the Eurocorps, which is due to perform as such (rather than as national troops from the five constituting countries), under NATO control in Kosovo from the spring or summer 2000. The degree to which France and Germany have together contributed to the elaboration of the CFSP is difficult to assess, because that is the very area where national interests appear at the most variance, and where declarations far outnumber deeds. The statement that 'German foreign policy is much more Euro-centric, while France has more widespread interests as a result of its colonial legacy and perceived global role' is almost common-place, yet may become open to questioning should Germany become a permanent member of the United Nations' Security Council, and develop a foreign policy more overtly supportive of her world-wide export performance. Franco-German relations in the field of European security have been notoriously conditioned by the Cold War, and within this context by relations with the United Kingdom and above all with the United States. France and the United Kingdom are nuclear powers, which Germany is not. Conversely, Germany and the United Kingdom have been staunch supporters of NATO, even at the cost of relinquishing ultimate decision-taking power to Washington, which France has opposed to the point of leaving NATO's integrated command in 1966 and not yet rejoining it in spite of recent moves in that direction. However, the Nuremberg 'common strategic concept' was based on the postulate that French and German security interests are indivisible. The 'common concept' reiterated the principles of security enunciated by the UN and the OSCE, and clarified the status of the Atlantic Alliance and WEU as mere military alliances, not political alliances, thus permitting a convergence of points of view. The Saint-Malo declaration[7] could have generated some uneasiness in the Federal Republic by reasserting a community of Anglo-French objectives and resources for Europe without prior consultations with or advance notice to Germany. In practice, it had the opposite effect and (almost chemically) precipitated the solution of the relationship between the Atlantic Alliance and the Western European Union adopted in Cologne in June 1999, thus complementing and clarifying the provision contained in Art. 17 (ex Art. J.7) of the Amsterdam Treaty. The Declaration of the European Council (3 and 4 June 1999) develops the Saint-Malo Declaration by expressing its 'intention' to provide the EU with 'the necessary means and capabilities' for 'conflict prevention and crisis management', so that it can adopt 'measures' to 'contribute to international peace and security in accordance with the Principles of the UN Charter without prejudice to actions by NATO'.[8] Interestingly enough, the French Permanent Representative to NATO, at a private function on 28 October 1999 made the following remark: 'What is new about Saint-Malo is not directly connected with defence, but with a determination to make the CFSP credible', adding that: 'by relocating European cooperation on security within the context of CFSP, Saint-Malo gave it the legitimacy and political dynamism which it could not have within the WEU framework'.[9]

In other words, the prospect of the development of a European Security and Defence Identity serves European political integration as much as it serves Western security interests. This trend was endorsed and reinforced by the Cologne European Council, and the task is now to follow the guidelines of Cologne, and to evolve a common security and defence policy which is truly European without appearing to compete with NATO, and without overlooking the interests of those member states of the Union which are neutral and/or non-members of WEU. Germany having overcome her reluctance, first to loosen her exclusive commitment to NATO, second to become involved in extra-territorial military operations, will now be expected to play, alongside France and Great Britain, a leading part in developing the European Security and Defence identity. This trend was confirmed at the Helsinki European Council of December 1999, when Germany, Italy and Spain followed the lead given by France and Britain at Saint-Malo and approved the Finnish Presidency's reports on defence and security. These reports flesh out the plans to create decision-making bodies such as a Political and Security Committee, and to proceed with the development of military capabilities, a rapid reaction force of about 60 000 troops, which would enable the European Union to carry out autonomous actions from 2003.

The third project, that of enlargement, still raises questions of method, with a division between those who, following the Commission, would treat each candidate according to its own progress towards absorbing the *acquis communautaire* and showing financial sustainability, and those like Mitterrand's former adviser, Jacques Attali, who advocate immediate and comprehensive enlargement, with long transitions periods and concessions to time-consuming adjustments. Whatever method is adopted, it is unanimously agreed that a European Union of twenty-eight or thirty member states needs drastic institutional reforms. But there the unanimity stops. And the 2000 Intergovernmental Conference had the invidious task of pushing those drastic reforms towards unanimous acceptance by member states who have so far repeatedly failed seriously to contemplate them.

The Cologne European Council not only set on train the establishment of a European defence system, it also demanded that the Intergovernmental Conference cover the following topics: size and composition of the Commission; weighting of votes in the Council (re-weighting, introduction of a dual majority and threshold for qualified-majority decision-making); possible extension of qualified-majority voting in the Council. The European Commission then asked, in the summer of 1999, three 'wise men', Jean-Luc Dehaene (former Prime Minister of Belgium), Lord Simon (former head of British Petroleum) and Richard von Weizsäcker (former President of the Federal Republic) to advise on the institutional implications of enlargement. Their report was published on 18 October 1999, and considered a range of reforms relating to policy- and decision-making, structure of the Treaties and organisation of EU institutions. The Helsinki European Council of 10–11 December then gave the green light for the Intergovernmental Conference to start its work on 14 February 2000. In principle, both France and Germany support the Commission's agenda for institutional reform, and the French, who assumed the Presidency of the European Union on 1 July 2000, have been keen to obtain positive results of the negotiation. What may be missing, however, is a common understanding of what long-term objectives an enlarged Europe should reach to attain in somewhat more significant terms than the portmanteau rhetoric of stability and prosperity.

Once more, the debate is open as to the finality of European integration and the constitutional form most likely to provide the means towards it. Prominent voices from both Germany and France have recently been heard on this matter. On a visit to the Paris French Institute of International Relations (IFRI) in November 1999, the President of the Federal Republic, Johannes Rau, defended his vision of a federal Europe as the ultimate stage of European unification.[10] This is the traditional point of view of the federalists, and like them, he advocated a 'succinct and comprehensible' written constitution clearly outlining the fields of competence of the Union and those of the member states, and into which a charter of human rights would be incorporated. He hinted rather optimistically that, as usual, the 'Franco-German couple' would give the lead and would once more be worthy of the task assigned to it by history.

A French voice with particular resonance in international fora is that of the former President of the Commission Jacques Delors. In an interview published in *Le Monde* of 19 January 2000, he warned of the danger of paternalistic behaviour towards the applicant countries, who should be listened to when they publicise their own views on the future of Europe, Eastern Europe being historically and culturally as European as Western Europe. He then continued, predictably, by expressing his own preference. Opposed to the principle of 'enhanced cooperation' as determined by the Amsterdam Treaty for reasons not dissimilar to those advanced earlier in this chapter, Delors advocates the establishment of what he calls a 'federation of nation-states' which is a nice conflation of the contrary doctrines of federalism and intergovernmentalism! 'What I consider from the federal method is that it makes it possible to know who does what, and therefore enables citizens to sanction what seems to them to diverge from the mandate they have given to their leaders. And what I consider from history, is that nation-states are there to stay.' In other words, Delors wants to keep the Community method, but make sure that it is given the means to work effectively, that it can cover new, relevant spheres of activities such as security of food supplies and environmental security, and that it must be given clear boundaries by the proper application of the principle of subsidiarity. This neo-federalism is of the functional rather than the constitutional type, and could develop a new pragmatism well in accord with a time suspicious of ideologies. It also offers a nice compromise between traditional German and French patterns of governance.

From a totally different perspective, that of an academic, Douglas Webber concludes a collective study of Franco-German cooperation in a number of policy areas by noting that 'other things being equal, the influence of the Franco-German relationship on the outcome of "intergovernmental" issues is strong.'[11] This is hardly surprising: when dealing at the level of governments, France and Germany benefit from the strong governmental and administrative links created over the years between the two countries because at that level implementation of the 1963 treaty has worked well. But in areas where the Community method applies, i.e. multilateral negotiations chaired either by the Commission or the Council over issues where well-informed, powerful interest groups put pressure and where differences of perception may be widely publicised, the two governments' strategies are much more fissile, and deals much more difficult to conclude. Moreover, in areas where the Franco-German treaty has not been followed by active implementation (such as armaments cooperation) or has suffered the weariness of the long-distance runner (such as efforts to enhance the other's language teaching, which is in retreat), the Franco-German partnership is at its least effective level, and might even shortly reach its nadir if the two countries do not quickly repair their public images tarnished by well-publicised dissents and scandals.

Is a weakening of the Franco-German relationship likely in an enlarged Europe also enmeshed in global networks and issues? And would that weakening be detrimental to the interests of that enlarged Europe? How is an enlarged Europe going to accommodate a single monetary policy which is, at the time of writing, the product of the Franco-German stubborn determination to further economic and political integration, but which is subjected to predictable teething troubles with a weak EURO and lingering disagreements over leadership of the ECB and democratic control of 'the bankers'? How will Germany and France be able to maintain the fragile but necessary balance between achieving an 'autonomous' European defence capability (France's ambition) and continuing to develop this capability within the framework and with the approval of NATO (Germany's preference) as agreed in the Amsterdam Treaty and reaffirmed at the Cologne European Council? Those are but a few of the questions which must be exercising not just France and Germany, but all member states of the European Union, the applicant countries, and the American Administration. It is widely acknowledged that France, and Germany, the 'cooperative hegemon',[12] have on balance served European integration well so far. Their task remains to use insight and pragmatic realism to manage an enlarged Europe which will, this century more than ever, aspire to unity within diversity.

NOTES

1. The radical potential of the Schuman Plan was exhaustively analysed by American scholars who constructed the theory of neo-functionalism from the experience of the 1950s and gave their studies such telling titles as *Beyond the Nation-State* (Ernest Haas) or *Europe's Would-be Polity* (L. Lindberg and S. Scheingold).
2. Hence the feeling of bitter disappointment when the Italians discovered that Italy had been excluded from the 'European core' of further integration advocated in the CDU Lamers-Schäuble Paper of 1994.
3. See Michel Albert (1991), *Capitalisme contre Capitalisme*, Collection 'L'Histoire Immédiate', le Seuil, Paris, p. 315.
4. The one exception is the withdrawal of Greenland in 1984, but Greenland can hardly have been considered European in the first place. Nor does it have, since 1979, the same relationship with Denmark that the DOM-TOMs have with France.
5. Preamble of the Treaty of Rome creating the European Economic Community, first paragraph.
6. Françoise DeLa Serre (1999), 'Une Europe ou plusieurs?', *Politique Etrangère*, Tome1, Vol. 64, pp. 21–33. Tim Lansford (1996), 'The Question of France: French Security Choices at Century's End', *International Security*, **5** (1), 45.
7. The Saint-Malo Communiqué of 4 December 1998, stated (1) that the provisions of the Amsterdam Treaty must be implemented fully and swiftly, (2) that the European Union must have a military capability enabling the Union to carry out autonomous actions to fulfil

obligations within NATO, (3) that the European Union must therefore have logistic means in order to take necessary decisions, (4) that Europe needs to be able to use forces responding rapidly to situations, and relying on a technologically advanced defence industrial base.

8. For a commentary on the implications of the Cologne European Council Declaration, see Lothar Rühl (1999), 'Condition and options for an autonomous 'Common European policy on Security and Defence' in and by the European Union in the post-Amsterdam perspective opened at Cologne in June 1999', Discussion Paper, *C 54*, ZEI, Bonn.

9. Authors' private notes on speech given by Philippe Guelluy to 'Cassiodore' group in Paris; private and limited distribution.

10. 'Une Constitution fédérale pour l'Europe?', *Le Monde*, 4 November 1999.

11. Douglas Webber (ed.) (1999), *The Franco-German relationship in the European Union*, Routledge, London, p. 172.

12. Thomas Pedersen, *op. cit.*, (see Chapter 6).

8. Postscript

Roger Morgan

Visiting Fellow, European Institute, London School of Economics and Political Science

As this book shows, the Franco-German special relationship assumed its remarkable characteristics during the period of European history that began with the Schuman Plan and ended forty years later with the conclusion of the Cold War. This relationship between Paris and Bonn played a decisive part in shaping the institutions and the policy priorities of the European Community, and in influencing the position of Western Europe in the East-West confrontation of that time.

The Franco-German relationship also played a significant role in the internal development of each of the two peoples whose deep historic interconnections had been traded by writers as diverse as Madame de Staël, Theodor Fontane, Jacques Bainville, Friedrich Sieburg and Vercors. At high political levels in Paris and in Bonn, once the immediate post-Liberation period was over, there were clear and pressing motives for the reconciliation which was insistently proclaimed as turning over a new leaf in Europe's history, and bringing together a renovated France and a new Germany in the task of constructing a new Europe. This endeavour – the pursuit partly of a vision and partly of hard-headed self-interest – was to place the two major continental states of Western Europe in a position of formal equality under innovative common institutions, and thus to make their commitment to this Europe, and to working with each other, part of the *raison d'être* (or as the Germans would say, the *Staatsräson*) of the new Fourth Republic as well as of the new Federal Republic.

It did not matter that there were potentially wide discrepancies between French and German ideas of what 'Europe' was about. Geopolitically, Frenchmen saw 'Europe' in part as a way of containing the power of Germany, while Germans saw it as a means of lifting their country to a position of equal status with their neighbours. Economically, the French tended to see the 'Community model' as something like France's national economic planning system transposed to the European level, whereas Germans tended to see it as consecrating free trade and the market economy.

What counted was that the two countries were working together in a common enterprise.

At the level of popular perceptions, this official drive for reconciliation naturally met with mixed reactions. It was all very well for political leaders to proclaim that 'our hereditary enemy is becoming our hereditary friend'. For many in France their country's sufferings under the German occupation could be neither forgiven nor forgotten; and in Germany, ten years after the war, a political leader was able to rouse a crowd to loud applause by deriding the way 'France was retrospectively declared a victor'. However for a significant number of French and German individuals, the experience of contact in wartime Europe had left memories that were not all negative. The argument to be used later by British 'Euro-sceptics', that Franco-German collaboration in the EC was no more and no less than a continuation of the wartime collaboration between Vichy and the Third Reich, is of course ridiculous and contemptible. However the day-to-day contacts of wartime Europe certainly helped to make many ordinary German and French people receptive to contact and cooperation in the very different Europe which lay ahead.

Why was it that France and Germany came to regard the European Community (later Union) as the automatic choice as the framework for pursuing many of their respective national purposes? Part of the answer must be that they had designed it themselves, to meet their own needs. Like the British in the UN, the OEEC, or NATO, they were not only present at the creation, but were able to play a decisive role in the shaping and development of the new organisation. Whereas in Britain in the year 2000 it was apparently a matter for serious political debate whether the country should withdraw altogether from the EU (which it originally boycotted, then tried to undermine, then joined only half-heartedly, to become a persistently awkward member), such an argument would be unthinkable in France or Germany. The ways in which they have consistently worked to maintain and develop 'their' European institutions for over half a century are well illustrated in the present book.

As well as their spontaneously generated reasons for wanting to bury some of the recent past, France and Germany were of course making their decisions about 'the construction of Europe' in the oppressive context of the Cold War. What Shakespeare said of greatness – 'some men are born great; some achieve greatness; and some have greatness thrust upon them' – could be adapted to characterise partnerships between states in the international system. Some partnerships are born harmonious; some achieve harmony, and some have harmony thrust upon them. There was nothing innately harmonious about the Franco-German partnership, but the two countries certainly worked tenaciously to achieve it, and the need for it was pressingly 'thrust upon them' by Western Europe's geopolitical predicament after 1945.

On this, as on other things, the situations of France and Germany were not identical. Germany, divided and occupied, and confronted from 1945 by the Red Army and from 1961 by the Berlin Wall, saw an urgent need to protect its security through political ties with its Western neighbours, as well as through military alliance with the United States. For France, by contrast, the threat to national security was less immediate and pressed (it took the form partly of colonial revolts in Indo-China and then in Algeria), and also the temptation to proclaim Europe's need for defence against American as well as Soviet influence was too strong to be resisted, especially by de Gaulle. Despite these differences, however, there can be no doubt that the perceived Soviet threat was a powerful 'external federator', which originally impelled France and Germany to undertake the task of building strong Western European institutions, and then kept their attention fairly firmly on the need to maintain and strengthen them.

The disappearance of this 'external federator' since 1990, combined with the simultaneous process of German unification which has in a sense solved 'the German problem', have naturally raised the question of how far the old motivations for 'constructing Europe' will continue to be effective. As this book has shown, although France and Germany, in their transformed circumstances, have thrown themselves vigorously into at least one gigantic European project, EMU, they have been rather more hesitant about enlarging the Union to the East, endowing it with a credible CFSP, and proceeding with the wisely assorted range of institutional and substantive changes debated for years under the catch-all heading of 'Political Union'.

The tempo of any advance in these projects – and some advance there will certainly be – cannot but be affected by the changes in France's, Germany's and Europe's fates since the dramatic events of 1989–90. This new situation is well captured in a slogan popular among German politicians in the 1990s: 'We Germans want Western neighbours in the East as well.' Yes, the collapse of the Soviet bloc gives Germany, and the West in general, the previously scarcely imagined prospect of extending the area covered by peaceable, stable, market-oriented democracies far to the East of the old Iron Curtain. This brings the prospect of freeing Western Europe both from the old Soviet menace and also from the less specific but still alarming threats arising from ethnic and territorial conflicts, drug-trafficking and other organised crime, and uncontrolled immigration from the potential earthquake-zone to the East.

However, a Europe stabilised by the eastward expansion of the Union (and of NATO) cannot be the same as the Europe inspired by the Franco-German tandem of the past. Instead of a Europe with its main institutions neatly strung out along a line east of Paris and west of Bonn – in Brussels, Luxembourg and Strasbourg – the Union of the early twenty-first century is one with its focus on a German capital, Berlin, much further East, and beyond that on relations with new member states extending up to (and even within) the frontiers of the old Soviet Union. In a Union whose membership embraces not only Central Europe from Warsaw to Budapest, but also most of the Baltic littoral and large stretches of the Balkans, the economic, cultural, and geopolitical weight of Germany is likely to be formidable. Even though France has worked to establish counterweights by securing commitments that the EU will continue to devote political and financial resources to its 'Euro-Mediterranean' dimension, and by establishing the German-French-Polish Weimar Triangle to institutionalise France's place in Central Europe, the situation is clear: one effect of the eastward enlargement of the Union is to increase the influence of Germany.

However, before sounding alarms about the threat of a renewed *Drang nach Osten* by an imperialistic *Reich*, we should try to define more precisely what the influence of a nation actually means, in the Europe of today and tomorrow. In the early twentieth century, the concept of a national 'sphere of influence' meant direct control over territory, or the use of political power to bend the will of subordinate governments to one's own: the struggle for influence in Western Europe since 1945 – and now in the enlarged Europe to be subject of the same communitarian rules and norms – it's a struggle for economic, civilian influence. The competition between states relates to market-shares, exports, contracts, investment and jobs. It follows that this competition will sometimes seem – especially to the losers – like a new form of conquest by a superior power, and the natural predominance of Germany's economy may be seen by others as merely a new version of political hegemony. Such a view, however would be superficially erroneous. The EU's objective of securing a 'level playing-field', already largely achieved, should ensure, over time, that economic benefits are earned on the basis of genuine competitiveness, and not of the backing of national governments; and the opening-up of a single market, one largely using a single currency which will bring transparency in costs and prices, should ensure that political conflicts between states continue to decline in importance compared with economic competition between firms.

Naturally the further opening up of Europe to market forces will bring not only new opportunities but also new problems, and different national traditions will give rise to different remedies. The contrast in approach between Gerhard Schröder and Lionel Jospin are a clear enough example of this. On the other hand, the fact that France, Germany and their European partners are firmly committed to promoting their national interests and resolving their differences within the framework of the EU suggests that adjustments and resolution of disputes will be carried out in more peaceful ways than in the Europe of the past.

French and German interests are clearly not identical, but are they fundamentally compatible? As this book shows, the two countries have succeeded, often after considerable efforts, in agreeing on common lines of action in relation to three extremely ambitious European projects; EMU, CFSP, and enlargement. When we consider how far apart their respective positions were at the start of the process, it is hardly surprising that they still show some differences of approach as these momentous undertakings come to be put into practice, and that the final results are still uncertain. However, the fact of so much agreement surely remains impressive and encouraging for the future.

As is shown by a recent study edited by Douglas Webber (*The Franco-German Relationship in the European Union*, Routledge, London, 1999), French and German governments have sometimes found it easier, in the end, to reach agreement on the ambitious 'constitution-making' projects such as monetary union, immigration policy or to some extent foreign policy or EU enlargement, than in more 'technical' sectors such as social welfare policy, telecommunications, energy policy, or scientific and technical research. These 'sectoral' areas have often remained the subject of Franco-German disagreement for years, partly because the national ministries handling them are essentially responsible to domestic interests, and only reach international agreements – even with a very close foreign partner, as in this case – when they are pressed into line by foreign ministers or heads of governments. These more elevated office-holders, indeed, have a more continuous sense of the importance of joint actions with foreign partners, and the progress of Franco-German cooperation in moving forward on the really big issues has been due essentially to initiatives and to agreements at these levels.

But will the future resemble the past in this respect, and will the main source of progress in the EU continue to be joint planning by France and Germany? One effect of the new and more relaxed condition of Western Europe has been that France and Germany, having worked heroically together to lead the EU from its pre-Mastricht to its post-Amsterdam phase, no longer feel the need to stress so emphatically the special significance of their bilateral relationship. In the era after Kohl and Mitterrand, such influential public figures as Rudolf von Thadden, the Federal Government's official Co-ordinator for German-French Relations, and Alain Lamassouce, France's former minister for European affairs, have each declared publicly that his country needs closer dialogues with a wider range of partners. On sections of the EU's future agenda, indeed, other member states are bound to be included in the inner circle of policy-making: on defence, obviously, the United Kingdom; and on enlargement, an array of states especially concerned, including Sweden, Finland, Italy and Austria.

Yet in the end, despite this widening of the circle of member states involved in more intensive bilateral or multilateral consulting and bargaining, and despite the eastward shift of the Union's centre of gravity, the Franco-German partnership seems likely to retain a good deal of its special and influential quality. It would indeed be surprising if it were to continue unchanged in the distinctly different Europe of the coming century; for the EU as a whole and for each of the two partners, to become irrelevant or insignificant.

Index